▼

ADVANCE PRAISE

"Steve Jones showed us how to brand like a rock star in his first book. Now he cranks the amp all the way to eleven with *Start You Up*, a book packed with fascinating behind-the-scenes stories of musical legends. These are stories with a purpose—they have much to teach us about persistence, leadership, and excellence—but they're also a heck of a lot of fun to read."

—Daniel H. Pink, author of *To Sell Is Human*

"I know firsthand how a strong personal brand opens doors and how a weak personal brand can kill a career before it starts. Steve's book uses music industry insights that will make you more successful, and you'll actually have fun reading it."

—Mike Michalowicz, author of *The Toilet Paper Entrepreneur* and *The Pumpkin Plan*

"Working with Fleetwood Mac, I witnessed the meteoric rise of a legendary brand. In this book, you'll observe the experiences of rock's elite, and if you're smart you'll put these lessons to work in your career, creating a personal brand that stands out—and rocks."

—Ken Caillat, coproducer of Fleetwood Mac's *Rumours* album and author of *Making Rumours*

"The essential ingredients in a creating a successful personal or business brand are the same. You must discover how to differentiate and embrace what makes you different and unique from the rest. Many individuals and companies are in constant search for perfection, but top music artists teach us that the secret to perfection is embracing the right imperfections that make you stand out and grow. This book shows the way to creating a differentiated brand that customers will love."

—Bolivar J. Bueno, coauthor
of *The Power of Cult Branding*

"Your name, whether on the front door of a company or the top of a resume, speaks volumes about you. How people perceive you can be the difference between a wildly successful business and a lifetime of missed opportunities."

—Don Seymour, managing director
at DMS Offshore Investment Services

"Steve has declared war on the all-too-common life of quiet desperation, the unfulfilled spirit, and the ho-hum career. Rock on."

—Hugh MacLeod (@gapingvoid), author of
Ignore Everybody and blogger at gapingvoid.com

START YOU UP

ROCK STAR SECRETS TO UNLEASH YOUR
PERSONAL BRAND & SET YOUR CAREER ON FIRE

STEVE JONES

GREENLEAF
BOOK GROUP PRESS

Published by Greenleaf Book Group Press
Austin, Texas
www.greenleafbookgroup.com

Distributed by Greenleaf Book Group LLC

For ordering information or special discounts for bulk purchases, please contact Greenleaf Book Group LLC at PO Box 91869, Austin, TX 78709, 512.891.6100.

Design and composition by Greenleaf Book Group LLC
Cover design by Greenleaf Book Group LLC
Cover image: ©iStockphoto.com/BlueMoonPics

Publisher's Cataloging-In-Publication Data
Jones, Steve (Stephen Andrew), 1970–
    Start you up : rock star secrets to unleash your personal brand & set your career on fire / Steve Jones.—First edition.
        pages ; cm
    Issued also as an ebook.
    Includes bibliographical references.
    ISBN: 978-1-62634-069-5
    1. Branding (Marketing) 2. Success in business. 3. Rock musicians—Marketing—Case studies. 4. Music trade—Marketing—Case studies. I. Title.

HF5415.1255 .J662 2014

658.8/27   2013954952

Part of the Tree Neutral® program, which offsets the number of trees consumed in the production and printing of this book by taking proactive steps, such as planting trees in direct proportion to the number of trees used: www.treeneutral.com

Printed in the United States of America on acid-free paper

14 15 16 17 18 19   10 9 8 7 6 5 4 3 2 1

First Edition

To my wife Susan, and our sons Isaac and Matthew:
You are my rock stars, and I am forever your biggest fan.

CONTENTS

Introduction   1

PART ONE: POSITIONING

Chapter 1: Why You Need a Rock Star
Personal Brand   13

Chapter 2: Who Are You? Discovering, Refining, and
Telling Your Unique Story   24

Chapter 3: Work Your Ass Off: There Is No Shortcut
to Success   37

Chapter 4: Running with the Devil (in the Details):
How Van Halen Turned Candy into Cash   49

Chapter 5: None of Us Know What We're Doing: How U2
Learned Everything While on the Job   59

Chapter 6: Focus: The Cult of Little Steven   69

PART TWO: PRESENTATION

Chapter 7: Be Different or Be Invisible: How Rock Stars
Stand Out   83

Chapter 8: Just Like Buddy Holly: Defining Your Rock Star
Visual Identity   96

Chapter 9: Make Rock Star Mistakes: Not Screwing Up Is
Proof You Aren't Trying Hard Enough   108

Chapter 10: The Game of Risk: How to Take the Right
Risks (And Make the Most of Them)   121

Chapter 11: Weird Works: How Joe Walsh Turned Quirky
into Cash   131

PART THREE: PASSION

Chapter 12: Embrace the Chaos: Turning Absolute
Insanity into Awesome Opportunity   147

Chapter 13: Finding Perfect Harmony: How David Crosby
Made Himself and Others Better   159

Chapter 14: Go with Your Gut: The Beatles Prove
That Some Things Cannot Easily Be
Predicted   171

Chapter 15: There Is No Plan B: Failure Is Not
an Option   182

Chapter 16: Making Every Person Count: How the Boss
Treats His Customers and Employees   192

Chapter 17: Diversify Yourself: How Nikki Sixx Built a
Personal Brand That Rocks   203

Chapter 18: Breaking Out on Your Own: How to
Forge Your Own Identity in the Shadow
of Greatness   215

PART FOUR: PURPOSE

Chapter 19: Finding Purpose: How Bob Geldof Made
Millions by Helping Others   231

Chapter 20: Give a Little Bit (or Even a Lot): How the Grateful Dead Cashed in on Their Generosity   244

Chapter 21: Find Your Mentor: You'll Never Walk Alone   257

Chapter 22: The Rock 'n' Roll Comeback: Every State Is Temporary   267

Chapter 23: Knowing When to Quit: Avoiding the Curse of INXS   283

PART FIVE: PROFITS

Chapter 24: Your Obstacles Will Define You: How a One-Armed Drummer Is Changing the World   295

Chapter 25: Rock Star Leaders: How Jagger, Bono, Grohl, and Bon Jovi Rank on the CEO Scale   307

Acknowledgments   321

About the Author   325

INTRODUCTION

In high school, I spent far too much time listening to music instead of studying.

Yeah, I wasn't the world's greatest student.

Textbooks bored me. Teachers put me to sleep. But music engaged me and brought out emotions and excitement. My high school marks weren't terribly bad, but year after year my report card always contained comments from teachers like "needs to work to his potential." I really didn't know what that meant. So for years, I figured that either school was really hard or I wasn't very smart.

My ninth-grade history teacher changed that. He didn't read from a textbook. He didn't write on the chalkboard. He simply told us stories. He told grandiose tales about explorers and revolutions, wars and battles, and presidents and coups. While textbooks took all of this information and made it boring, he made it all come to life. My ninth-grade history mark was fantastic, and suddenly school wasn't quite so tough.

I hope that the backstage rock 'n' roll stories that follow in the pages ahead help bring the concept of personal branding and career growth to life for you the way my ninth-grade teacher brought history to life for me. Stories are so much better than the facts and figures; they are the cornerstone to all communication, including personal branding. Instead of facts and figures, this book is simply a collection of stories about rock stars, the crazy stuff they did, and how we can use their experiences to build our own personal brands and become, in essence, rock stars at whatever it is we want to do in life.

My 2011 book, *Brand Like a Rock Star: Lessons from Rock 'n' Roll to Make Your Business Rich and Famous* connected with people because of those types of stories. I applied the lesson learned from my ninth-grade history teacher and shared stories about the bands I love. Combining my experience in marketing and music, the book examined branding from the perspective of rock music legends. Instead of dry information in a textbook, the book shared business wisdom through the many backstage stories from rock 'n' roll.

What could AC/DC teach businesses about building a consistent brand? What could Bob Marley's short but brilliant career teach entrepreneurs about niche marketing? What could the bold punk rock experience of the Sex Pistols show us about using PR to get attention? As it turns out, the answer to all of those questions is "quite a lot." As I researched chapter after chapter, I discovered that rock 'n' roll provided an incredible template for building stronger brands and creating more profitable businesses in the process. I also began to notice that the same lessons applied to individuals, often more directly than they did to businesses. These lessons can be applied to all of us, helping us to build personal brands that can elevate us from weekend-loving, Monday-dreading worker drones into rock stars, complete with fans and a bright spotlight shining on us on stage. At that point, *Start You Up* began to take shape.

Rock 'n' Roll gives us uplifting, against-all-odds success stories, like Rick Allen of Def Leppard, a drummer who—at the height of his band's rise to fame—lost his left arm in a horrific car accident.

There are tales of growth and learning, such as U2, a band forced to write their own songs because when they started out *they weren't good enough* to accurately play cover versions.

There are profiles of people with purpose, like Bob Geldof, who found a way to turn good work into good pay.

Some of the stories are just plain fun, like Al Kooper's sneaky role in helping to create a Bob Dylan classic, and the lesson it can teach us about taking risks.

And it wouldn't be rock 'n' roll without comeback stories, like Meat Loaf's rise from obscurity to stardom, then to bankruptcy, and back to stardom sixteen years after his first breakthrough.

The personal branding and career development lessons of rock stars are not always positive. Axl Rose comes across as a petulant poster child for the damage that overinflated ego can do to raw talent. Mötley Crüe bass player Nikki Sixx let his addiction to heroin kill him—literally—before he finally overcame it and built a legendary personal brand in music, photography, fashion, literature, and media.

You can learn a lot from the musicians and bands you love. You can learn what to do and what not to do in order to build a rock-solid personal brand that will help you thrive in today's competitive world.

While the chapters in *Start You Up* are not sequential and you can pick up and start reading pretty much anywhere, the book is divided into five sections based on what I call "The Five Ps of Personal Branding": Positioning, Presentation, Passion, Purpose, and Profits. Like Maslow's Hierarchy of Needs, this hierarchy prioritizes the growth of a strong personal brand.

POSITIONING

The first six chapters of the book start with the building blocks of personal branding: exploring what the concept means, defining why it is so important, and explaining how to start to develop a personal brand that can launch your career to new heights. "Positioning" is about discovering your unique story and understanding how it contributes to your personal brand.

PRESENTATION

The next five chapters delve into how to communicate your personal brand, really demonstrating what makes you unique and desirable. Using the foundation in the first six chapters, we will add some essential elements to your growing personal brand. "Presentation" is about how your personal brand is seen, heard, and sensed, and how you can build and enhance it as you grow.

PASSION

In the third section, we will put some exciting tools in your personal branding toolkit, diving into areas often driven by emotions. Passionate topics covered include creativity, the ups and downs of partnerships, stress, planning, and how to use your gut instinct. "Passion" goes beyond the basics to explore how to turn doing what you love into your life's work.

PURPOSE

The next five chapters take personal branding beyond the basics and explore how to leave a powerful impact on the world around you by putting your personal purpose to work in your career. Topics like generosity, empathy, and mentorship highlight this section. "Purpose" is essentially about finding greater meaning in what you do and allowing your values to guide you and grow your brand and career.

PROFITS

Ultimately, success or failure is measured by profit. Thinking beyond the traditional financial definition of profit, your success may be measured by emotional profit or personal satisfaction profit. "Profits," the final section of *Start You Up*, will show you how to turn your personal brand into long-term profit through leadership, a never-say-die attitude, and the ability to overcome any obstacle you encounter.

PUTTING THESE LESSONS TO USE

While I didn't realize it at the time, with hindsight I can clearly see that I have successfully applied many of these rock 'n' roll lessons to my own career. Like so many of us these days, my career path is far from normal. Growing up in the late '70s and early '80s, my friends and I loved music. I listened to the radio nonstop. But unlike most kids, I wasn't listening for just the music. I was also listening for the DJs who came on between the songs! I loved the way they talked and laughed and connected with me as I listened alone in my room at night while I should have been doing homework. I lived in Toronto, and my favorite station was a legendary but now long-gone Top 40 station called 1050 CHUM.

When I was thirteen, my dad, a wildlife biologist, took a job in the extremely small, remote northern Canadian town of Marathon, Ontario: population 2,500. There wasn't much going on in Marathon in 1983. It was a lonely mill town—cursed with the frequent stench of sulphur. There wasn't another town for an hour in either direction along the Trans-Canada Highway, which bypassed the town a few miles to the north. The interchange there gave you no reason to consider stopping unless you were low on gas or too sleepy to continue driving. Directly through the center of town ran the railway tracks, and our house backed onto them. Our entire home would literally shake as trains whipped through town with no more reason to stop than the drivers on the highway. Marathon was, and remains, a hidden gem. It is a town that you need to seek out in order to know it even exists. If you're looking for peace and quiet, Marathon is a great place. But that wasn't what I was looking for in 1983.

It was a massive culture shock, leaving a huge, bustling city for a sleepy, tiny town seemingly in the middle of nowhere. I didn't deal tremendously well with the transition, but one thing saved me from complete meltdown. There was a newly opened radio station, a tiny touch of show biz in a backwoods outpost! It became my personal quest to get a job there.

I sent the manager a proposal to host an after-school radio show, just for the high school kids. He politely brushed me off. I followed that up with a proposal for a night show, just for the high school kids. Another polite rejection followed. But I was relentless. I typed up and submitted proposal after proposal until he finally hired me. My new job may have been a ploy by the manager to end the harassment, but I didn't care. My foot was in the door.

My assignment was to play recorded segments on the

air late at night on the weekends, when none of the DJs were working. The DJs would record their voice parts, and I would play them back between records and commercials to make them sound like they were live on the air. For $3 an hour, I was in heaven, and the hard-working DJs got some time off.

After about a year pressing "play" on recorded tapes, I could no longer fight the urge to turn on the microphone. So I paid one of the DJs ten bucks to "forget" to record his portion of the late-night broadcast. At 11:40 p.m. on a warm summer Sunday night, I turned on the microphone for the first time. I was fourteen. Wow . . . I was terrible. I think I knew it then, but I was too high on the emotion of being on the radio to grasp just how bad I was!

I spent the next decade playing music and talking on the radio (and gradually getting *slightly* better at it) at various radio stations. Some played Top 40 hits, others played rock, and a few played country music. It didn't matter much to me, because I lived for the moment the songs ended and I turned the microphone on. Over the years, I transitioned from being a DJ to managing DJs, then to managing radio stations, and finally to consulting and overseeing various radio station brands around the world.

My career has taken me to radio stations in the US, Canada, and the Caribbean. Just like the lyrics in the theme song to the TV show *WKPR in Cincinnati*, I've been up and down the dial during my broadcast career. In thirty years on and off the air, I have had the pleasure of meeting some of the biggest rock stars on the planet, working with their teams to launch albums and promote concerts. I was there to watch their careers rise, sometimes fall, and—for some—even rise again. To paraphrase the Grateful Dead, it indeed has been a long, strange trip.

I've watched musical careers hit brick walls, despite tremendous talent. And I've also seen careers flourish, despite mediocre talent. I have been extremely fortunate to learn some hard lessons without having to spend my own money to do it! For three decades, I have watched as record labels spent hundreds of millions of dollars attempting to launch and sustain the careers of bands. I have also witnessed businesses of all types spend hundreds of millions of dollars to advertise, promote, and launch new products on the radio stations where I worked. The money spent wasn't mine, but the lessons I learned certainly are. Their successes and failures were my teachers, and I'm honored that you've allowed me to share some of what I have learned with you.

As you read *Start You Up* I'd love to hear from you. If you have comments, questions, or want to expand on the ideas, please contact me on Twitter @rockstarbrands, or by email at steve@startyouupbook.com. You can also connect with me on Facebook at www.facebook.com/startyouupbook.com.

▼

PART ONE:

POSITIONING

CHAPTER ONE

WHY YOU NEED A ROCK STAR PERSONAL BRAND

Your life is too short to dread 4,420 Monday mornings. That's how many times you'll wake up on a Monday, assuming you live to be eighty-five. The vast majority of us will greet those Monday mornings with loathing, drowning out the pain with copious amounts of coffee and the knowledge that, if we can just survive another four sleeps, Friday will once again grace us with her promise of a weekend of freedom from the shackles of our jobs.

That's no way to wake up 4,420 times. It is a terrible way to spend 1/7 of your life.

Despite Loverboy's early '80s assertion, not everybody is actually working with the weekend as their goal. Most people are. But become a rock star, and you break out of that cycle and build a life and career where Monday mornings are as exciting as Friday afternoons. The reality is that rock stars don't care what day it is. And of course being a rock star in this case doesn't mean literally playing music on stage. It means being famous for whatever it is you do, no matter how exciting or mundane it may seem. I believe there are rock star salespeople, rock star waitresses, rock star small business owners, and rock star trash collectors. Being a rock star simply means being among the very best at what you do, having an absolute blast doing it, making people very happy with the end result, and hopefully pocketing a handsome reward for your efforts.

Rock stars understand that they aren't just people; they aren't just a name and a face. Rock stars realize that they are real-life brands. Just like Coke, Mercedes-Benz, and Ben & Jerry's, rock stars are famous for something. They represent something special to their fans. When people think of famous musicians—and even the singers and bands that they dislike—they immediately conjure together a clear and very specific image of how that rock star looks and sounds, how the rock star acts, and what the rock star stands for.

Mention Kiss, and nearly everyone identifies their comic book makeup, pyrotechnics, and Gene Simmons's famous tongue.

Ask people about Lady Gaga, and they will almost universally talk about her outrageous costumes and her very public views on gay rights and anti-bullying.

Bob Dylan is a poet and troubadour with a nasal voice, a love-or-hate generational sound of change.

P!nk represents feminine power and positivity, with a look and message that encourages her fans to celebrate their individuality.

The Rolling Stones? The elder[ly] statesmen of rock, famous for Mick Jagger's moves (and lips!) and Keith Richards's legendary ability to survive whatever abuse he could subject his body to.

Adele stands for substance over style, an astonishingly powerful voice combined with a refreshingly everywoman look and attitude that endears her to fans.

Think of any famous rock star and you can instantly hear their music, see them on stage, and even picture how they act offstage, even though you've probably never met them. You often know what they stand for politically and how they feel about important issues. In some cases, just thinking of a famous rock star can often ignite all of your senses! Aside from sight and sound (the obvious ones), think about how would it feel, smell, and taste to crack open an ice-cold Landshark Lager on a hot summer day with Jimmy Buffett at a hole-in-the-wall bar on Duval Street in Key West. That's a personal brand at work, turning on all of your senses at once.

The power of these rock-star personal brands extends beyond mere sensory reactions. Strong personal brands are *emotional* reactions. How would Bono break up a fight instigated by a bully? What would Bruce Springsteen say to the owner of a company who wants to move his American factory to China? What would Jack Johnson be doing if you met up with him on a beach in Hale'iwa?

That's what personal branding is all about. At the mere mention of a name, a complete image is formed and decisions are subconsciously made about whether you like them or not. It happens when you think of rock stars, and it happens when other people think about you; you are a brand! Your challenge is to understand and build your personal brand in such a way as to open up career opportunities, increase your level of happiness and productivity, make more money, and become famous for what you do.

WHAT IS A BRAND?

When you think of a brand, what comes to mind first?

If you're like most people, you think about visuals and logos. Maybe it is because the concept of "branding" extends back to cattle ranchers marking their herds. Most of us think of a brand as a look, a logo, and a set of colors that identify a company. However, that is just scratching the surface.

To understand what a brand really is, think about some logos. All of them are famous brands. When you consider the logo, make note of how you feel about the brand. See the logo in your mind's eye, and then close your eyes and consider what your brain and your heart are telling you about that company.

Sit back, close your eyes, and visualize the following well-known logos for these famous brands: The Apple™ computer logo, with the famous bite (or is it a byte?) on the right side; the rugged Harley-Davidson™ shield; British Petroleum—BP™—and its white, yellow, and green sunburst; BMW™, with its clean, black ring, embossed with the company's initials, encircling the four white and blue quadrants; and the interlocked "N" and "Y" of the New York Yankees organization.

When you think about the Apple logo, you might first recall the Apple devices that you use. Now think about why you use those devices. What do you love about your iPhone or iPad? What can you accomplish with them? How does it feel when you use them? Apple makes electronic devices and computers, for sure. But what the brand stands for is innovation, progress, and intuitive technology.

Similarly, Harley-Davidson makes motorcycles, but the essence of the brand goes far deeper. Harley buyers are purchasing more than just a bike; they are purchasing the lifestyle that goes with a Harley. They are buying into the rebel attitude and buying a bike that tells the world that they aren't like everybody else.

BP, or British Petroleum, likely stands for one thing in the minds of most North Americans. Despite the company's efforts to erase the perception, BP still represents the worst environmental disaster in decades, the 2010 Gulf of Mexico oil spill. When you see their logo, there is a very good chance that the oil spill and its impact immediately come to mind.

BMW has built a brand based on performance. While there are safer cars, faster cars, more expensive cars, and tougher cars, BMW is the car people turn to when they want a performance vehicle.

If I let my inner Red Sox fan speak, the New York Yankees represent everything that is wrong with baseball. No doubt that the Yankees logo sparks a reaction in any ball fan, but that emotional reaction varies based on whether you root for the pinstripes or not. Looking at the logo, Yankees fans see the most valuable franchise in baseball, a team that has won more championships than anyone else, and a team that everyone wants to play for. Sox fans and others see a team that has used its deep pockets to buy pennants. It depends which side of the fence you're on.

In every case, the real essence of the brand isn't the logo itself, but rather the emotional reactions that happen when you see the logo or interact with the brand. Rather than the logo, the slogan, or the color scheme, the brand is the emotional reaction that takes place in the heart of the customer—it is how your customer "feels" a product. Likewise, your personal brand is how other people feel about you.

THE HEART OF THE MATTER

The heart really is what all this branding stuff is all about. The heart rules everything! How you feel determines how you act. In fact, I believe that nearly every purchasing decision is made with the heart, not the head. The brain has a role, for sure, but it is a far smaller role than we think. The brain is simply there to back up the heart's decision.

You've probably had the experience before of finding yourself wanting something that you logically know you don't really need. You know you can live without it, but you buy it anyway. Think about your last vacation and the use-less souvenirs you bought that are now stuffed in a closet somewhere. If your brain made the buying decision, it would have said to you, "Those sombreros are useless and you'll never wear them." But it didn't happen that way. Your heart said, "This vacation has been so amazing that I want to take a piece of Cancun home with me, and these sombreros are perfect. I'll wear them on a patio this summer and drink Corona, and memories of this vacation will come flooding back." Once your heart made its intentions clear, your head simply justified. "Sounds good to me," your brain said.

When summer came, the sombreros were collecting dust. You should have listened to your brain, but you didn't because you couldn't. Your heart buys . . . your head justifies.

When I was in my early twenties, I desperately wanted a soft-top, four-wheel-drive Jeep. The desire in my heart was so strong that it was able to convince my head that a Jeep was the best purchase for me. It didn't have the best fuel economy or the best safety rating—in fact it was terrible on both counts. It had two useful seats, because accessing the back seats was torture. There was essentially no cargo space in the back. In the winter, it was freezing cold, with only a thin layer of fabric saving me from the frigid weather. On so many criteria, the Jeep was a terrible idea.

So I bought a Jeep. My heart was able to convince my head. I didn't drive long distances, so fuel economy didn't matter. At twenty-two I was invincible, so safety didn't concern me. With only my wife and me to worry about, who needed back seats? And I could buy an extra heater for the cold winter days. Most of all, I wanted that Jeep because it was a cool-looking off-road machine that sent a message to the world that I was the kind of person who didn't follow the beaten path. The Jeep spoke to my heart.

The heart buys. The head justifies.

One cold winter day a few months later, shortly after the soft top was sliced open and the heater stolen, my wife and I discovered that we would be having our first child. We were going to need that back seat. And working heat.

We sold the Jeep and bought a minivan.

GETTING PERSONAL

So what does my story about trading in my Jeep for a Dodge Grand Caravan have to do with your career? Well, just like the Jeep represented something in my heart and mind, you represent something in the hearts and minds of those around you. Just like owning a Jeep said something about me, the friendships and relationships people have with you say something about them.

When your name is mentioned or when you walk in a room, people instantly conjure up feelings and images associated with you. Just as they do with products, people decide almost instantaneously if they like you or not and whether they will engage you or not. You are a brand.

Just as the world-famous corporate brands do, you advertise, promote, and market your brand. Every day, the things you do, the way you act, the words you choose, and the people you associate with help to shape, positively or negatively, how brand "you" is perceived by others. That is the core of your personal brand . . . *how others perceive you*. It might not line up with reality, and it might not be exactly what you want it to be, but it exists in the minds of everyone who meets you or comes into contact with you: in person, online, via stories and rumors, or through work you've done.

To put it succinctly, you are what they think you are. Perceptions are realities.

When you are looking for a job, your personal brand can often be the difference between a lucrative, life-changing offer and another résumé tossed in the scrap heap. When you already have a job, a strong personal brand can be your key to fast-track the corporate ladder, gaining more security and financial reward as you go. In interpersonal relationships, your personal brand is essential in establishing trust and determining what kind of friend you are to others. In every aspect of your personal and professional life, your personal brand influences how people treat you.

Like it or not, you are constantly being judged on your looks, words, actions, and intentions. *Everything you do is being judged!* It is a frightening and seriously unfair reality, but it is reality nonetheless. The food you order at a business lunch, the color of your socks, the jokes you tell, your hairstyle, the friends you keep, and the car you drive are just a few of the ways you are being judged every single day. The good news is that you have some degree of control over all of them. The bad news is that once someone makes up their mind about you, changing it is nearly impossible. Indeed, the stakes are very high.

You need a rock-star personal brand. You need to clearly and powerfully represent something to people. You cannot afford to be ambiguous.

What will people feel when they meet you?

"Even if you want to hate me, I'm okay with it. Just fucking feel something." —Nikki Sixx

The Rock Star Playlist: Five Songs That Mention Actual Brands

1. **"Little Red Corvette" by Prince.** This song sounds like an ode to the classic American sports car, but in reality the "corvette" Prince is singing about is a woman with whom he has just had a one-night stand. In typical Prince fashion, he works in plenty of double-entendre throughout the song. Newlywed Fleetwood Mac singer Stevie Nicks wrote her hit "Stand Back" in her honeymoon suite after hearing "Little Red Corvette" on the radio on her wedding day. Prince is officially listed as a cowriter on the song and made a cameo keyboard appearance in the studio.

2. **"Cadillac Ranch" by Bruce Springsteen.** The song was never a single in America, but it remains one of his fan favorites. Despite sounding fun and innocent, the message, according to music critic Dave Marsh, is really all about the inevitability of death. It was one of the key tracks on Springsteen's 1980 album *The River*.

3. **"Smells Like Teen Spirit" by Nirvana.** When a friend spray-painted "Kurt smells like teen spirit" on his apartment wall, Kurt Cobain interpreted it as a message about youth

and rebellion. What Kathleen Hanna really meant to do was ridicule him for smelling like the deodorant Teen Spirit, which his then-girlfriend used. Instead, she inspired one of the greatest rock songs ever made. Kurt claims he wasn't aware of the brand association until months after the song was recorded.

4. **"The Jump Off" by Lil' Kim.** Although not a major pop hit, Lil' Kim does accomplish quite a feat in this song, mentioning thirteen different brands in the tune, an unofficial record for a song. She mentions, Bacardi, Barbie, Bvlgari, Ferrari, Bentley, Hummer, Mercedes Benz, Escalade, Jaguar, Woolrich, Sprite, Playboy, and Range Rover.

5. **"Take Me Out To The Ball Game."** Probably one of the first mentions of a brand in a popular song is this 1908 baseball classic written by Jack Norworth and Albert Von Tilzer. Although neither of them had ever been to a baseball game, the song would go on to become the unofficial anthem of the sport. Today, you'll hear it in nearly every major and minor league ballpark during the seventh inning stretch. The brand mentioned? Cracker Jack, of course. (And by the way, on Crosby, Stills, Nash, and Young's "CSNY2K" tour in 2000, they played this song, complete with a video of legendary sportscaster Harry Caray, during a break in their music.)

▼

CHAPTER TWO

WHO ARE YOU?: DISCOVERING, REFINING, AND TELLING YOUR UNIQUE STORY

Your quest to establish a rock star personal brand begins with your story. What makes you so remarkable? What makes you different from the person in the cubicle next to you? With seven billion people roaming the planet, what makes you stand out from the rest of us?

Maybe you are a rags-to-riches story like Warren Buffett, or maybe you tell a David vs. Goliath saga of triumph: an everyday man taking on the big guys, as did vacuum maker James Dyson. Perhaps your story is that you are a risk-taking big thinker like Richard Branson. While you may think you are unremarkable compared to these accomplished and high-profile names, there is no question that you are unique. You have a story to tell; you simply haven't yet clearly defined it and understood how to tell it. You don't have to have millions of dollars or a track record of high-profile successes to have a great story.

Don't underestimate the importance of your story. Stories are the cornerstone of human communication. On cave walls we painted drawings to share tales of successful hunts or plentiful crops. Those drawings evolved into fables, songs, and folklore in order to teach important morals and values to our youth and carry on our traditions and religions. Stories were told through actors, singers, and jesters, not simply for entertainment but for the genuine value in passing lessons from person to person, generation to generation. With the advent of the printing press, stories became accessible to even greater masses. From paper, stories hit the screen, first in movies and then on TV, and today on computers and tablets and smartphones. We human beings are obsessed with stories! No wonder your story has such a tremendous impact on how people perceive you. Everything starts with your story.

THE TALE OF TWO ROCK STARS

He was a young boy growing up in postwar New Jersey in a family who struggled to make ends meet, and he didn't fit in at the Catholic school where his parents sent him. They transferred him to another school, but that didn't help the problem. His only solace was his guitar, which he played voraciously. After dropping out of college, he watched his friends get drafted into the war in Vietnam, many of them never to return home. He swore he'd never go. When his number came up in the draft, he used a concussion sustained in a motorcycle accident, along with intentional erratic and hungover behavior, to get a medical exemption from having a rifle put in his hand. While he avoided the Vietnam War, another different kind of war was being fought around him. The industries that defined his hometown started to crumble and collapse, leaving honest and hardworking people—his people—fighting for their own survival.

That's the story of Bruce Springsteen, a story reflected in Bruce's music and his personal brand.

His breakthrough hit "Born To Run" is a first-person love letter to his girlfriend "Wendy," inviting her to get on his motorbike and escape the decaying factories and dead-end opportunities of a small New Jersey town.

"The River" is a haunting tale of a man coming to terms with a life that didn't turn out as he imagined, despite having done all the things he was supposed to do. He got a good job at the factory, joined the union, married his high school sweetheart, and did just as society expected him to.

His famous anthem, "Born in the USA," despite mistakenly being used in several political campaigns as a pro-American rallying cry, is actually a commentary on the failings of the country Bruce loves, as told through the eyes of a returning veteran with none of the parades, respect, and job prospects he expected to find.

All of those Bruce Springsteen songs are powerful, emotional, and deeply connective stories. They are stories that many people can relate to, and they are stories that many people want to share with their friends—remarkable stories. While the songs are not autobiographical, they are all reflective of the values embedded in Bruce Springsteen's personal story. Today, while Bruce Springsteen has more personal wealth than he could ever possibly spend, we continue to relate to him as an "everyman" figure. Isn't that amazing? Despite an immense fortune, people look at Bruce Springsteen as a spokesperson for the blue-collar worker, the underdog, and the honest but unfortunate among us.

When you examine Bruce Springsteen's life, both onstage and off, he consistently reflects the identity his story has crafted. He is hardworking, often playing for more than three hours on stage with his band. He is a dedicated family man who carefully protects the privacy of his children. He has campaigned alongside Barack Obama and supported the Democratic Party, a party that is connected to labor unions, minority rights, and liberal values. When tragedy hit his hometown, Bruce got involved, playing benefit concerts in New York in 2001 after the 9/11 terrorist attacks and in New Jersey in the wake of Superstorm Sandy in 2012.

In a strange way, it seems almost as if Bruce Springsteen can read the mind of America. When the nation needed a voice after the shock of 9/11, it was Bruce who came forward to sing "The Rising," a soaring ode to a firefighter climbing the steps of a burning building, never to return. The first time I saw him perform that song live, it was an emotional moment. I remember more than a few of us grown men wiping away tears at the raw power of the song played live. A few years later, in the wake of the devastating recession of 2009, Bruce sang "We Take Care of Our Own," a song calling upon the nation to look after the least-fortunate citizens.

That's the Bruce Springsteen story. He shares it in everything he says and does. It is a vital part of what defines Bruce Springsteen among hundreds of other musicians. He owns those values to the point where any other blue-collar, politically minded singer will inevitably draw a comparison to The Boss.

Another musician has an equally well-defined personal story, although a very different one. His story replaces the shore of New Jersey with the Gulf Coast. He was born in Mississippi and raised in Alabama, wrapped in the warm waters and breezes of the Gulf of Mexico. Growing up by the sea gave him a view of the world sculpted by ocean waves, tides, and the wake of boats coming and going from the harbor. After graduating from college, he earned money busking for tourists in New Orleans and then headed farther south to Key West to do the same. Geography influenced the music he was exposed to, and he began to cultivate a type of music that brought together country, folk, pop, and island music. He is a happy-go-lucky man in perpetual pursuit of a good time and a sandy beach.

That's the story of Jimmy Buffett.

His only big hit, "Margaritaville," tells the tale of a man

alone in a tropical paradise, wasting away and trying to find a woman to blame for his lonely state.

Nearly all of Jimmy Buffett's most well-known songs are similar stories of beaches, boats, unusual characters, and tropical breezes. He sings about life lived in flip-flops without a care in the world, and millions of fans relate to his music.

Just like Springsteen, the values that define the Jimmy Buffett story continue to be reflected in everything he does, on and off the stage. He is a private pilot, captain of his own yacht, and an avid surfer. He has been known to drop in unexpectedly to remote locations where the surf is predicted to be especially strong so that he can surf alongside the locals. His charity work is extensive and most often focuses on causes close to his home and heart. He played benefit shows to raise money for the victims of Hurricane Katrina in 2005 and to help with the cleanup of the Gulf coast following the epic BP oil spill of 2010.

These days Jimmy Buffett doesn't need to busk for change on Duval Street in The Conch Republic of Key West. Like Bruce Springsteen, Buffett lives a life of immense luxury. He has homes in Palm Beach, Florida, and St. Barts in the Caribbean. His wealth allows him to often pilot his personal Dassault Falcon 900 around the world on tour. This luxury executive jet airplane, on the low end, will cost you nearly $20 million to purchase—used. His business empire includes clothing, restaurants, hotels, casinos, alcohol brands, and sports franchises. Yet we continue to see Jimmy Buffett as the busker on the beach.

How do artists like Bruce Springsteen and Jimmy Buffett

continue to relate to normal nine-to-five people, despite their immense wealth? They tell us a story that is powerful, personal, and compelling. Their actions consistently reflect the values that define their story. They seldom stray from their story or go off-script. Because their story is relatable, engaging, and based on everyday values, we see them as relatable, engaging, everyday people.

So what's your story? How can you find it? And how can you make it work to help further your career and your business?

SMART AS A FOX

Mark Fox is the author of *Da Vinci and the Forty Answers*, a cool little book that forces you to rethink how problems can be solved. He's a very smart guy. While in his early thirties, Mark took a job with NASA and became the youngest chief engineer on the space shuttle project. While we toss around the phrase, "it doesn't take a rocket scientist," Mark Fox *really* is a rocket scientist.

Today Mark is an author, speaker, and business consultant. He helps businesses, very few of them related in any way to the space program, solve their problems and attract more customers through creative thinking. Mark has no shortage of customers today, and many of those people hire him because of his amazing story. When you hire Mark Fox to help overcome your business challenges, you aren't hiring any other consultant . . . you are hiring the man who was the youngest chief engineer in NASA's space shuttle program! You are hiring a guy who helped put people into space to help inspire your team to think more creatively. How incredibly cool is that? Clients like Morgan Stanley, Century 21, 3M, and Universal Studios have turned to a former rocket scientist to help their people with creative thinking and problem solving.

By using his NASA story, Mark Fox has built a powerful personal brand. There are countless consultants offering creative problem-solving workshops, but companies are drawn to Mark Fox because he tells a powerful, personal, and compelling story. He was a rocket scientist at NASA, and the youngest one at that.

A PRESIDENTIAL STORY

The president of the United States is a great example of a powerful personal story. The child of a white girl from Kansas and a black man from Kenya, Barack Obama grew up in a single-parent home. He was born in Hawaii and grew up for a period in Indonesia. He later graduated from Harvard Law School and worked on behalf of the urban poor in Chicago as a community organizer.

Barack Obama was able to use his story to help create a strong personal brand. He has an international perspective, thanks to his unusual upbringing. He was born into relatively little money and worked hard for everything he earned. With only a mother to raise him in his childhood home, he can relate to the plight of single parents and the challenges that they face. All of those factors contribute to the unique and powerful story that helped Barack Obama become the first black president in the history of the United States.

Even if Barack Obama had never become president, his story remains a very authentic and honest one that forms the foundation of a powerful personal brand.

BUT WHAT ABOUT ME?

So you didn't come from nothing to become president?

You aren't a rocket scientist?

And you don't write fantastic hit songs about breaking free from the shackles of a small decaying New Jersey town or sing-along songs about living on a Caribbean beach and searching for your lost shaker of salt?

You still have a story to tell.

It Doesn't Need to Be Complicated

Maybe your story is something simple, like the way you dress.

Gary is a fifty-nine-year-old developer in suburban New York. Gary doesn't build houses; he creates entire communities of multimillion-dollar mansions. He is responsible for hundreds of high-end luxury homes all over New York, New Jersey, and Connecticut. Every day, Gary does million-dollar deals with clients, suppliers, and real estate agents. From April to October, you won't find Gary wearing shoes; only sandals will do. And they match up with his shorts and T-shirt. When the temperatures turn cooler in the fall, Gary trades shorts and sandals for jeans and casual shoes. Even when sitting down to negotiate major deals in oak-paneled boardrooms, Gary doesn't give in. He never wears a suit. It's always jeans and a T-shirt.

Early in his career, Gary was concerned that his casual look would hold him back, until a particular business deal convinced him that his anti-suit reputation was a potential gold mine. "I was bidding on a major deal with an older guy who was ex-military," Gary explains. "This guy had a reputation for being fanatical about well-polished shoes, suits, and ties. And I was actually thinking that maybe I would need to break my vow to never wear a suit and tie in order to get the job done. That was until I called his secretary to set up a meeting. She had an indifferent tone in her voice when I called, but as soon as I said my name, she said 'Now, you're not going to show up here in shorts and a Hawaiian shirt, are you?' That's when I knew I was onto something. Here was a guy with dozens of meetings every day with guys just like me, but he knew who I was before I even walked in the door."

By refusing to comply with the expected norm, Gary established a reputation. Even people who didn't know Gary knew *of* Gary. "There were probably many times along the way when my nonconformity may have cost me money and opportunity, but the long-term benefit of just being known for something far outweighs any negative," says Gary.

A Guide To Finding Your Story

Keep it real. Your personal story begins with your personal reality. Sure, you can create a mythical fable about your greatness, but it is certain to be discovered. And even if your lie is never revealed, people will always spot a fake. Bruce Springsteen really did grow up that way, as did Jimmy Buffett. Is there something in your upbringing or your geographic background that is unique to you? Is there something in there that influences your view of the world?

Make it personal. After all, this is your personal story. It should contain elements that are personally revealing. Jimmy Buffett really was a busker in Key West, and for a period of time he actually lived on a boat tied to a dock. Much of his story and his music can be reflected in that one simple but personal fact. If Jimmy were afraid to reveal personal details, his story would not carry the power that it does. Your personal story should always be the real you.

Accept the consequences. Sometimes personal stories are uncomfortable and come with negative consequences. Springsteen avoided the Vietnam draft on medical grounds that even he admits were marginal. He isn't afraid to tell that story, even though it may alienate him from some people who find those actions offensive. In a less dramatic way, our contractor from New York, Gary, was willing to walk away from business because he refused to wear a suit and tie. Both were able to accept that telling a compelling personal story comes with consequences, and they aren't always immediately positive.

Make it compelling. There's no question that Mark Fox's story of being the youngest chief engineer in the history of NASA's space shuttle program is compelling. Certainly one of the things that makes his story compelling is our collective fascination with the space program, but there is another reason it is compelling: Mark's story is unexpected. Unexpected stories are more interesting. You don't expect a left-brain rocket scientist from NASA to be teaching your company about right-brain creative problem solving. That's compelling because it is unexpected.

Embed it in everything you do. You need to be consistent in order for your story to resonate with people. The fact that Jimmy Buffett really does captain a yacht, pilot a plane, and search the world for surfing hotspots are all consistent with his story. His business ventures are nearly all based on his story, including Margaritaville restaurants, stores, casinos, and hotels, as well as Landshark Lager and his Margaritaville drink mix. The story is reflected in every aspect of his life.

Shut up! Spend more time listening to other people share their stories than you do telling your own. The world's greatest storytellers are often among the world's greatest listeners, because they want to understand those around them so that their stories can better relate and connect with people.

The Rock Star Playlist: Five Quintessential Storytelling Songs

1. **"Coward of the County" by Kenny Rogers.** "Coward of the County" is about a young man dealing with his father's advice to always turn the other cheek. He is bullied repeatedly until he proves his father wrong, resorting to violence to solve his problems. The story was compelling enough to inspire a movie that starred Rogers in the lead role.

2. **"Well Respected Man" by The Kinks.** The Kinks had a unique knack for telling simple yet powerful stories in their songs. "Well Respected Man" does exactly that, sharing the story of a simple man who is doing everything in the most conservative manner. After visiting a luxury resort, Ray Davies wrote the song as a commentary on how the rich view the honest and hardworking middle class.

3. **"Alice's Restaurant" by Arlo Guthrie.** This story/song runs over sixteen minutes long, but it is worth every second. It chronicles the garbage-disposing antics of a group of hippies in New England who find themselves in trouble with the law over Thanksgiving, and how that encounter with the police leads to Arlo being rejected from the Vietnam draft.

4. **"Cat's in the Cradle" by Harry Chapin.** It is impossible for any father to listen to this song and not take an inner vow to be a better parent. The song is the story of a boy who idolizes his absentee father and sadly grows up to be just like him. As a father, I dare you to listen carefully to the words and not well up.

5. **"Stan" by Eminem.** Featuring the haunting vocals of Dido, "Stan" is the tale of an obsessed fan who cannot understand why his favorite singer won't reply to his letters. In the end, the lengths that Stan goes to get Eminem's attention are disturbing.

▼

CHAPTER THREE

WORK YOUR ASS OFF: THERE IS NO SHORTCUT TO SUCCESS

He didn't stumble into his nickname. He earned it, night after night, city after city, and show after show. He sweated, he danced, he sang, he grooved, and he rocked. He gave his fans everything he had and made it his personal mission to make sure that every fan left happy. He worked his ass off. That's how James Brown became known as "the hardest-working man in show business."

James Brown brought more than a concert to town; he brought a show. His band was notoriously big, often with several people playing each instrument. When James Brown showed up, he brought upwards of forty people with him. He didn't bring that many people because he liked their company; he brought forty people in his revue because that's what he felt it took to create an extravaganza that fans would remember for the rest of their lives.

His fans were black and white, rich and poor. They were drawn to his music for its intensity and passion, for its groove and funk. When Martin Luther King Jr. was assassinated in 1965, it was James Brown who received credit for helping to diffuse racial tensions in Boston by playing for his fans and bringing people together as one.

Maybe it was appropriate that it was James Brown's heart that gave out, because without question he had played his heart out countless times in cities all around the world with shows lasting several hours and highlighted by numerous costume changes, performance skits, jumps, splits, acrobatics, and, of course, the music. He toured relentlessly, playing over three hundred nights in a single year. James gave everything to his fans night after night because, as he said, "that's what they came for."

At nearly every show, James would perform a cape routine that involved singing himself to exhaustion, to the point where the show's MC would come out on stage, drape a cape around the singer, and help him off the stage. His band would continue playing, and the background singers would continue singing. Every night, the fans would call for James's return, and every night, just before he left the stage under that massive cape, he would throw the cape away and turn back to the microphone to perform one more encore. Theatrical? Absolutely, but amazingly honest at the very same time.

He had a tumultuous personal life, frequently running into trouble with the law from his teenage years until he died. There were high-speed chases, assaults, and weapons charges that put Brown behind bars more than a few times. For the last thirty years of his life he battled drug addiction, spending time in rehab as he attempted to clean up. And by all accounts he was not a great husband—arrested numerous times for domestic violence. He fathered at least twelve children, nine from his three marriages and three others outside of wedlock. There are plenty of aspects of James Brown's character that you don't want to emulate.

But you can't deny the man's work ethic. Even as he aged and battled diabetes and prostate cancer, he kept up his rigorous touring schedule. In 2004, while fighting cancer, he played major festivals like Bonnaroo and Glastonbury and toured Europe and South America. His fans were never let down, no matter what kind of physical pain James Brown was going through. He worked like an athlete, playing through the pain, because that's simply what he did. Until the day he died, James Brown was the hardest-working man in show business. He rocked night after night, because that's the only way he knew. He was working his ass off almost right up until the day he died. One of his final shows, an Irish concert in fall of 2006, saw him play in front of eighty thousand people. He died a few months later, on Christmas Day.

The relationship between hard work and success isn't up for debate. While there are people who work hard and fail, your odds of being successful in your chosen field go up in proportion to your work ethic. The harder you work at something, the more likely you are to be successful at it—no question. What is debatable is how much of a role natural, God-given talent plays in that success. Can a hardworking person with little talent compete with a naturally gifted, lazy person?

In his fantastic 2008 book *Outliers* (Back Bay Books, 2011), Malcolm Gladwell suggested that time spent working a chosen craft was the essential key to mastering nearly anything. He didn't discount the role of natural talent and aptitude, but Gladwell put forth the intriguing idea that almost any person can master almost any challenge by putting in ten thousand hours of hard work. Gladwell came up with some excellent examples, including the Beatles. Many people consider the Beatles an overnight success, rising from obscurity to world fame in just a few years. What is often forgotten is that the Beatles played the bars of Hamburg, Germany, relentlessly from 1960 to 1963, playing over 1,200 backbreaking shows, often playing two eight-hour shows in a single day! As a result, the band played for more than ten thousand hours together before ever trying to conquer America.

Bill Gates was exposed to a computer in 1968, when he was just thirteen. While very few other children his age had the chance to do it, Bill Gates spent his teen years programming computers, logging well over ten thousand hours before most people had ever touched a hard drive.

I can relate on a personal level. I became obsessed with the radio as a teenager. Just like plenty of other kids growing up in the 1970s and '80s, I was fascinated and captivated by the voices and music coming out of the speakers and the incredible ability of audio to set the mood of a room. The difference is that I lucked into a job at an actual radio station when I was just thirteen years old. Throughout high school, every evening and weekend, I was at the radio station, either working or just hanging around. By the time my friends and I were graduating and deciding what to do with our lives, I had already logged my ten thousand hours in a radio station. My career in media, marketing, writing, speaking, and communication is a natural by-product of where I spent my ten thousand hours.

Film producer Samuel Goldwyn understood that hard work in and of itself wouldn't lead to success. He was famously quoted as saying, "The harder I work, the luckier I get." He's right. Hard work didn't lead to overnight success. Hard work gave Goldwyn more experience, and more experience led to more connections and opportunities, which in turn led to more breaks. Those experiences also led to more trial-and-error situations in which hard lessons were learned, saving him from future mistakes that other, less hardworking people would make. They also led to Goldwyn's exposure to other people's ideas and concepts, which over the long run led to more unique ideas and concepts. The harder you work, the more opportunity you create for yourself, the more connections you make, and the more exposure you will have to game-changing people and ideas. In essence, you create your luck (or what other people see as luck) by working your ass off.

So is hard work really the key? Can anyone, with ten thousand hours of experience, do almost anything at an elite level? Of course not. Talent matters. We are all born with certain skills and attributes. We have different aptitudes and IQs. Throughout life, all of us are exposed to different factors that influence how we perceive the world around us and how we react to it. Because none of us are exactly alike, we all do certain things better or worse than others.

In a 2011 article in *Psychology Today*, "Hard Work Beats Talent (But Only If Talent Doesn't Work Hard)," Piers Steel, a PhD in industrial organizational psychology, noted that while hard work will beat raw talent, the killer combination of hardworking talent always wins. In other words, not every band that spends ten thousand hours playing in a bar in Hamburg will become the best-selling rock band in history. Not every child who spends ten thousand hours playing video games will become the richest software developer in the world. And frankly, any teenager who spends ten thousand hours hanging around a radio station is probably fortunate to emerge sane and sober, let alone successful! The hard work and time are absolutely essential, but having natural talent is important, too.

Steel examined the relationship between cognitive skill (talent) and pure effort (hard work), and the evidence was overwhelming. Even if you were born without genius in your genes, you can outperform the smartest person if you work hard, but only under one condition: if you work hard . . . *and they do not*. But the moment the person with higher cognitive skill puts in equal effort, the game changes. Natural skill, talent, intelligence, and aptitude, combined with hard work, results in the ultimate killer combination.

For the benefit of those of us who were not blessed with abnormally high IQ scores, there is still some good news. According to Steel, hard work can create a much more even playing field between those with natural talent and those with more modest abilities. With enough effort, even the lesser skilled can be pretty damn good and compete well with the hardworking, skilled people!

BEING FUNNY IS HARD WORK

We think of someone like Jerry Seinfeld as being gifted with natural talent, and there's no doubt that he is. But one of the hallmarks of Seinfeld is his incomparable work ethic. He sat down with a reporter for the *New York Times* in December 2012 and talked about the glacial way that he writes a single joke. He chronicled a particular joke about marriage that he loved doing, but it seemed to lose his audience a tiny bit when he told it. The joke subtly evolved over three years, with Jerry changing the pacing, choice of words, and body language ever so slightly until one night, he hit on the exact body motion to match the punch line, and suddenly the joke came together. "If it takes me three years, I'll wait," he told the *Times*. "If I love the joke, I'll wait."

Seinfeld's work ethic is legendary. When he first scored a spot on *The Tonight Show with Johnny Carson* in 1981, he practiced his five-minute routine more than two hundred times before going on the show. Today, despite a net worth estimated by Forbes at $800 million, he continues to tour endlessly, playing venues in cities large and small. "If I don't do a set in two weeks," he said, "I feel it."

Jerry Seinfeld is a perfect combination of hard work and natural talent, but there is no question that his work ethic has enhanced his gift for humor and refined his ability to use it effectively. Like Samuel Goldwyn, Seinfeld's hard work has resulted in good luck.

Thomas Edison famously downplayed the role of intelligence. "Genius," said Edison, "is 99 percent perspiration." While 99 percent is clearly hyperbole, he's not wrong about the vital role of hard work, sweat, and effort. If you are determined enough and willing to put in the time to perfect your craft, you can be great. You may never be as great as an equally motivated hard worker with a natural talent, but you'll be in the game; you'll compete. And with a few well-earned lucky bounces, you might just win.

Besides James Brown, who are the hardest-working bands in rock 'n' roll?

The Grateful Dead broke up following Jerry Garcia's death in 1995. But between 1965 and their final show, the band played 2,333 concerts. That's an average of nearly eighty shows a year. They never took a full year off and in some years played relentlessly. Without a doubt, the Grateful Dead rank among rock's hardest workers.

Bruce Springsteen has taken a few years off now and then, but when he hits the road he does so like nobody else. While most rock concerts last between ninety minutes and two hours, Springsteen concerts routinely run past three hours. I've been at some that nearly hit the four-hour mark! On

July 30, 2012, Bruce set an all-time record in Helsinki, Finland. His show there lasted four hours and six minutes. The band cranked out thirty-three songs that night, including five that had not been previously played on the "Wrecking Ball" world tour. That's pretty impressive, especially for a sixty-two-year-old musician who long ago paid his dues and earned the right to take a night off now and then.

In terms of number of years playing together, the Rolling Stones deserve a little credit. They've been together since the early 1960s and recently celebrated their fiftieth anniversary as a band with a major concert tour. During those fifty years together they've embarked on some pretty amazing tours, working their asses off on the road playing stadiums all around the world. But at the same time, they've also had lengthy periods of downtime where they didn't play at all together. Their "A Bigger Bang" tour from late 2005 to late 2007 remains their largest, comprising 147 shows and bringing in over $558 million in ticket sales.

If you equate hard work with the bottom line results, you've got to consider U2. The all-time record for the most profitable tour ever is held by their "360" tour, which ran from June 2009 through July 2011. With 110 concerts, the band sold over $736 million in tickets. The tour would have wrapped up much sooner, but the band was forced to take a one-year hiatus when Bono needed back surgery partway through the tour.

A more recent example of the sheer power of hard work is the unexpected success of Mumford & Sons, the quirky British folk-rock group that first hit the charts in 2010 with

"Little Lion Man." They have since gone on to win Grammy Awards, sell millions of albums, and quickly establish themselves as one of today's great new bands. Much of that success can be traced back to hard work. After first forming in 2007, the band made playing live as often as possible their top priority. They played anywhere and everywhere. In those first three years before breaking into the mainstream, they toured the US ten separate times, often bypassing the biggest cities and playing smaller secondary markets and college towns. In those smaller cities they were more likely to make a splash, not competing for attention with bigger acts playing on the same night. Mumford & Sons found fans wherever they went, winning them over one song at a time. While it takes work ethic to play dingy clubs in Hamburg night after night like the Beatles did, it also takes a similar commitment to play thirty concerts in sixty days—playing every second night as Mumford & Sons did—on a tour that stretched from Perth, Australia, to Dublin, Ireland. With that much geography and that many time zones to traverse, the task of entertaining fans for hours every night becomes even more challenging.

Being hardworking today, for a rock band as well as the rest of us, extends beyond the traditional definitions and into the digital realm. For Mumford & Sons, hard work happens behind the scenes, attending to social media, responding to fans, and immersing themselves in the nuts and bolts of their career. In an interview in *The Guardian* in 2012, Tom Lamont observed the band backstage. Bassist Ted Dwane had claimed the dressing room bathroom, where he was recreating a darkroom to develop photographs. Vocalist and multi-instrumentalist Ben Lovett was connected into the Wi-Fi, replying to email and tending to the business of his London-based record label Communion Records. Even though they weren't performing, the band was hard at work.

Hard work is vital. There are rare overnight success stories, but most of them disappear as quickly as they appeared. They are short-lived, one-hit wonders. There really is no shortcut to long-term success. What rock stars have done that we can all learn from is to find that magical sweet spot where hard work meets natural talent. When you work incredibly hard at something that you have a natural aptitude for, you can rise to be among the elite at your chosen craft.

The Rock Star Playlist: Rock's Hardest-Working Bands

1. **"I Got You (I Feel Good)" by James Brown.** They didn't call him the hardest-working man in show business for nothing. He worked his ass off for his fans every night up. His offstage turmoil was overshadowed by his reputation as an incredible entertainer.

2. **"Badlands" by Bruce Springsteen.** The man famous for playing for hours at a time often makes this song a highlight of his show. As the chorus builds, the fans are engulfed in bright white lights that pulsate to the beat as they fist-pump to the song's driving chorus.

3. **"Iko Iko" by The Grateful Dead.** Playing over 2,300 shows in thirty years is a pretty amazing accomplishment. The band hardly took any time off between forming in 1965 and calling it quits when Jerry Garcia died in 1995. Add to the total the countless post-Garcia incarnations of Furthur and The Dead, and that number grows even higher.

4. **"40" by U2.** When the band played the final show of their massive "360" Tour in the eastern Canadian city of Moncton, they surprised fans with several unusual songs. They played "Out of Control" and "I Will Follow," two songs from the *Boy* album that are seldom played live. Another live rarity in recent years, "40" wrapped up the night as the final song on the band's record-setting tour.

5. **"You Can't Always Get What You Want" by The Rolling Stones.** During one of the early dates on their fiftieth anniversary tour, The Stones played a moving version of this song with the help of the Trinity Wall Street Choir from New York City.

▼

CHAPTER FOUR

RUNNING WITH THE DEVIL (IN THE DETAILS): HOW VAN HALEN TURNED CANDY INTO CASH

Van Halen was famous for plenty of things in their career, including Eddie's one-of-a-kind tapping guitar solos, Alex's throbbing double-bass kick drum, their inability to retain a lead singer, and David Lee Roth's flamboyance and flexibility. But one of the most famous Van Halen stories isn't about the guys in the band or the great music they made. It is about their rider.

In concert terminology, the rider is the part of the contract that stipulates what the band needs for their performance and who will provide it. It usually contains a wealth of information that varies from the vital—such as specific equipment requirements and band member food allergies—to the trivial—such as the preferred brand of vodka that the drummer demands. Van Halen was known for featuring one of the most seemingly trivial rider clauses in rock music history. It was a simple clause that stated that no brown M&M candies were to be found in the backstage area.

Thanks to that clause, personnel had to be hired by each concert promoter to separate the various colors of M&M candies to make sure that no brown ones ended up in the backstage candy bowls. The task needed to be performed with surgical gloves and surgical precision, because if even a single brown M&M was discovered backstage, the consequences were dire. Not only would lead singer David Lee Roth throw a temper tantrum and trash the dressing room, but the band also had the option of not playing the concert and billing the promoter the full cost of the show. A promoter could potentially lose millions of dollars for not diligently removing every last brown M&M.

For decades the M&M clause, and the trashed dressing rooms that resulted, came to symbolize the self-absorbed nature of the band and of rock 'n' roll in general. What kind of petulant baby would trash a dressing room because of a stupid brown M&M candy?

It turns out that David Lee Roth and Van Halen, while they may have been petulant babies, weren't biased against brown M&M candies. They didn't have an allergy to brown food coloring. In fact, they really didn't care one way or another about brown M&M candies. Instead, the brown M&Ms were simply a tool the band used to test the promoter's diligence.

In the late 1970s, Van Halen was one of the first rock bands to bring massive stage and lighting rigging into aging arenas and stadiums. Quite often the buildings were not able to handle the weight of the gear, and changes needed to be made to accommodate the equipment and ensure the safety of both the band and their thousands of fans. If the equipment wasn't properly installed and accounted for, the results could be catastrophic and expensive. In one case, the weight of the band's gear on stage crushed a soft basketball court to the tune of hundreds of thousands of dollars. It turns out that the promoter didn't account for the weight of the band's sound gear. He didn't read the rider and realize that he would need a reinforced floor.

So Van Halen added the clause that demanded no brown M&M candies were to be found backstage. When the guys would arrive at a new venue, the first thing they would do is head to the candy bowl and look for brown M&Ms. If they found one, it was a signal that the promoter hadn't completely read the rider, and the crew immediately began an inspection of everything. The brown M&Ms served as a canary in a coalmine for Van Halen. If there were brown M&Ms, something wasn't right. David Lee Roth's penchant for destroying dressing rooms when he found the annoying brown candies was simply a hobby. He claims he trashed them just for fun, to send a message to the promoter.

The behavior sent a message to more people than just the concert promoter. Fans got word of the M&M clause and Roth's temperamental backstage antics, and the legend surrounding Van Halen grew exponentially. Knowing that the M&M clause and the backstage dressing room destruction was making the band look bad, why didn't they just clear things up and issue a public statement revealing the truth? Because, as David Lee Roth says, "Who am I to deny a good rumor?" Roth knew that Van Halen's bad-boy image would only be enhanced by backstage antics and ridiculous demands, so the band left the rumor alone and only bothered to clear up the confusion decades later.

The M&M clause was a smart move on two counts. First, it was a great PR tool for the band. It enhanced their reputation and helped to build their brand. Second, it provided them with a system of checks and balances to make sure that their own safety and the safety of their fans wasn't compromised by promoters taking shortcuts to save money. It was a brilliant way to gauge the promoter's ability to get all of the tiny details just right. Those tiny details, while they may seem like nothing at all, could have been life-and-death details for Van Halen, and they needed to know they were looked after.

THE LITTLE DETAILS ARE EVERYTHING

In building your personal brand and growing your career, do you pay enough attention to the tiny details? The little things may appear trivial, but it is important to remember that impressions and reputations are cumulative. How we perceive people really comes down to hundreds of tiny details that add up to one overall perception.

I know of HR managers who will discard an otherwise excellent résumé because of a single spelling mistake. That's all it might take to disqualify you from your dream job, a job that you may actually be brilliant at. But there are HR managers who see a single spelling mistake as a brown M&M: a signal that something isn't right about you. They have a point, don't they? If your résumé has even a single spelling mistake on it, they can safely assume that you can't spell, you can't use spell check, or you didn't bother to have someone proofread your work. What does that say about you as a potential employee?

Another tiny detail that is often overlooked in the development of your personal brand is your social media presence. While not all bosses will admit it, there is hardly an executive today who doesn't use social media to examine potential hires. By simply keying your name into Google, a potential (or current) employer can instantly learn a tremendous amount about you. He or she can read your tweets, look at your Facebook timeline, and see where you've checked in on Foursquare. If your social media presence is immature, profane, or controversial, you could be putting your future at risk. An early mentor in my career, broadcasting executive Bob Templeton, once told me to never put anything online that I wouldn't want to see plastered across the front page of the *New York Times* the next day. Bob was referring to email, long before social media came along. Today's instant connectivity and frequent sharing make the issues much more pressing. The rule is, if you say it online, don't expect an ounce of confidentiality, and don't be surprised when it comes back to haunt you.

Some people look at social media as something to be cleaned up and refined in order to not damage your personal brand, but that's the wrong way to look at it. Rather than cleaning up your social media presence, rebuild it from the ground up. Your social media presence should be built strategically in order to reflect who you are and what you stand for. As you create your Facebook profile, Twitter feed, and LinkedIn account, think carefully about what each post and tweet says about you and your brand. You should be using each social media platform with purpose and poise, reflecting your personal brand at all times. If you have something angry to say, fight the urge to immediately blast your social media channels with it! Take a deep breath and wait a few hours. Consider the potential impact on your career before you hit "post."

Even your email address should be carefully examined. When an HR executive receives an application for a position from an email address that is silly or offensive, they are very likely to hit "delete" and send your resume to the trash bin without even reading it. If you have a silly-named email account, don't use it for professional communication. Use it between friends, but create a new professional-looking email account, ideally your name or a variation on it, that leaves a positive impression. If you're really serious, reserve your name as a URL and create an email like yourname@yourname.com.

GARY CRUSHES PERSONAL BRANDING

Author and businessman Gary Vaynerchuk has built up a brilliant personal brand online, and that brand has helped to propel his books *Crush It* and *The Thank You Economy* to bestseller status. Gary's brand is really the culmination of a whole bunch of little things, all delivered with consistency. If you watch Gary's videos, read his blog, or see him speak at conferences, you'll see someone who is deeply personal in how he communicates. He isn't afraid to tell you about his life story, often in very personal terms. He swears a lot, and he never wears a suit. He talks about his desire to buy the New York Jets one day, and he wears his passion for the team proudly. When Gary speaks onstage he doesn't use cue cards or PowerPoint, and when he speaks on camera he speaks from the heart and not from a teleprompter. Gary's initial area of expertise was wine, but he has parlayed the success of his online wine store, Wine Library, into a career in social media and brand management.

Like every brand, Gary's personal brand is the culmination of a wealth of little details that all fit together, like pieces of a puzzle, to create a perception. In Gary's case, the puzzle pieces include irreverence and attitude. His New Jersey swagger and come-from-nothing work ethic permeates everything he does. Not only can he get away with a few F-bombs, people expect that sort of thing from him. Dropping a loud "fuck" in a room full of suits is a Gary Vaynerchuk specialty. But if you try the same thing at your next corporate retreat, don't expect the same result! Unless you have or are building a personal brand driven by that kind of attitude and language, it probably won't work for you quite as well as it does for Gary. All of the little details in Gary Vaynerchuk's brand have given him the ability to do what he does. The little details, the puzzle pieces, all fit together.

A TALE OF TWO TWANGS

For a musical comparison, consider two country singers: Willie Nelson and Taylor Swift. Both are strong brands, and for both of these artists, all of the little puzzle pieces fit together to create two cohesive images. Willie is the aging outlaw country singer who never really fit in. He was always a bit too edgy for the country purists, and he didn't go the conservative "God, Mom, and apple pie" route that many country singers opt for. Yet Willie was always too country to be a rock star. He wore his country badge proudly and never watered down his twang. Along with contemporaries like Waylon Jennings, Kris Kristofferson, and Johnny Cash, Willie Nelson was a different kind of country singer. He was rebel country.

Meanwhile, Taylor Swift has cultivated a different brand. She's a youthful and wholesome country singer who does things her own way. She doesn't have people write songs for her, as many country singers do. Taylor writes her own songs, and she writes them about her personal experiences. She has joked that it is hard for her to find a date, because men all fear that they'll eventually end up as the topic of one of her songs when the relationship ends. And they're right! Taylor writes very personal songs about very personal experiences. She projects a clean-cut, honest, and family-friendly image to her massive legions of mostly young fans.

Let's imagine that one of them gets arrested for marijuana possession. Actually, we don't have to imagine it! Willie Nelson has been arrested with pot, many times. When Willie gets busted for possession, it is a mere footnote in the news; nobody really notices. People have come to expect Willie Nelson to get arrested for pot, because he makes no secret that he uses it—a lot! He's written songs about it. His biography is even called *Roll Me up and Smoke Me When I Die*. He has recorded music with Snoop Dogg, another notorious pot fan. And Toby Keith recorded a parody song called "I'll Never Smoke Weed with Willy Again." Marijuana is a key little piece in the puzzle that is the Willie Nelson brand.

If Taylor Swift got arrested for marijuana possession, it would be big news. The Taylor Swift pot scandal would be on the front page of the paper, all over the show business gossip websites, and the talk of the music business. Analysts would examine how it might impact her career and how it might alienate her young female fan base. They would instantly compare her to other good-girls-gone-bad like Lindsay Lohan and Miley Cyrus. There's no doubt that a Taylor Swift pot bust would create major buzz, because that puzzle piece doesn't fit with her image. When the pieces don't fit, everyone notices . . . and not in a good way.

The little details matter. The puzzle pieces have to fit together. Examine all of your little details like your social media trail, your email address, and the spelling on your résumé. Are there brown M&M's in there waiting to be discovered by those judging you for opportunities and jobs? Get rid of them.

The Rock Star Playlist: My Five Personal Favorite Van Halen Songs

1. **"Panama."** "Panama" brings together all of the elements that made Van Halen great: pounding drums, screaming guitars, seriously sexual innuendo, and the requirement to crank up the volume as loud as it goes.

2. **"Dance the Night Away."** As their first Top 20 hit song, "Dance the Night Away" introduced Van Halen to a broader audience. Despite the song's commercial appeal, it doesn't shy away from typical Van Halen touches. I personally love the cowbell, bass line, and massive chorus.

3. **"Jump."** "Jump" showed a new side of Van Halen, as Eddie traded in the guitar for a keyboard. Although somewhat dated-sounding as we look back, at the time "Jump" combined '80s pop sounds with traditional Van Halen hard rock. To this day, it is a hard song to not turn up when it comes on the radio.

4. **"Eruption / You Really Got Me."** Although a slight cheat to combine two songs, most fans can't hear one without the other. "Eruption" showcased what Eddie could do on his own and then instantly gave way to the power and punch of the whole band covering the Kinks' "You Really Got Me."

5. **"Right Now."** Those who gave up on Van Halen when Sammy Hagar replaced David Lee Roth missed out on a fantastic song in "Right Now." Hagar himself believes that the song is his best lyrical work with the band, turning away from "cheap sex songs" and getting "serious and talking about world issues."

CHAPTER FIVE

NONE OF US KNOW WHAT WE'RE DOING: HOW U2 LEARNED EVERYTHING WHILE ON THE JOB

We know them today as one of rock's all-time greatest bands, a group that has withstood the changing times and fads since the late 1970s, surviving through disco, punk, new wave, hair bands, and grunge. They own the record for the most profitable tour of all time, have won twenty-two Grammy Awards, and continue to record, tour, and influence musicians worldwide. Beyond music, they are a political force and a voice of change. They are U2. With Bono's passionate vocals, Edge's jangling guitar, and the tight, pulsating rhythm of Larry Mullen Jr. and Adam Clayton, U2 appears to be a band of musicians who were born with a ridiculous amount of talent. But that's not the case at all. When the boys first started playing together, they . . . well . . . sort of sucked.

When fourteen-year-old drummer Larry Mullen Jr. put a notice on the school bulletin board that he was looking for musicians to form a band, it was 1976, and the big musical style of the day in Ireland was punk rock. The punk sound had captivated frustrated young people all over the UK and was spreading around the world. Punk bands like the Sex Pistols and the Clash were loud and angry. Musical skill seemed very secondary. So when Bono, Edge, and Adam responded to the ad, they weren't all that concerned about having any significant musical talent. If their punk rock heroes didn't seem to exude any obvious proficiency at their instruments, why should they?

It turned out that even the seemingly simple punk songs were harder to replicate than they thought. U2, or Feedback as they initially called their band, wasn't good enough to do other bands' songs. So they wisely came to the conclusion that in order to be a band, they would have to write their own songs, easier ones that they could perform.

Just two years after first jamming together in Larry Mullen's kitchen, U2 won a talent contest. Aside from the much-needed £500 cash, one of the prizes was recording studio time and a guarantee that their demo would be heard by CBS Records. CBS liked what they heard enough to release the band's first songs to the Irish public in 1979. It would only be another year or two before the band started to grow beyond Ireland, eventually becoming one of the most successful rock bands on the planet. It is hard to imagine any band starting from less and achieving so much.

Nearly all of us are just like U2 in their early days: we don't really know what we're doing! We have a clue for sure, and we want to succeed, but we are full of self-doubt. We are convinced that other people know much more than we do. It becomes our mission to prevent people from catching on to our dirty little secret . . . that we really don't know what the hell we are doing.

Certainly most of us know what we are doing for the most part, *most of the time*. But nobody, even the most seasoned expert, has all of the answers all of the time. What separates rock stars is their ability to learn on the job, ask the right questions, seek out direction, and, to a degree, "fake it until they make it," because they intrinsically know that they will make it, and make it big.

U2 decided to be a band. They were undoubtedly unqualified, and learned quickly that they lacked the skill needed to be a band. So they learned on the job. They didn't decide *not* to be a band because they lacked skill. Instead, they acquired skill as they went. They rehearsed hard. They played gigs for free at high schools and churches, and they immersed themselves irrevocably into their craft. With so much practice and hard work, U2 gradually got much, much better. When they won that talent contest and got their music in front of CBS, the ball was rolling for U2. But it only started rolling because they committed to improvement and never stopped improving. Giving up because they were unqualified would have been the easy way out. Deciding to not be a band until they were world-class musicians would also have failed miserably. Becoming qualified while already on the job was hard but came with a much bigger payoff.

LEARNING NEVER ENDS

Learning doesn't stop after you get hired. Any successful person in any career field will tell you that they are lifelong learners and perpetual students. For U2, learning was, and remains, a continual process. After the success of their debut album, *Boy,* and the world tour that followed, expectations were high for the band's second album. That album, *October*, came out in 1981, but the expected momentum wasn't there. *October* didn't sell nearly as many copies as the band and their record label anticipated.

U2 recorded *October* under tremendous pressure from their record company, hoping to capitalize on the popularity of the first album. Recording the dreaded sophomore album is always a tough act for any band, but adding to the challenge was a lack of songs to record. They already had studio time booked when a briefcase containing lyrics to many completed songs was stolen backstage while the band played a concert in Portland, Oregon. That meant that they went into the studio without any finished songs. Bono had to re-create and sometimes improvise lyrics to many of the songs as the clock ticked away on expensive studio time. Another wrinkle in the recording of *October* was that both Bono and The Edge had become more involved in the church around the time of the album's recording, leaving it with an underlying theme of faith, religion, and spirituality. The overtly Christian themes didn't resonate with mass audiences the way the teen angst themes on the debut album did.

The lack of success that greeted *October* led U2 to once again focus on learning and improving. Giving up was never an option. Their songwriting skills improved. Their focus was narrowed. Their live show got even tighter. The band was determined to make the follow-up album, *War*, a massive success. The album was more political and rugged and less obviously spiritual. Songs from *War* connected with fans in a big way, and songs from that album, like "Sunday Bloody Sunday" and "New Year's Day" continue to be vital elements of the U2 collection.

They had to learn on the job once again when creating their breakthrough album *The Unforgettable Fire*. They learned how to layer and texture their sound, creating the foundation for their massive album *The Joshua Tree* a few years later. After that album established them as the biggest band of the '80s, they spent time educating themselves about the history of rock 'n' roll in America and created *Rattle and Hum*, an album and movie that explored roots and blues music, collaborating with B. B. King and Bob Dylan. With every new album, the band was learning and growing while on the job.

Those on-the-job experiments and evolutions didn't always go well. In the 1990s, the band got carried away with electronic and industrial elements and started to alienate some longtime, core fans. After a few years of making less commercially successful music, U2 regrouped and decided to return to their roots. Bono was very vocal about the band's lack of focus and publicly declared that U2 needed to change in order to "reapply for the job as best band in the world." They did reapply for that job, and by all accounts they landed the gig. Since that statement was made in 1999, U2 has gone on to record classic songs like "Beautiful Day," "Stuck in a Moment You Can't Get Out Of," and "Sometimes You Can't Make It on Your Own." They were inducted into the Rock and Roll Hall of Fame, and they completed the highest-grossing tour ever, the twenty-four-month-long "360" tour. The band was also an early promoter of the now-ubiquitous iPod, licensing their song "Vertigo" for Apple commercials and partnering with the company to release a special iTunes boxed set of the band's music.

Learning on the job was a hallmark of U2 from their very first jam session.

LEARNING FROM A VIRGIN

Richard Branson didn't know everything about publishing when he started his first business, a magazine called *Student*, when he was sixteen years old. But he was passionate for the idea and did it anyway, learning what he needed to learn while on the job. By age twenty he was running a mail-order record business, and two years later he founded a chain of record stores and a record label called Virgin.

What education did Richard Branson have in the music business when he started out? None. Branson hardly had any education at all. He was dyslexic and found traditional school challenging. He left school at sixteen and started into business. Even the name of his company, Virgin, was chosen in part because it reflected the fact that he was entirely new to business and had little clue as to what he was doing. He learned a lot on the job in those early days of publishing and turned the profits he earned and the knowledge he gained from the record store into a record label. And so it went with Sir Richard Branson, a man who is now, according to a 2011 list in *Forbes* magazine, the fourth richest man in the UK. Not bad for having learned nearly everything while on the job!

GETTING THE KNOWLEDGE YOU NEED

In 2008, a twenty-five-year-old rising young product designer named Jake Fischer was hired by a manufacturing company to oversee product design at their Cincinnati, Ohio, plant. His resume certainly credited him with the experience required for the job, and Jake aced the one-on-one interviews with the confidence and composure of a veteran. Even Jake was convinced he had the knowledge and talent to do the job.

That balloon of self-confidence was pierced quickly the first week he was on the job. The company was planning to launch a new product, and Jake was put in charge of overseeing large-scale customer research and consumer analysis that would determine many of the defining characteristics of the end product. Jake had overseen research studies before, but nothing this massive—not even close. At first, he was overwhelmed with the scope of the challenge and considered asking his new supervisor to put someone else in charge of it.

Fortunately, Jake took a deep breath and decided to move forward in the same way that U2 and Richard Branson did. First, he learned absolutely everything he could about the project and his role in it. He met with key people, both above and below him in the corporate structure, and asked endless questions, some of them wise and some of them probably pretty basic. "I kept reminding myself that it didn't matter if some of my questions were stupid," said Jake. "My only goal was to completely understand the task ahead of me. People would eventually forget that I asked stupid questions, but they would never forget it if I completely blew the project."

Jake also stepped outside of his company and spoke to a trusted network of friends and advisers. Without breaking company confidence, he was able to learn more about how others handled similar projects in the past. Jake's biggest takeaway from those discussions wasn't a clear-cut path to success, but instead it was the knowledge that there was no clear-cut path to success. "The most important thing I learned from those conversations was that there was no single right way to do things. I learned that there are all kinds of different nuances and styles, and none of them are 100 percent right or 100 percent wrong."

Once Jake had acquired enough information, he established a core group of smart people that he could consult with along the way. Decisions were never made by committee, but they were also never made without consultation and discussion. When decisions were made, Jake was able to confidently make them with authority and conviction.

In the end, the project was a success, and Jake gained tremendous confidence, both within himself and within his company. He also created a model that he continues to employ to this day. "Even though I did those things out of necessity at first, I still do them. I still have those conversations, create those advisory teams, ask those basic questions, and consult with people who know more than I do."

The Rock Star Playlist: Five Classic Anti-Education Anthems

1. **"Another Brick in the Wall Part Two" by Pink Floyd.** There isn't a more famous anti-school song anywhere. Roger Waters wrote it as a protest song against the rigid confines of the British school system. Students worldwide have since adopted it as the de facto anti-school anthem.

2. **"School's Out" by Alice Cooper.** This classic rock song became the first hit single for Alice Cooper, and it continues to be a favorite of students. School isn't just out "for summer," sings Cooper, but it is out "forever." The song was revitalized in 2004 as a back-to-school commercial for Staples, in which Cooper appeared as himself.

3. **"High School Confidential" by Rough Trade.** Relatively unknown outside of Canada, this sexually charged hit tells the story of an attractive young female student who is having a sexual affair with her high school principal. This was one of the most sexually explicit songs to ever reach the Canadian charts.

4. **"Smokin' In The Boys' Room" by Brownsville Station (1973) and Mötley Crüe (1985).** This was the only Top 40 hit by Brownsville Station and the first Top 40 hit for Mötley Crüe. It is a simple anti-school anthem protesting a high school's smoking ban.

5. **"Teacher, Teacher" by .38 Special.** Instead of being anti-school or anti-learning, this rock song took a different approach, encouraging teachers to prepare students for real life beyond the high school doors. It was included in the 1984 movie *Teachers* starring Nick Nolte.

▼

CHAPTER SIX

FOCUS: THE CULT OF LITTLE STEVEN

Although he's never really caught on as a solo performer, there's a very good chance that you've heard, watched, or been influenced by the man known by various pseudonyms, including Miami Steve, Little Steven, and Steven Van Zandt.

He was born Steven Lento in Winthrop, just north of Boston, a seaside town you may have unknowingly seen outside the left-hand side of the plane as you approach runway 22L/R at Boston's Logan Airport. When he was just seven, his family moved to Middletown Township, New Jersey, another seaside town in the shadow of a major city.

He came of age along the Jersey Shore in the 1960s, deeply moved by the music that crackled through his AM radio from the big stations up in New York City. He fell in love with the raw rock 'n' roll of the British Invasion, the soulful emotions of the Stax and Motown sound, and the powerful chords emerging from basements and garages everywhere as young people plugged in guitars and turned up their amplifiers. He studied every band and analyzed every note, soaking up these great new sounds. Steven was part of the first generation to have its youth directly influenced by the dangerous new sound of rock 'n' roll.

Another Jersey boy growing up in the same place at the same time would forever impact Steven's career. When he first met Bruce Springsteen, the two connected instantly. Both loved the same music and shared a common dream to spend their lives playing it. As they grew up, their paths crossed often in rehearsal spaces, clubs, bars, and jam sessions. The early 1970s music scene in New Jersey was tightly connected, and even when they were in separate bands the two musicians jammed, wrote, and performed together regularly.

Steven officially joined Bruce Springsteen's E Street Band in 1975, when he helped Bruce create his epic breakthrough album *Born to Run*. For the next decade he would essentially be Bruce's right-hand man, playing lead guitar and singing background vocals on some of Springsteen's most popular material. He left the band in 1984, after recording *Born in the USA*, and embarked on a solo career, returning to join the E Street Band again in the mid-1990s when Bruce brought the original team together again. To this day, Steven Van Zandt remains a pillar in the E Street Band.

Despite having no acting experience whatsoever, in 1999 Steven was asked to audition for a role in the HBO series *The Sopranos*. Series creator David Chase had seen Van Zandt don a '60s costume and very humorously induct The Rascals into the Rock and Roll Hall of Fame in 1997. Right away, Chase felt that Van Zandt, even with no experience as an actor, would be perfect to play cool-but-deadly strip club owner Silvio Dante. He was right. Van Zandt nailed the role, and for six seasons he received tremendous acclaim for his work on the series.

His radio show, *Little Steven's Underground Garage*, is heard on more than two hundred radio stations in the US and many more around the world. The quirky weekly program profiles a wide breadth of garage band rock 'n' roll from the early 1960s through the modern day. He also supervises two channels for Sirius/XM satellite radio, the *Underground Garage* channel and the *Outlaw Country* channel.

As a musical entrepreneur, Steven oversees his own record label, Wicked Cool Records, which nurtures the careers of emerging garage rock bands. He has also been very active in helping to chronicle the history of rock 'n' roll and its impact on politics and history.

His personal impact on music and entertainment has been tremendous, yet a relatively small number of people are true fans of Little Steven. There are many far less influential artists who have far greater fan followings. Steven Van Zandt has created a dedicated tribe of followers that has allowed him to build a career doing what he loves to do. The tribe doesn't need to be massive. As long as the tribe is dedicated, Van Zandt can continue to uncompromisingly do what satisfies his soul.

There is a wonderful aspect to the "uncompromising" side of the equation. A certain level of job satisfaction comes from being able to make a living doing what you love to do, without having to compromise your values along the way. The vast majority of us have spent most of our lives compromising, trading in two days of freedom for five days of steady pay. The example set by Steven Van Zandt illustrates how you can use your personal brand to start to build a career with less compromise.

Three important factors have helped Van Zandt create the freedom to be uncompromising.

First, he is immensely talented. There is no question about his musical abilities. He is a world-class multi-instrumentalist. His ear for production in the studio is first-rate. Steve Van Zandt is exceptional at what he does. The good news is that you are probably exceptional at what you do as well.

Second, he is well connected in his field. Through years of hard work, Van Zandt has established a network of people who know him and what he is capable of. When Bruce Springsteen needed help arranging the horns on the *Born to Run* album, he knew exactly who to call.

Third, and most important, he is focused. Steven Van Zandt is singular. He is the raw garage rock guy from Jersey. That's why Sirius/XM tapped him to program their *Underground Garage* and *Outlaw Country* channels, but they didn't ask him to oversee their show tunes channel or the all-'90s alternative rock channel. It explains why HBO didn't ask him to play a shoe salesman on *Sex and the City*. They asked him to play a mobster, born and raised in Jersey, a real-life character that Steven probably saw plenty of in his younger years.

ONE THING

In their stellar 2012 book *The ONE Thing: The Surprisingly Simple Truth behind Extraordinary Results* (Bard Press, 2013), Gary Keller and Jay Papasan identify how focus on one singular thing drives the success of nearly every successful individual. Focusing on one thing, according to Keller and Papasan, forces you to eliminate other distractions from your life, distractions that mislead and derail you. One of the cool theories in the book is the suggestion that you should regularly ask yourself this one focusing question: "What's the one thing I can do such that by doing it everything else will be easier or unnecessary?"

That's precisely what Steven Van Zandt did in his career. By becoming the "garage rock guy," he has created a work life that makes doing everything else easier or unnecessary. He was able to easily transition into a side career as an actor in *The Sopranos* because of his very personal, funny, and engaging Rock and Roll Hall of Fame induction speech for The Rascals. His role hosting *Little Steven's Underground Garage* on radio stations worldwide was made infinitely easier because of his never-ending garage rock focus. Nobody else has the credibility to host such a show, and nobody could ever host it in the same personal way that Little Steven does. He has staked his claim as king of the garage rock mountain, and he will not be dethroned. Thanks to that status, all of the other things he does are easier, and many of them are ultimately unnecessary. The wealth Little Steven has accumulated (by being singularly focused!) makes it such that he doesn't need to do them . . . he does them because he wants to.

In the rock star world, all of this may seem simple. Little Steven plays with Bruce Springsteen's E Street Band; he has toured the globe and played on some of rock 'n' roll's greatest songs and albums. When you're that established, focusing on one thing is easy, because you no longer need to worry about putting food on the table and making next month's car payment. But the real world isn't so different from the rock star world! We only make it different because we believe that we need to in order to become successful. We believe we need to juggle things, multitask, and be all things to all people in our lives. That simply isn't the case, and coming to terms with this—and applying focus to your life—will be a key part of building your rock-star personal brand. Focus in your personal brand comes from successfully applying the Pareto principle.

APPLYING PARETO

Italian economist Vilfredo Pareto first put forth his theory in 1906, when he noticed that 80 percent of the land in his country was owned by 20 percent of the people. He studied other countries and soon discovered that this 80/20 phenomenon wasn't unique to Italy. The 80/20 principle confirmed Pareto's suspicion that the majority of every country's wealth belonged to a small minority of its citizens. The principle stands today, more than a century later. In today's world, the richest 20 percent of the population owns 82.7 percent of the world's wealth. Even among the extremely ungodly rich, the ratio is pretty close. For example, the three richest people in the world in 2013 (Carlos Slim Helú, Bill Gates, and Amancio Ortega), hold as much wealth as the next seven richest people in the world combined. Looking back at past years, the same ratio exists, no matter who is the richest person and how much net worth they have.

What's really scary is how well the Pareto principle holds up when you look beyond economics and apply it to our businesses, careers, and personal lives. You've probably heard before that 80 percent of your sales come from 20 percent of your customers. Most experts would agree that this is as close to a business universal as you'll find. But 80 percent of your complaints will also come from 20 percent of your customers. Eighty percent of your sales will be made by 20 percent of your sales staff. And the list goes on.

There is an extremely good chance that you wear 20 percent of the clothes in your closet, in various combinations, 80 percent of the time. Odds are high that 80 percent of the fun you have will be had with 20 percent of your closest friends. In a classroom, 80 percent of the discipline issues a teacher deals with will generally come from 20 percent of the students. Of the things that stress you out, 80 percent of your angst will be generated from 20 percent of your stress factors. And the list goes on.

How can you apply the Pareto principle and the lessons of Steven Van Zandt's garage band focus to your personal brand?

First, understand that 80 percent of your personal brand—your reputation—will by driven by 20 percent of what you actually do. Little Steven's musical interests span well beyond Springsteen songs and garage rock, but his reputation and personal brand is firmly rooted in his garage rock. That may only account for 20 percent of what he loves, but it generates 80 percent of what his personal brand does for him.

Your personal brand will be similar. By focusing on the 20 percent of your work that builds 80 percent of your reputation, you can begin to better grasp what needs to be eliminated, delegated, or outsourced in order for you to be even more successful. The more effort and focus that you place on the 20 percent will make your 80 percent more memorable and powerful.

In the workplace, that means carefully examining your daily routine. What are you doing on a regular basis that doesn't contribute to your long-term success? What kind of tasks can be delegated or eliminated in order to allow you more time to be insanely great at your 20 percent, the things you do that build your brand, increase your productivity, and make you happy?

Meetings can be shortened, based on the Pareto principle. You can get 80 percent of the vital information you need from attending 20 percent of the meeting. Since it would probably not go over well if you singularly choose to leave after 20 percent of each meeting, work with your colleagues to shorten meetings and focus on the important 20 percent. The less time you spend on the mostly irrelevant remainder, the better.

The road to better physical health goes through the Pareto principle, too. It is very likely that 20 percent of your physical activity generates 80 percent of your fitness results, and that 20 percent of the food you eat is responsible for 80 percent of your weight gain.

It is important to remember that the Pareto principle is just that: a principle, not a hard-and-fast rule. The math isn't always exact, but the principle applies almost universally: *The vast majority of your desired results are generated from a small minority of your actions.* The Pareto principle forces you to focus.

FOCUS BRINGS OPPORTUNITY

Heightened focus feeds your personal brand, opening up more opportunities for you. Little Steven became well known in New Jersey for his raw rock 'n' roll style, and he spent much of the early 1970s jamming with the eventual members of Bruce Springsteen's E Street Band. But Little Steven didn't officially join the E Street Band until 1975, three years after Bruce Springsteen's debut album. The story, according to Dave Marsh's Springsteen biography *Born to Run*, is that Bruce had hit a brick wall trying to perfect the horns in the song "Born To Run." He called his long-time friend Steven Van Zandt because of his incredible wealth of knowledge when it came to R&B and soul music. Van Zandt came to the rescue, not only helping arrange the horn section but also coming up with the signature guitar sound in the song. That guitar sound, according to Bruce, was one of Little Steven's greatest contributions to

Bruce's music. From that point until 1984, Little Steven was a rock-solid member of the E Street Band.

After leaving the E Street Band in 1984, Little Steven created a project that left a lasting legacy on the world. Although it wasn't the kind of massive success that songs like "We Are The World" and "Do They Know It's Christmas" were, Little Steven's political song "Sun City" is, in hindsight, credited with helping to end apartheid in South Africa. The song, recorded as the group Artists United Against Apartheid, brought together rockers like Springsteen, Tom Petty, Bob Dylan, Joey Ramone, Peter Gabriel, Jimmy Cliff, Bob Dylan, Run-DMC, Keith Richards, U2, Afrika Bambaataa, and many others. Their collaborative effort raised awareness about the racial segregation in South Africa and also served as a pledge by these artists to never play Sun City, a luxury casino resort about two hours outside of Johannesburg. Although it was only sporadically played on American radio stations, music critics applauded the song and its powerful message. It only peaked at #38 on the *Billboard Hot 100* chart, but it was a bigger hit in countries like the UK, Canada, and Australia, where it cracked the Top 10. In South Africa, however, the song was banned.

Ask anyone in the music industry, and they know what Little Steven stands for: garage rock, the soulful honesty of rock 'n' roll, and musical integrity.

In your field, can people do the same thing for you? When you ask those who know you, will they all answer with the same consistency and confidence when they talk about what you stand for?

The Rock Star Playlist:
Five Songs Little Steven Helped Create

1. **"Born to Run" by Bruce Springsteen.** When he couldn't find the perfect horn sound for his 1975 song, Bruce called upon his old friend and frequent collaborator, Little Steven. He called him because nobody knew how to make soulful rock 'n' roll like Steven. The result wasn't just a great horn part, but a legendary guitar sound and a lasting partnership that endures forty years later.

2. **"I Don't Wanna Go Home" by Southside Johnny and the Asbury Jukes.** Little Steven and Southside Johnny were partners in this famous Jersey Shore band that played with and influenced countless artists from the area. Their debut album in 1976 included this song that Little Steven wrote, which became one of their signature songs.

3. **"Bobby Jean" by Bruce Springsteen.** One of the final songs cut for the album *Born in the USA* appears to be a tribute to Little Steven, who was leaving the E Street Band at the time. The song was never released as a single, but it has become a cornerstone of Springsteen's live set and has been played live well over five hundred times since the "Born in the USA" tour.

4. **"I Am a Patriot" by Jackson Browne.** This song from 1983 remains a sort of underground American political classic. Many artists have performed their own versions of it, including the most well-known version by Jackson Browne. The song downplays political associations, instead pledging allegiance to country and family over any party or belief.

5. **"Sun City" by Artists United Against Apartheid.** Bucking the feel-good tone of group efforts like "We Are The World,"

continued on following page

Little Steven brought together diverse artists to record a biting and powerful song that called attention to the racial segregation in South Africa. The song was a turning point, helping to bring attention to and alter opinions toward South Africa and its apartheid system. In the years following the song's release, under internal and external pressure, the South African government began steps to reform the system. Apartheid officially ended in 1990, but the balance of power between blacks and whites did not change until the 1994 democratic elections.

▼

PART TWO:

PRESENTATION

CHAPTER SEVEN

BE DIFFERENT OR BE INVISIBLE: HOW ROCK STARS STAND OUT

In a sea of cubicles, how can you possibly stand out? When there are hundreds of other equally competent people doing the exact same job that you do, how can you ever hope to emerge as a rock star in your field? For most of us, the answer lies in working harder to try and do our job better than those around us. If that's your plan, good luck. Good luck getting noticed as you arrive earlier, leave later, and sweat harder than everyone else around you. Good luck giving up precious family and personal time to prove that you're the best. Good luck fighting off the younger and hungrier generation who want to steal your job and are willing to work harder for less money. And good luck trying to figure out what "better" really means!

To one employer, the best employees might very well be the ones who arrive earliest, work through lunch, and stay late. There are still plenty of employers who measure hours worked with quality of work. To another employer, the best employees might be the ones that make the least noise, cause the least hassle, and create the least amount of work for them. Some employers seek out people who can forge relationships, shake hands, and schmooze. Others are looking for the antisocial type who can sit for hours in front of a computer screen without losing focus. And some measure success based entirely on results, paying very little attention to what their employees are up to on a minute-by-minute basis. There is no single way to define "better," so if your mission is to succeed by being better, you are in for a long struggle.

In rock 'n' roll, the connection between talent and success is a tenuous one at best. Rock is littered with musicians who could barely play their instruments. Possibly the most notorious story is that of Milli Vanilli, the Grammy award–winning duo who took the world by storm with hits like "Girl You Know It's True" and "Blame It on the Rain" in the late 1980s. But it wasn't long before a skipping CD at a concert revealed the fraud. They were lip-synching everything! When they played live, not a single note was being sung. On its own, that isn't so unusual. Many artists use backing tracks to help augment their live performances. This fraud went far deeper. As the scam unraveled, we learned that none of the members of Milli

Vanilli wrote, sang, or played their songs, either on stage or on their albums. The entire Milli Vanilli act was created by Frank Farian, the German producer behind the success of 1970s disco band Boney M. The two guys whose faces graced the album covers and who toured the world were simply actors playing their roles. Milli Vanilli was soon disgraced and stripped of their Grammy award.

THE WORST MUSICIAN IN THE HALL OF FAME

On the other hand, there are truly incompetent musicians who have even been enshrined in the Rock and Roll Hall of Fame! Consider the Sex Pistols. Granted, the Sex Pistols were never really about complex and challenging chord progressions. They weren't really even about music per se. The Sex Pistols were a reflection of social discontent, the creation of music and fashion mastermind Malcolm McLaren, who put the band together in his vision. Their antiestablishment attitude and hard-edged, noisy punk rock captured the spirit of England's angry working lower class at the time, and the band became a massive success. Despite their short time together and the limited amount of music they made, the band was inducted into the Rock and Roll Hall of Fame in February 2006. In keeping with their image, nobody from the band attended the ceremony, calling the shrine to rock greats "a piss stain."

Although the band is forever in the Rock and Roll Hall of Fame, there is little debate that bass guitarist Sid Vicious was a terrible musician. The only debate might be just how bad. When Sid Vicious joined the Sex Pistols in 1977, the band was already becoming a major force in the UK. Although the band was growing in popularity, they didn't choose Vicious because his musical talent made the band better. He won the job because he had the right attitude and look. In fact, according to McLaren, Vicious "couldn't play guitar, but his craziness fit into the structure of the band."

He couldn't play guitar.

Note that McLaren didn't say that Vicious was a poor bass guitar player or a mediocre guitar player. He categorically stated that the band's guitar player, the one he recruited and the one that is in the Rock and Roll Hall of Fame, "couldn't play guitar."

The rest of the band was well aware of Vicious's shortcomings. Singer John Lydon said, "Everyone agreed he had the look, but his musical skill was another matter." The first rehearsals with their new guitarist were, according to Lydon, "hellish," despite the fact that the new guy tried really hard and rehearsed as much as possible.

Vicious's lack of musical skill was compounded by health problems and serious drug addictions, to the point that when the band went into the studio to record their 1977 album *Never Mind the Bullocks*, Sid Vicious was hardly involved. Legend has it that his bass guitar work can be heard on one song, barely audible beneath the overdubs. The band didn't last much longer, and neither did Vicious. His short and tragic life spiraled out of control, and he died of a heroin overdose on February 1, 1979.

Sid Vicious wasn't a musician; he was a showman. He was unlike any other showman in rock 'n' roll. But he certainly wasn't a great musician. He is, however, in the Rock and Roll Hall of Fame because he, and the band he was part of, stood out. They were unlike anything else we had ever seen. They were, despite Sid's lack of bass-playing talent, rock stars.

Sex Pistols aside, generally rock stars are pretty damn good musicians. They might not be the very best, but in most cases they are very, very good at what they do. But are the most successful rock stars actually the musicians with the greatest talent? As you examine many of rock's greatest success stories, you start to see a pattern emerge: while being excellent at what you do is important, most true rock stars aren't necessarily better than their not-so-famous counterparts . . . they are just dramatically different.

GETTING THE WORLD'S ATTENTION

Wicked Lester was like a thousand other rock bands in the early 1970s. They were popular in their hometown of New York but no more popular than any other bar band. A few record executives sniffed around at them, but those sniffs never amounted to much. Wicked Lester was just another rock band, and the fame and fortune they were seeking was nowhere in sight. As discouraging as their lack of success was, it wasn't enough to completely deter the two principal members of the band. Before calling it quits, they decided to change their name, focus their sound, and create a comic book image using elaborate makeup and stage pyrotechnics. Kiss was born, and within two years Gene Simmons and Paul Stanley were leading their band on their first world tour.

Now here's the question worth considering: In their evolution from Wicked Lester to Kiss—from obscurity to massive super-stardom in a few short years—did Gene Simmons and Paul Stanley make the leap from being terrible musicians to the world's best musicians? Did they go from being brutal songwriters to world-class songwriters in twenty-four months flat? Of course not. When Gene and Paul were in Wicked Lester, they were already reasonably solid musicians. They spent countless hours playing live, practicing, and honing their craft. Despite their futile efforts as Wicked Lester, they were not bad musicians. So what variable changed? What happened to take Kiss from zero to sixty? The answer is that by putting on makeup and blowing stuff up on stage, Kiss showed the world something it had never, ever seen before. Kiss forced people to sit up and take notice. Kiss was dramatically different, and by being dramatically different, they were able to get people's attention very quickly.

As Wicked Lester, they were solid musicians. As Kiss, forty-odd years later, they remain solid musicians. The difference was not musical skill. Kiss wasn't better at making music, they were better at making you notice them . . . because they were so different.

In rock 'n' roll, as in life itself, the main problem with trying to be *better* than everyone else is that there are a million different opinions about what "better" really means. The concept is entirely subjective! One person's better is another person's worse.

THE MONEYBALL DIFFERENCE

Consider Billy Beane, the General Manager of the Oakland Athletics baseball team, and the subject of the book and movie *Moneyball*. I love Billy Beane's story, and it isn't because I'm envious that he had Brad Pitt play him in a movie. (Personally, I'm lobbying to have Bruce Willis play me when my life story makes it to the big screen.) What I love about Billy Beane is that he has demonstrated beyond any doubt that what constitutes "best" and "better" is entirely subjective. Beane has put together some very successful baseball teams built on players overlooked by other teams. His teams have been extremely successful on relatively small payrolls by using a different system of player evaluation. To Billy Beane and others using the Sabermetric system of player evaluation, a completely different set of criteria is used to determine the so-called best player for any given position. Instead of traditional baseball measurements of effectiveness, like batting average or RBIs (runs batted in), Beane and his counterparts evaluate players on a different set of measurements, allowing them to find players who are undervalued (and therefore underpaid) by other teams. The player Billy Beane looks at as the best for his team could very well be a player that another team looks at as a liability, or at the very least as a disposable player, allowing Beane to pick up talented players at a bargain. So in baseball, the "best" player for the job depends very much on what set of statistics you decide to use to evaluate the player. It is exactly the same in job hunting, career advancement, and personal brand development. One person's "best" is another person's "meh."

Don't get me wrong. You can't rise to the top without a certain level of quality. Billy Beane's story of creating winning teams using undervalued baseball players wouldn't have become an Oscar-nominated movie if his teams perpetually finished last. Being unique and different on its own is not enough to make you a rock star in your field. You absolutely need to perform at a certain level of quality *and* stand out from the crowd. But once you've achieved an acceptable level of quality, being unique and different is absolutely essential to grow your career from virtual unknown to worldwide superstar.

And that brings us back to the story of Kiss. As Wicked Lester, they had achieved that acceptable level of quality. They were good at what they did. But it took doing something dramatically different, in the form of Kiss, to get the world to pay attention to them. The combination of a dramatic difference and an acceptable level of quality created an explosion of popularity that continues for Kiss to this day.

THE SAFETY DANCE

How can you apply this to your career and your personal brand?

Look at the real-world example of David Holmes, one of

thousands of flight attendants working for Southwest Airlines. If you've flown Southwest, you are no doubt familiar with the casual and fun approach the flight attendants take to the normally boring and dry safety announcements. Southwest flight attendants have been known to sing, rhyme, and generally have fun delivering boring information like the inflight safety announcements. David Holmes is the man who turned the usual safety message into a rap song. A cell phone video taken of his in-flight rapping went viral on YouTube, making David an Internet celebrity. After millions of people watched his safety message rap on line, he was invited by the company to make an appearance at the Southwest Airlines annual general meeting, where he explained—in a rap, of course—the company's financial results.

Frequent fliers seldom even hear the safety announcements on most airlines. They board the plane and immediately all of that droning on and on about seat backs up and tray tables stowed and oxygen masks dropping becomes white noise. Not so when David Holmes is on duty. David makes you pay attention . . . not because you are scared for your safety, but because you are intrigued by something you've never seen or experienced before. Flight attendants like David are impossible to ignore! Because they are unique, David, and other Southwest crew members like him, become memorable and make flying a little bit more fun. That attitude and memorability has become a cornerstone of the remarkable success of Southwest.

Is David Holmes the greatest flight attendant ever? Are Southwest flight attendants, who have fun with the safety announcements, somehow better than those on other airlines? Probably not, depending on how you define better, of course. Commercial aviation is a heavily regulated industry, and there is no question that legislated training and procedures are similar across all airlines. Thanks to those tight regulations, there should be no tangible difference between any airline when it comes to emergency and safety procedures. With regard to the less critical aspects of the job, like serving drinks, answering questions, or taking care of customers' needs in-flight, there's no reason why a United or American or Emirates flight attendant cannot be every bit as efficient and helpful as a Southwest flight attendant. But Southwest is unique. Southwest encourages their flight attendants to be dramatically different, and the result is an outstanding personal brand like David Holmes.

When you are dramatically different and you become known for it, something very powerful happens. In the case of Kiss, no other band can ever put on makeup without drawing comparisons to them. Any band wearing that kind of makeup will inevitably be called "Kiss-like." Any airline that has singing flight attendants who laugh, rap, and make jokes on the intercom will be compared to Southwest. And any major league sports executive who finds a new way to evaluate players and create winning teams will no doubt be compared to Billy Beane. In other words, when you become well-known for your dramatic difference, you become the king of your own hill. No longer are you just another band, airline, or baseball manager. Now you are the pioneer of something entirely new. When you are the leader, everyone else who does something similar to what you do becomes a follower. The impact that being a leader can have on your career cannot possibly be overstated. Everyone wants to hire leaders; everyone wants innovators on their team. Followers are easy to find, but recruiting leaders is always a challenge.

A STERN DIFFERENCE

Being dramatically different means standing out from the crowd, and that doesn't come without its share of risks. How-ard Stern was fired from WNBC Radio in September of 1985 because he was so dramatically different. Despite his immense popularity, WNBC couldn't reconcile Stern's dra-matic difference—raw honesty and sexually, politically, and racially charged humor—with their radio station's image. So they fired him. Of course, Howard Stern went on to become the most popular and highly paid radio personality in history. He would never have achieved that level of success if he had sounded and acted like every other radio personality. Don't forget that even though Stern was successful because he was dramatically different, he was also fired because he was dra-matically different. The lesson is that your difference, while it may be your eventual ticket to success, comes with a price and a risk that you need to be willing to take. Standing out from the crowd isn't always popular or easy, and sometimes it means walking away (or being asked to walk away) from certain jobs. When Stern eventually found the right station for his style, his unique difference made him rich and famous.

In order to stand out amid the numerous cubicles and

offices and résumés, you can and should be different. If you are at least as good as those around you at what you do (and hopefully even better), your best opportunity for success will come from being dramatically different, not from trying to get incrementally better.

Ultimately the reality you are faced with is that no matter how great you are at your job, if you are just like everyone else—except better—the odds that anyone will notice your brilliance are phenomenally low. You'll never get the chance to demonstrate your genius to the world unless you somehow stand out from those around you. You need to be dramatically different. If you choose to make your quality work into your only point of differentiation, success will be a much bigger challenge.

The Rock Star Playlist: Five Dramatically Different Songs That Got Noticed

1. **"God Save the Queen" by The Sex Pistols.** Despite being a musically simple song, "God Save The Queen" was like nothing else on the radio in the UK at the time. It tapped into the powerful antiestablishment sentiment being felt among British youth and instantly became a rock 'n' roll classic.

2. **"Don't Worry, Be Happy" by Bobby McFerrin.** Few songs have been used more often in movies, commercials, and popular culture. "Don't Worry, Be Happy" stands out because it is so dramatically different. Using no instruments whatsoever, the song includes only voice sounds made by Bobby McFerrin himself.

3. **"Someone Like You" by Adele.** This song was a breath of fresh air on the radio in 2010, when every song seemed to sound like Katy Perry or Lady Gaga. Hearing a song that included nothing but piano and a powerful voice delivering a heart-wrenching lyric made the world pay attention to Adele.

4. **"99 Luftballoons" by Nena.** Hearing a song in German on American radio was unusual enough, but an apocalyptic song about a nuclear war triggered by floating helium balloons was truly bizarre. Nena's only hit went all the way to #2 on the US charts. It was re-recorded in English and became a hit in the UK, Canada, and Australia.

5. **"Strutter" by Kiss.** There are plenty of songs that could well capture the career of Kiss, but I chose this song because it is the first song on the band's first album. For millions of fans, this was their introduction to the band that used comic book imagery, makeup, and extensive pyrotechnics to stand out in a major way. There's no doubt that Kiss was dramatically different.

▼

CHAPTER EIGHT

JUST LIKE BUDDY HOLLY: DEFINING YOUR ROCK STAR VISUAL IDENTITY

He tried going on stage without them, in order to be cool. But it was a failed experiment. One night he dropped his guitar pick and couldn't find it. You can't be a rock star when you're on your hands and knees trying to find a one-inch piece of plastic on a stage. Then again, with 20/800 vision in both eyes, finding an elephant on stage would have been difficult for him, let alone tracking down a stray guitar pick. So Buddy Holly went to see his local optometrist, Dr. J. Davis Armistead of Lubbock, Texas, who recommended that the young rock star try a pair of black, thick-framed glasses he had found in Mexico.

The look stuck. When Buddy Holly became famous, his

look was as much a part of his identity as his sound. Very few musicians wore glasses on stage, and those who did tried to downplay the look with nondescript frames. Glasses weren't cool in rock 'n' roll in the 1950s.

Buddy Holly changed all of that. His distinctive glasses became a fashion sensation, and optometrists across America struggled to find the thick "Buddy Holly glasses" to meet the demand from young fans who wanted to look like Buddy Holly—many of them with perfect vision! Across the ocean, teenagers growing up in England even took notice. One of those impressionable young Brits was John Lennon. Not only did John name his band, the Beatles, in homage to Holly's Crickets, but he also took away some of Buddy Holly's fashion sense. He wore glasses on stage. To this day the round-rimmed glasses remain an essential element of John Lennon's legacy. Just as we have taken to calling black, thick-rimmed glasses "Buddy Holly glasses," we have also come to know round-rimmed, thin granny glasses as "John Lennon glasses." When a fashion accessory bears your name, there is a good chance you have a powerful visual identity!

John Lennon wasn't the only British boy to be influenced by Buddy Holly's glasses. Reginald Dwight had perfect vision but wore glasses on stage in honor of Holly and Lennon. After changing his name to Elton John and rising to worldwide fame, he realized that all the years of unnecessarily wearing glasses had taken a toll on his eyes, deteriorating his vision, and making prescription glasses a must. Although they started out as a fashion accessory, they became a medical necessity. Over the years, Elton's flamboyant glasses have become a key part of his image.

Decades later, the Buddy Holly visual identity lives on. Rivers Cuomo of the rock band Weezer has adopted similar retro, black horn-rimmed glasses, and even sang about it on the band's first hit, "Buddy Holly," in 1994.

Buddy Holly wasn't a success *because* of his glasses. He was a brilliant musician who came along at a pivotal time in rock and roll music, and in his short career he left an indelible imprint on musicians in rock, country, blues, and soul music. He was a landmark musician, but there is no denying that Buddy Holly's unique and bold eyewear helped make him memorable to millions of people. Being memorable is generally a very good thing when it comes to developing a strong personal brand and making a lasting impact on people.

THE DANGER OF BEING THE SAME

The human brain, dramatically simplified, has a filter to prevent you from being driven crazy by constant exposure to the same things over and over again. Imagine if you were forced to read and understand every single traffic sign, advertisement, bumper sticker, logo, and sign that you were exposed to in a given day! Attempting to digest and process all of it would waste an inordinate amount of time and brain function. To alleviate this, the brain simply filters out what it has seen before and understands, like the highway speed signs you see every day on your commute to and from work or the billboard that you drive past every morning. The eyes see the sign, but the brain files it away in a "been there, seen that" folder where it puts stuff that doesn't really matter much. This phenomenon can be extended to your visual image. If you look, sound, and act like a million other people, you'll never get noticed. You'll probably be filed away in the "been there, seen that" folder, just like highway signs and stale billboards.

Yet at the same time, business creates immense pressure to conform to standards and norms. Certain jobs require uniforms; others require a suit and tie. Some are okay with your piercings, and others are not. In some cases, businesses attempting to create a certain aura around their brand will want to have a team that keeps a consistent look or feel. All of these factors play into how you develop your visual style and build your personal brand.

Your visual look is a walking billboard for who you are. For those meeting you for the first time, your visual image is likely to be the first basis upon which you are judged. That doesn't mean you necessarily need to compromise your values in order to get ahead . . . it just means that you need to be aware of what your visual look says about you.

The message your visual identity sends is critical to developing your personal brand. First impressions, as they say, are lasting impressions. Do you want to be perceived as stylish and contemporary, or would you rather be known as traditional and dependable? Do you strive to be seen as intense and focused, or is it your mission to be looked at as relaxed and easygoing? Each of those images requires a different visual. You might not trust a new doctor if you walk into her office and she's wearing ripped jeans. It is hard to take someone seriously in a high-stakes real estate deal when they are wearing flip-flops and shorts. On the other hand, you expect (and hope) your surfing instructor will be wearing something by Hurley or Billabong when you first meet. He or she would lose credibility wearing an Armani suit.

The power of first visual impressions is universal, but the messages each look sends vary greatly by geography. I discovered this firsthand in the summer of 2012 when I was hired to deliver a branding talk at a convention in Honolulu, Hawaii. The audience was mostly local business people who lived and worked in Hawaii. Just before I was to leave for Hawaii, my friend Geoff Bate from Imagine Words & Music called with some advice. Geoff had been doing business in Hawaii via his West Coast production company for decades.

"Don't bring your suit," he cautioned me. "When you get to Hawaii, go straight to Macy's and buy yourself a really nice designer Hawaiian shirt." He warned me against buying a cheap one, telling me that a decent Hawaiian shirt could run north of $100, and that the locals could tell the difference. Geoff went on to explain that business in Hawaii is conducted casually, and it is much easier to develop a rapport of trust when you aren't dressed in a New York City power suit and tie. I already intuitively knew that I could dress more casually than usual for the Hawaiian convention, but I didn't think that a true Hawaiian shirt would be appropriate. As it turned out, my friend's advice was accurate. I picked up a cool Tommy Bahama shirt that fit in perfectly with local business attire. And fortunately, the new shirt matched perfectly with the colors in the very manly kukui nut lei I was given when I arrived at the event.

As people filed into the room, I realized that business attire in Honolulu was different from business attire in New York or Toronto or Frankfurt. Colorful Hawaiian shirts were normal, as were brightly colored collared shirts, often worn untucked. Everything was more casual and laid back, a look and feel that I could definitely get used to.

That fantastic Hawaiian shirt now hangs in my closet for ten months a year, making an appearance for summertime parties and for winter escapes to the islands. But it was worth every penny—an instant trust-builder. Since I didn't look like an outsider, I wasn't treated as an outsider. In order to connect and build trust with the business people I was speaking to in Hawaii, it was wise to adapt to local customs.

On the other hand, fitting in too much can be extremely dangerous. When you blend in with everyone else, you become invisible—just another face in the crowd. As much as you want to fit in, it is far more important to your career that you stand out. How can you accomplish both?

THE LITTLE DIFFERENCES

The challenge is that standing out and being memorable usually involves being different, which goes directly against the need to look the part. The secret is finding a way to be memorable and stand out from the crowd while still fitting in. Is that even possible? Or are these goals mutually exclusive? Absolutely not. Consider Buddy Holly, where only one small aspect of his visual image was dramatically different. Aside from the glasses, Holly, like his musical contemporaries, generally wore a suit and tie on stage. His hair was short and well kept. Buddy Holly stood out, and he was able to do so with without a complete and outright rejection of accepted styles. For Buddy Holly to stand out from the crowd, he simply made a small but bold twist and proudly wore a pair of unusual glasses.

Former lawyer-turned-personal-branding-expert, author, and national speaker on this subject, Katy Goshtasbi, CEO and founder of Puris Image in San Diego, agrees that you don't have to change the world in order to stand out and be memorable. While she claims that the visual brand element is only about 20 percent of the overall personal brand built for her clientele, it matters very much to your overall personal brand projection. "It can be a shirt color that is a little different in color or style than everyone else; it can be a pair of red or animal print shoes; it can be a great necklace or earrings; or it can be a bright necktie or scarf or bag," says Katy on her blog at www.purisimage.com. "All that matters is that your item catches someone's eye, draws them to you because of the warmth and energy it gives off, and leads to a meaningful interaction with that person."

Ah. Your unique visual look isn't just there to create recall! Done right, it can be a conversation starter and an icebreaker. Your look itself can be a sort of social object around which discussions can begin. It can be the catalyst to meeting new and intriguing people and making connections that can benefit you in countless ways.

THE SOCIAL OBJECT

On a snowy day in March 2013, deep in one of the dreariest winters in New England history, I was meeting with Dr. Phil Feldberg, a dentist near Hartford, and a group of local business people. Phil always dresses well, wearing a shirt and tie to the office every single day. On that snowy day, Phil wore a bright tropical shirt instead. He did it because until that winter day, Phil and I had only ever met in sunny locations. By breaking the norm and wearing a colorful Hawaiian shirt, Phil created a social object. Buying bagels in the morning at the coffee shop, the clerk commented on how Phil's tropical shirt was the perfect thing to take her mind off the snow. At the office, both the staff and his patients asked Phil why he was wearing a crazy shirt instead of his usual button-down shirt and tie. All it took was a one-day break from the norm to turn a shirt into an icebreaker around which conversations could flourish. When conversations flourish, relationships are built and good things happen.

What aspects of your own visual identity can you

personalize while still fitting in with the expectations of your role? How can you put a powerful but simple twist on the ordinary to make it extraordinary and make it your own? Once you determine what it is that you can make your own, be consistent. If you plan to make wildly colorful socks a part of your personal brand, wear them every day. You never saw Buddy Holly without his famous glasses. Today, most of us would probably not recognize a picture of him without them!

A BIG HAIRY DEAL

There are few rock bands with a more consistent visual identity than ZZ Top. For these guys it wasn't a particular fashion accessory that made them unique; it was the ridiculously cool, long beards that two-thirds of the band sported. That look, combined with slick videos, helped make ZZ Top impossible to avoid in the early 1980s. MTV was just starting out, and ZZ Top was one of the first bands to benefit from people's newfound infatuation with videos. While most of the bands and singers on MTV were made up and stylized, ZZ Top appeared with beards to their bellies and caught everyone by surprise. And while the long facial hair may have been unusual in rock 'n' roll in the early 1980s, it was perfectly in line with their image as a badass Texas blues band. They fit in and stood out, simultaneously.

To this day, the long beards remain an iconic part of ZZ Top's image. There are only a few legendary rock artists who have made facial hair part of their visual identity. Freddie Mercury rocked a slick moustache for many years as the frontman for Queen. Jerry Garcia of the Grateful Dead made the Santa Claus beard a key part of his image. For grunge artists like Kurt Cobain, a few days' growth of stubble helped reinforce the perception that his generation didn't care much about anything. Then there were the numerous stars that made sideburns famous, including Elvis Presley and Jim Morrison. Finally, there was Lemmy, the lead singer of Motorhead, who trademarked the mutton-chop in rock 'n' roll. But nobody made facial hair a key element of a brand the way ZZ Top did!

DEFINING YOUR VISUAL IDENTITY

As you go about creating a visual identity to enhance your personal brand, ask yourself these key questions:

1. What is my ultimate goal? If you are self-employed you may have a totally different set of goals than someone climbing the corporate ladder, as author Hugh McLeod reminds us in the title of his second book, *Freedom Is Blogging in Your Underwear*. If you're a blogger working from home, the underwear-only look rocks . . . but not so much if you're a police officer.

2. What does this look say about me? Does my look enhance or take away from the message I am trying to send about myself? Ideally, every aspect of your look contributes to the message you want to send about yourself and what you do.

3. Who will reject this look? Try to put yourself in the shoes of others and understand who will dislike your

look. It is impossible to please everyone, so rather than attempting to, think about who you are displeasing. If you are going to be offputting to those who are critical to your career development, you might want to rethink your look.

4. Does this look honestly reflect who I am? It is fine to have aspirations and goals and to develop a look to help you achieve them, but if your look doesn't ultimately reflect an honest version of who you are, maintaining your image successfully will be painful and difficult at best. Sincerity is vital in personal branding, and a look that doesn't feel sincere will set you back. Ask yourself if you can pull this off, day in and day out, while remaining true to who you are. Bruce Springsteen's jeans and T-shirt look supports his blue-collar personal brand, but it is also firmly rooted in his upbringing and his comfort zone.

5. Who might others compare me to? We naturally try to categorize new things in our lives, and that can help or hinder you. If you are drawing fashion comparisons to George Clooney, you are likely to leave a more favorable impression. On the other hand, if your look appears to be inspired by Charles Manson, you could be in trouble. And despite the great work of Charlie Chaplin, growing a Chaplin-like moustache will not draw favorable comparisons to the great silent-movie actor.

The Rock Star Playlist:
Five Rock Stars with Unique Visual Images

1. **"Peggy Sue" by Buddy Holly.** He inspired so many with his look, but his music was equally inspiring. One of his biggest hits, "Peggy Sue," also had a great song, "Everyday," on the B-side of the single. Both are among Buddy Holly's ultimate classics.

2. **"Imagine" by John Lennon.** John named his band in honor of Holly, calling them the Beatles in homage to Holly's Crickets. His look, wearing glasses on stage, was also a direct influence of the late Buddy Holly. Lennon went for round granny glasses, unlike Holly, who opted for horn-rimmed.

3. **"Bennie and the Jets" by Elton John.** Inspired by John Lennon, who was inspired by Buddy Holly, Elton John adopted glasses as a signature part of his look. Instead of wire glasses like John or horn-rimmed like Buddy, Elton John instead made his glasses extravagant, helping to build his larger-than-life image.

4. **"Buddy Holly" by Weezer.** Rivers Cuomo cites John Lennon as a musical influence, but his horn-rimmed glasses definitely evoke Buddy Holly. So did the song by his band, Weezer, named after the iconic singer. However, it wasn't originally about Buddy Holly. Early versions of the song included references to Ginger Rogers and Fred Astaine, not Buddy Holly and Mary Tyler Moore.

5. **"Numb" by U2.** Although The Edge didn't wear glasses, like Buddy Holly he forged his own unique look through perpetually wearing a knit cap or tuque. As his hair started to thin, The Edge started wearing the caps. They've become a core part of his visual image. This song, "Numb," is one of the rare U2 songs on which he sings lead vocals.

CHAPTER NINE

MAKE ROCK STAR MISTAKES: NOT SCREWING UP IS PROOF YOU AREN'T TRYING HARD ENOUGH

"Rehearsing is for cowards," Jackson Browne is quoted as once saying.

That's because rehearsing gets you closer and closer to perfect, and perfect makes you boring. "You know, music really isn't supposed to be perfect," said Tom Petty in the Dave Grohl documentary *Sound City*. "It's all about people relating to each other and doing something that's really from the soul."

Artists like Tom Petty, Dave Grohl, and Jackson Browne crave the accidental magic that happens when talented musicians pick up their instruments and just play. The natural imperfections that permeate the music become part of what makes the songs powerful. It is those very flaws, some nearly inaudible and some quite obvious, that allow the songs to connect with human beings on a very personal level.

The freedom to make mistakes, explore, and jam, leads to new discoveries and new sounds. Sure, practice makes perfect, and rehearsal is important. But endless rehearsal makes for perfect music, and perfect music is boring music.

So much of rock's soul is rooted in mistakes, flubs, and screwups. Many great songs began unintentionally, as jam sessions where the musicians just related to each other, playing and improvising on the spot. And some were filled without outright errors that, for one reason or another, somehow unexpectedly contributed to the song and were preserved for all to appreciate.

MY FAVORITE MISTAKES

Van Halen's quintessential guitar solo song "Eruption" was actually just Eddie Van Halen playing in the studio, noodling on his guitar the way musicians do during their down time. Eddie was playing a blistering guitar piece that he had been doing in their live shows. Unbeknownst to Eddie, the tapes were rolling, and producer Ted Templeman realized right away that he had recorded a piece of guitar brilliance. Eddie wasn't so sure, because he felt he could, with practice and rehearsal, play the piece better. Templeman knew it wasn't going to get any better. "Eruption," as recorded live in the studio, became one of Van Halen's most revered songs . . . despite having what Eddie Van Halen felt was a clear mistake right at the beginning.

Can you pick out the mistake? I've heard the song a thousand times and I certainly can't. Maybe the most seasoned guitar virtuoso could find it, but the average ear could never pick it out. "Eruption" is a powerful guitar song that dares you to turn it up even louder. It is perfect exactly as it is.

How about the famous opening eight-note piano lick in "Old Time Rock and Roll" that plays twice before Bob Seger launches into the lyrics? Apparently that, too, was a mistake. It was only supposed to play once, but the producer accidentally recorded it twice, back to back. When they played it back in the studio, it sounded even better than the original plan. The result was the iconic opening notes to one of Bob Seger's signature songs. Would Tom Cruise, dancing in his underwear in *Risky Business*, be the same without those eight notes playing twice? I think not. Those doubled-up opening notes help make the song what it is.

My personal favorite rock 'n' roll flub happens in the first few bars of "Roxanne" by The Police. A few notes into the song, you can clearly hear a stray piano note, followed by laughter. The note jumps out because it is entirely disconnected from the song happening around it. Go and listen for it . . . you can't miss it. That piano note was played by Sting, but not on purpose and not by his hands! It was Sting's *ass* that created that odd note. He accidentally sat down on the piano, his backside hit the keys, and he laughed out loud at his clumsiness. Despite the obvious mistake, the band and their producer decided to leave the odd piano note in. It somehow made the song better.

THE NOT-SO-PERFECT INSTRUMENT

For lifetimes, the very best violins have been those made by legendary craftsmen Guadagnini and Stradivari. These seemingly perfect, multimillion-dollar violins are the choice of the world's greatest violinists. Unfortunately, Antonio Stradivari died just before Christmas in 1737, and Giovanni Guadagnini passed in the fall of 1786. Those two events have severely limited supply of the instruments. No new classic Stradivarius and Guadagnini violins are being manufactured, driving up the already-inflated value of the remaining ones. If you own one of the last 512 Stradivari and you're willing to part with it, you should be financially set for life. Even the ones in the poorest condition fetch millions.

Those who know the instrument well say that there is something almost magical about the Stradivarius and the Guadagnini. Other violins sound great, but they say that these special instruments have an almost unworldly quality to them. They could be called the perfect violins, and no manufacturer has ever been able to create anything quite like them. Does it not seem odd, that with so many high-tech tools at our disposal, we haven't been able to recreate that magical sound? Could we not utilize our collective knowledge, resources, and computer sciences to recreate these perfect violins?

Apparently not, because for centuries people have tried, and failed. The magic of these violins has eluded every manufacturer. The *Telegraph* reports that in 2012 a team of scientists used the absolute cutting-edge of cutting-edge technology to analyze the Stradivarius, attempting to determine what made it sound so sweet. They examined the violin using high-energy beams of light from a particle accelerator, the same technique used to unlock the secrets of atoms. What they found was surprising. As they looked under the paint and varnish, they found unusual asymmetrical patterns that no one had ever seen before. Contrary to what everyone believed, the Stradivarius wasn't perfect at all. Undetectable to the human eye were tiny imperfections, holes, and possibly even patches. The scientists theorize that it is these miniscule imperfections that create the so-called perfect sound of the instrument.

Physicist Dr. Franco Zanini, who led the study, believes the imperfections were intentional, designed to remove unpleasant harmonics that come from perfect symmetry. "Doing this is beyond a computer," he told the *Telegraph*. "Perhaps they were doing this by trial and error, but it is not impossible that these imperfections have been made on purpose to remove this imperfect sound."

Amazing. The world's most valuable and best-sounding violins are perfect by virtue of their imperfections.

YOU NEED TO BE IMPERFECT

In personal branding, can one really embrace imperfection? What works for the violin shouldn't necessarily apply to the individual. And if the old saying "you only get one chance to make a first impression" holds any water, then logic would suggest that rehearsal and the pursuit of perfection are the best ways to go about building your personal brand and your career. If people are making snap decisions about you the moment they shake your hand, it stands to reason that you should put forward an image of absolute perfection.

Not so fast . . . Former Massachusetts governor and 2012 presidential candidate Mitt Romney was frequently accused of appearing robotic and inhuman, and he had trouble connecting with people because of it. Watch video of Mitt Romney in action for just a few minutes, and you can easily see why. His hair is perfect. His clothes are perfect. He seldom stumbles and he delivers flawless speeches. Yet those seemingly flawless performances did not resonate with people. Nobody wanted to have a beer with Mitt Romney. He wasn't likeable in that human way. His overly rehearsed veneer was a problem for Mitt Romney! He was so polished that he came across as robotic. His look and sound reflected his immense wealth, which only further distanced him from ordinary voters. Now to be fair to Mr. Romney, there were many factors at play that resulted in his election loss in 2012. While it wasn't all about his image, it is an absolute certainty that his air of perfection failed to help him. As human beings, we don't bond with perfection. We bond with people who are like us: flawed, scarred, and insecure. While we look to our leaders to be somehow better than us, we also look to them to reflect our human qualities at the same time.

Leonardo Da Vinci was a master at understanding imperfections and flaws. In many of his paintings he used a technique called *sfumato* that, translated from Italian, essentially means "smoky." If you examine the lines of Da Vinci's famous *Mona Lisa*, you'll see lines that are anything but perfect. They are intentionally smoky and hazy, leaving the impression of a character in motion. The *Mona Lisa* does not look at all like a photograph, yet for generations people have found themselves drawn to this emotionally captivating painting. Could it be that her smoky lines and appearance of perpetual motion reflect the view from our own eyes, always observing the world in a state of motion? "Confused shapes arouse the mind," noted Da Vinci.

Even our pop culture heroes are flawed in some ways. We hear relentlessly of Oprah's battles with her weight and Jennifer Aniston's failed relationships. We watch *TMZ* and read *People* magazine to find out that our celebrity idols are just like us: going out to a restaurant for dinner, walking their dogs in the park, and taking their kids to the beach on a sunny afternoon. And having spent plenty of time backstage at rock concerts, the biggest compliment I hear a fan pay their favorite artist is "she was so down to earth." Yes, we indeed look for ourselves in others . . . and none of us are perfect. We all make mistakes, every day, and we respect those who do the same.

THE IMPERFECT APPLE

Steve Jobs was a legendary leader for a wide variety of reasons (and not all of them positive). One of his greatest assets was his speaking skill and his onstage presence. He had the magical ability to leave an audience completely wowed by what they had just witnessed. But among all the product launches and press conferences that Steve Jobs conducted, one stands out as game changing . . . because it was all about imperfections.

It was the summer of 2010, and Apple had just released their wildly successful iPhone 4. It was the fastest-selling product the company had ever rolled out. But there was a problem, and the problem was taking headlines away from the product. The issue was the phone's antenna, buried under a stylish metal rim. When the phone was held a certain way, the metal prevented the antenna from working properly, and calls were dropped. It was estimated that the phone dropped only one of one hundred calls, but it was enough to create a storm of anti-Apple sentiment in the technology media. According to the Walter Isaacson biography on Jobs, he was on vacation in Hawaii at the time and returned to California to deal with the crisis. He called together his inner circle to plan a press conference for that Friday. Steve Jobs stepped on stage that day in front of the media with a simple approach. "We're not perfect," he said. "Phones are not perfect. We all know that. But we want to make our users happy." He went on to offer a free return policy for anyone who was unhappy with the new iPhone 4.

What happened next was amazing. The wait list for the iPhone, which had been at two weeks, grew to three weeks. The return rate, even with Jobs's offer of a free return, *actually dropped*. The return rate of 1.7 percent was lower than any previous version of the iPhone and most other phones. Scott Adams, the creator of the *Dilbert* cartoon, wrote a glowing blog post about how the Steve Jobs PR maneuver was likely to be studied for years to come. He lamented that the situation was worth creating a humorous cartoon about until Steve Jobs defused it with his presentation. "Nothing kills humor," said Adams, "like a general and boring truth."

On stage that day, Steve Jobs was human. In a general and boring truth, he admitted to imperfection. He also displayed another very human trait: the desire to please. Displaying human vulnerabilities like that help endear a company and its leader to consumers. And clearly Apple has endeared itself to many, becoming one of the most valuable technology companies on earth.

What happens when you reveal your imperfections?

▸ **Relationships are formed.** We do not bond with perfection. As imperfect creatures, we have a mental and emotional disconnect with the idea of perfection. If you want to relate to people, reveal yourself to be one of them.

▸ **Trust is built.** Revealing imperfections is a sign of honesty, and we want to engage and connect with those who are honest. If you want people to trust you, don't be afraid to admit your flaws and mistakes.

▸ **Reputations are cemented.** Actor Hugh Grant, after being arrested with a prostitute in Hollywood, famously apologized on *The Tonight Show* in 1992. His career never missed a beat, because he was honest. On the other hand, Lance Armstrong attempted to cover up his lies for years, and when he finally came forward with the truth, his personal brand was already destroyed.

Unfortunately, North American culture hasn't always made it easy to be imperfect. If you read enough fashion magazines you could quickly be convinced that we should all have a rock hard six-pack and skin without blemishes. It is easy to get carried away chasing an unattainable level of so-called perfection. Clearly the happier and healthier path is to embrace our imperfections and give ourselves the freedom to be who we really are.

FREEDOM TO FAIL

In her book *Better By Mistake: The Unexpected Benefits of Being Wrong* (Penguin, 2012), Alina Tugend outlines how, by embracing imperfection, companies, students, and careers can grow and create a culture of freedom. Only in that kind of environment can people be unafraid to take calculated risks and learn from them. She suggests that when we are experimenting, innovating, and growing, we are naturally more likely to make mistakes. But when the fear of making a mistake becomes too much, we revert back to what is safe and known, making fewer errors . . . but also making fewer innovations. Making fewer mistakes doesn't advance humankind. Our world is moved forward by innovations.

Tugend analyzed the Japanese school system, a much different system from the traditional North American classroom. In Japan, students engage in more independent thought, and after each project they are encouraged to look at what worked and what didn't, learning from the mistakes they made along the way. In the North American culture, we are reluctant to accept mistakes from our students, let alone ourselves, in our professional lives.

You've probably heard the phrase, "If you aren't making mistakes, you aren't trying hard enough." It's true! Mistakes happen when you are pushing the boundaries and challenging the accepted ways of doing things. Mistakes are a natural by-product of changing the world. If you plan on making monumental change, you'd better get used to screwing up now and then. The key isn't avoiding mistakes; it's learning from them. Every time you make a mistake, you learn one of two things: You either learn to never do that particular thing again, or you learn something really cool and unexpected that was a direct result of the mistake. Both lessons are more valuable than never making a mistake at all.

Baseball sluggers often talk about "gripping the bat too tight" when they are in a hitting drought. They talk about the need to loosen up and let things happen naturally. They strive to find that mental "zone" where they can knock one ball after another out of the park. The funny thing about great hitters in baseball is that they need that freedom to swing hard. Almost universally, the best home run hitters have a high tendency to strike out. That's because they are swinging for the fences, unafraid of what might come if they fail to do it.

Success like that comes only when you give yourself the freedom to fail. The pressure of achieving success can be overwhelming, even smothering—cluttering up your mind and preventing you from arriving at great solutions to the problems you face. Instead of looking forward to the positive results of a job well done, the pressure to succeed creates a fixation on not making mistakes. In sports, that's called "playing not to lose" instead of "playing to win": when a team starts to try and prevent mistakes instead of scoring points.

Winston Churchill aptly noted that success is simply going from failure to failure without ever losing your sense of enthusiasm. Let go of the fear and embrace your mistakes. Jump from failure to failure, always eager for the next opportunity to screw around and try new things. When they go well, celebrate the results. When they don't, chalk it up to a learning experience and gracefully move on to the next challenge. Give yourself the freedom to make mistakes, and great things can happen.

The Rock Star Playlist: Five of Rock's Most Memorable Mistakes

1. **"No Woman, No Cry" by Bob Marley & The Wailers.** The classic 1975 version from the album *Live!* is one most often heard today, and it contains a mistake that could have, but fortunately wasn't, fixed. One minute and fifty seconds into the song, the speakers gently and hauntingly give feedback. It almost sounds like those lost friends are saying hello from the beyond. To me, that bit of feedback makes the song perfect.

2. **"Eruption" by Eddie Van Halen.** I can't hear it, but Eddie can. Apparently there is a mistake right off the top of the most famous guitar solo in rock history. Whatever. It's brilliant.

3. **"Old Time Rock 'n' Roll" by Bob Seger.** That famous piano solo at the beginning was only supposed to happen once. The second time was a mistake by the producer, and Seger decided it sounded better repeated.

4. **"Roxanne" by The Police.** Sting sits down on a piano and laughs, about six seconds into the song. The band believed the stray piano note added to the song's haunting nature.

5. **"Creep" by Radiohead.** The crunchy guitar that invades this soft song just before the chorus was an attempt by guitarist Jonny Greenwood to wreck the song. They were recording it in one take, and Greenwood didn't like how it was going, so he hit his guitar really hard, repeatedly. According to Eddie O'Brien of Radiohead, that guitar "is the sound of Jonny trying to fuck the song up."

CHAPTER TEN

THE GAME OF RISK: HOW TO TAKE THE RIGHT RISKS (AND MAKE THE MOST OF THEM)

*R*olling Stone magazine ranked it the "greatest song of all time," six-and-a-half minutes of the most famous minutes in rock history.

And it only turned out the way it did because one guy was brave and crazy enough to take the risk of a lifetime. It was a risk that could have gotten him kicked out of the studio and possibly blacklisted from the industry altogether. Instead, the risk of a lifetime resulted in one of the most iconic elements of "Like a Rolling Stone" by Bob Dylan.

Al Kooper told the story brilliantly in the 2005 Martin Scorcese documentary *No Direction Home: Bob Dylan*. Kooper was a guitar player who was fortunate enough to be invited in the studio to watch as Bob Dylan worked on "Like A Rolling Stone." Dylan's regular guitarist, Mike Bloomfield, was there, and there was no need for another guitar player, but Al Kooper was tuned up and ready to go if needed. But since he wasn't, he put his instrument away and sat down in the control booth with the producers to watch the recording in progress.

As the session went along, Kooper began to sense what a fantastic song they were recording, and he was itching to get involved, somehow. They certainly didn't need another guitar player, so Kooper suggested to the producer that he had a "great organ part" in mind for the song and he would like to try and play it on the Hammond organ. The producer shut him down, telling him that he was just a guitar player and not an organ player. That's when fate intervened. The phone rang, and the producer turned to answer it. While the producer was talking on the phone, Kooper quietly got up, walked into the studio, and sat down at the organ. He didn't ask any questions. He just sat down and got ready to play. As far as Al Kooper was concerned, the producer didn't say "no" outright. He only said "you're a guitar player," and as far as Kooper was concerned, that wasn't a "no." So, when the producer hung up the phone and the band began to play, a guitarist named Al Kooper was playing the Hammond organ.

There were two problems with the scenario. First, Al Kooper *didn't* actually have "a great organ part" in mind. That was complete and total BS! He lied and made up that story in order to work his way into the studio. In reality, Kooper had hardly ever played the organ . . . he was a guitar player! So he was going to have to come up with something reasonably interesting on the spot. Second, Al couldn't properly hear the band in his headphones. In order to play along with the other musicians he had to watch them for the chord changes. As a result, his organ parts consistently started about an eighth note behind the rest of the musicians. It wasn't intentional. It was the only way he could keep up!

When the band stopped to listen back to the tape of the session, Bob Dylan immediately asked about the unusual organ sound. Dylan demanded, apparently quite emphatically, that the organ be turned up. Dylan loved the organ, especially how it came in slightly behind the rest of the band. That signature sound, an eighth-note late because the so-called organ player couldn't hear the band, wasn't supposed to happen. Al Kooper wasn't even supposed to be in the room, but he was. His presence was a risk that left an indelible mark on one of rock's greatest songs.

Al Kooper calls that the day he became an organ player. Over the course of the next few decades, Al Kooper could be heard playing organ and guitar on countless rock 'n' roll classics. He became one of the top session players in the business, and it all began with a calculated risk.

Would "Like a Rolling Stone" be the song it is today without that organ part? Absolutely not. And would Al Kooper have gone on to such a prolific career without that risk? Absolutely not. The decision to walk into that studio without the producer's permission changed both Al Kooper's career and music history for the better.

FIRE YOUR CRAPPY CLIENTS!

Risks are scary. I'm pretty sure Al Kooper was a little nervous as he got up and walked into Bob Dylan's recording studio to improvise a part on an instrument he seldom ever played! But only through risk does reward ever follow, a lesson I learned from a friend named Tommy Kramer.

Tommy is in the Texas Radio Hall of Fame, so he's a pretty big deal in the Lone Star State. He had a lengthy and successful career as a radio host and turned that into a lengthy and successful career as a consultant to other radio hosts. When I first worked with Tommy, he took a risk. He outlined what he was all about and then he told me that he wasn't going to waste any time arguing with me. "If you are going to argue and debate all the time," he warned me, "I'll just fire your ass."

Wait a minute. Wasn't I hiring him? Shouldn't I be angry, being told how the relationship will work when I'm paying him good money? Tommy Kramer was willing to take that risk. He shared with me his experiences as a consultant and how much time he had wasted arguing with his clients in order to make his point. The combative clients, he found, seldom took his advice anyway. He discovered that he was wasting time, breath, and knowledge on people who weren't going to listen. So one by one, he started to fire his annoying clients. As new clients came on board, Tommy established the ground rules: they didn't have to take his advice, but he wasn't going to waste any time arguing with them.

That was a big risk. He could have killed his business by

firing his clients. However, for Tommy it was more important to find peace of mind and satisfaction in his job, and he wasn't getting that from clients who wanted to do nothing but fight with him. Tommy taught me a great lesson. Fire your crappy clients and take the risks that come from that. Your personal and professional happiness is too important to risk wasting on them.

THE BEST THING, NEXT BEST THING, AND WORST THING

In his book *Thinking Fast and Slow* (Farrar, Straus, and Giroux, 2013) Daniel Kahneman illustrates how we are wired to be twice as sensitive to potential losses as we are to potential gains. We are wired to be risk-averse! Fear is hardwired into our DNA to protect us from danger, yet in our modern world, that hardwired fear might be causing more harm that it is preventing.

Your natural state of risk averseness is itself a risk when change happens so quickly. In the digital age, with its perpetual and accelerating change, making decisions quickly is vital to career success. Yet in order to reduce our risk, we are inclined to hold off making decisions until we have all of the information. We don't want to make a mistake, so we wait. Choosing to wait—to do nothing—can be more dangerous than making a decision. And while that is especially true in today's fast-changing world, it isn't a new phenomenon. "In any moment of decision," said President Theodore

Roosevelt more than a century ago, "the best thing you can do is the right thing. The next best thing you can do is the wrong thing. And the worst thing you can do is nothing."

To do nothing is the worst thing, yet it is the natural state most of us find ourselves in. We are conditioned to hold off, wait for more information, and act only when we have absolute confidence in the outcome of our decisions. We are afraid of failure, which could lead to rejection and ridicule, so we stay in a holding pattern and wait for change to find us. Philip Bobbit from the University of Texas has given a name to our tendency to assume the present situation won't change. He's labeled it the "Parmenides Fallacy" after the Greek philosopher who argued for the existence of a single, eternal reality: that "all is one" and change is an illusion. Professor Bobbit's Parmenides Fallacy was profiled in Margie Warrell's book *Stop Playing Safe: Rethink Risk, Unlock the Power of Courage, Achieve Outstanding Success* (Wiley, 2013). Warrell wrote that while we like to think that in time things will get better, more often than not "the opposite is true: things that aren't working well now only get worse." According to Warrell, when we let fear prevent us from taking risks—asking for a promotion, taking on greater responsibilities, leaping into a new career opportunity, or changing the way things are done in our companies—we often fail to consider how our lack of action could be making things worse. Our inaction, fueled by fear of risk, often doesn't lead to the status quo, but instead contributes to a worsening situation. In a March 2013 piece in *Forbes*, Warrell suggests asking yourself one question when weighing your options: Is this choice driven more by what inspires me, or by what frightens me?

HOW BIG IS YOUR RISK?

Some risks are obviously bigger than others. The consequences of firing a few clients or planning a six-month leave of absence are relatively small compared to the consequences of quitting a job and making a wholesale career change. When you are unhappy at work, the risk of losing a steady paycheck every two weeks can be easily outweighed by the personal and health benefits of leaving a bad job behind.

As they do about their spouses, plenty of people bitch and moan about their work. Sadly, many of us complain about the hours and the people at work, but deep down the stresses are not enough to entice us to take a major risk like quitting. As human beings, we just like to find something to complain about. Other people are seriously stressed by the workplace, finding themselves in an unhealthy environment that needs to be corrected. When do you know when it is time to take a risk and leave your job? In a January 2012 article in *The Guardian*, journalist Laura Marcus compiled a checklist, based on her research, to help you determine if the risk of leaving your job is worth it. Here are Laura's criteria:

Don't Take the Risk! Stay If . . .

- ▶ You've always had regular work, what you do won't easily fit into freelance or self-employment, and there are few vacancies in your line.

▶ You've only become unhappy recently. Like parties, if you stay awhile longer, it could get better.

▶ You have debts and/or large commitments and responsibilities and your job is secure.

▶ You live in an area of high unemployment.

▶ You're the family's sole earner.

▶ You might be made redundant. Why not hang on for that payout?

▶ You hate insecurity, need routine in your life, and you're not very flexible.

Take the Risk and Leave If . . .

▶ Your job is making you ill.

▶ Your skills are in demand.

▶ You've started a business while employed and it's going well.

▶ You have plenty of savings or an inheritance.

▶ You have a working partner who's prepared to support you—and means this!

▶ You have great contacts, you love networking, and you have strong self-belief.

▶ You've done your research, you spotted a gap in the market, and you're the one to fill it.

The Rock Star Playlist: Five of the Riskiest Moves in Rock 'n' Roll

1. *In Rainbows* by Radiohead. This 2007 album was released as a digital download, and the band asked fans to "pay what you want" for the album. *New York Times* writer Jon Pareles called it the music industry's "most audacious experiment in years." With no official way for the industry to audit downloads, it is difficult to know if it was a success. According to the band, the average price paid was about $6.00. Although it was a risky move, it appears that it paid off for Radiohead, both in financial terms and in free publicity.

2. **Bob Marley Makes Jamaica Smile.** The 1976 Smile Jamaica concert comprised a few shows put on to help quell political violence that was spreading across the island. The show was sponsored by Jamaican Prime Minister Michael Manley, which led to controversy about the concert's true intent. Accused of supporting Manley, gunmen attacked Bob Marley in his home, shooting the singer twice. Despite his injuries and the attackers still being at large, Marley promised he would still play one song at the concert. He ended up performing for almost ninety minutes, risking his life for his fans and his country.

3. **James Brown Calms Boston.** Boston was a city already rife with racial tension in April 1968 when Martin Luther King Jr. was assassinated. With James Brown set to play the Boston Garden the following night, officials feared more violence would break out. James Brown played a risky but electrifying concert, making a public appeal to the audience to refrain from violence and work together to stay safe. Instead of increased violence, many credit Brown with defusing a volatile situation.

continued on following page

4. **Cat Stevens Converts.** After nearly drowning off the California coast in 1975, folk singer Cat Stevens began a journey of self-discovery that ultimately led to his conversion to Islam in 1977. Two years later he changed his name to Yusuf Islam and retreated from public life. That personal risk came with public backlash, especially after 9/11. As Cat Stevens, his music has lived on, and in recent years Yusuf has once again started making music.

5. **"Stan" by Eminem and Elton John.** After taking tremendous heat for writing lyrics perceived to be homophobic, Eminem was joined on stage at the 2001 Grammy Awards by the openly gay Elton John. Together the two sang a poignant version of Eminem's song "Stan." Hip-hop music is notorious for anti-gay lyrics, and Eminem took a risk appearing on stage holding hands with Elton John. The risk of a backlash was offset by a powerful demonstration of a new level of societal awareness in the hip-hop world.

▼

CHAPTER ELEVEN

WEIRD WORKS: HOW JOE WALSH TURNED QUIRKY INTO CASH

While nearly everyone in the world was trying to get ahead by proving they were normal, rock stars discovered something brilliant: weird works. Apparently, people like weird. Our minds are wired so that we notice and remember the unusual and ignore and forget the usual. At one point in our evolution, that wiring was essential to our survival; the unfamiliar could very well endanger our lives. Rock stars are notorious for unusual. Most rock stars don't look, dress, talk, or act like the rest of us. Driven by creativity and not by conformity, rock stars are, by their very nature, weird.

Joe Walsh is one of the weirdest ones. Joe is like your

strange uncle who comes to town and feeds beer to your dogs and lets your twelve-year-old drive the car. He laughs a lot, smiles a lot, and doesn't appear to take things too seriously. He lives life in a different world—a place of perpetual play, a world that plenty of us would benefit from visiting now and then. Despite his astonishing résumé, Joe Walsh isn't the household name that he should be.

What did Joe Walsh accomplish in rock 'n' roll? Well, without Joe, the Eagles album *Hotel California* doesn't exist, at least not in the way that we know and love it. That legendary 1976 album was the first record that The Eagles recorded after Joe replaced Bernie Leadon as the band's guitar player. Walsh, along with Don Felder, helped create an album that showcased a harder-rocking version of the band—not a coincidence, since Joe Walsh was well known for his edgy guitar work, his talk box, and his unusual technique of hot-wiring the pickup on his guitar.

Joe Walsh brought more than great guitar work to The Eagles, according to Bill Szymczyk, who produced *Hotel California* as well as Joe's solo work. "Joe brought a sense of levity to the band," said Szymczyk in the fantastic 2013 documentary *The History of The Eagles*. That levity may have helped extend the band's existence by a few years, as tensions were high in the late 1970s. Two Joe Walsh compositions made it onto *Hotel California*. One of those songs, "Life in the Fast Lane," remains one of the most powerful and popular Eagles songs ever. Many regard *Hotel California* as the defining album of the band's career. It has sold over sixteen million copies in the US alone. There's no doubt that Joe Walsh changed The Eagles, and most people would agree that he changed the band for the better. He wrote or co-wrote Eagles classics like "The Sad Café," "Pretty Maids All in a Row," and "In the City," on which he also sang.

On his own, Joe always let his quirky sense of humor permeate his music. His hit songs like "Rocky Mountain Way," "Life's Been Good," and "Ordinary Average Guy" showcase his odd take on life. Some of his more bizarre songs, like "All Night Laundromat Blues," "I.L.B.T's," and the hidden "Flock of Wah Wahs" on *But Seriously Folks . . .* are just pure nuttiness.

Aside from music, Joe Walsh's wonderful weirdness was highlighted by his mock campaign for the US presidency in 1980. Joe's platform included proclaiming the song "Life's Been Good" as the new national anthem and giving free gas to everyone. Over the years Joe Walsh has brought his quirkiness to the stage with a wide variety of musicians, from Eric Clapton to Jimi Hendrix, from Bruce Springsteen to Dave Grohl. He's also toured with his brother-in-law, Ringo Starr.

For fans of Joe Walsh, Joe is special *because* he is weird. He is interesting, engaging, and memorable because he's unlike anyone else on the planet; his fans wouldn't want him any other way. When he plays with The Eagles, there is a special section of fans—myself included—who cherish the moments when Joe Walsh steps up and sings his songs. Joe knows that he's weird and loved for it. As he told Howard Stern in 2012, he isn't a fan of the normal side of life. Instead, said Joe, "I like side B."

Sadly, outside of rock 'n' roll, weird gets a pretty bad rap.

THE SYSTEM OF NORMAL

We are taught to conform. We are pressured to look like everyone else, think the way our friends think, and to fit in with the group. From the earliest days when we enter the education system, conformity is rewarded and weird is shunned. We are seated in perfect rows, walk in single file, and follow a strict set of rules. Students are chastised for "wrong" answers and are generally discouraged from veering off-course in class. Not only is it difficult to be weird in our conformist system, but as a teenager it can be downright dangerous. Those who are labeled weird by their peer group are often bullied, verbally and physically, until they suppress their weirdness and fit in with the crowd.

As a result of this societal quest for conformity, companies and businesses today look remarkably similar to each other. Everyone at work dresses the same. Cubicles in Hong Kong look just like cubicles in Harrisburg, which look just like cubicles in Halifax. Business protocol is the same nearly everywhere in the world. We've created a world where everything is normal. When everything is normal, nothing is memorable.

WE ARE ALL WEIRD

Seth Godin wrote a fantastic book a couple of years ago called *We Are All Weird* (The Domino Project, 2011). In it, Seth encourages us to embark on a mission to add more weirdness to our working world. Weird, according to Godin, is more than just decorating your office with goofy trinkets. Weird is consciously choosing not to follow the "checklist of normal." Weird means being true to yourself, thinking beyond the usual ways people think, and deciding to voice your thoughts even when they make you or others feel uncomfortable.

In a July 2012 interview with the *Chicago Tribune*, Seth noted that the most successful among us didn't get there by being normal. "We succeed by doing something that everyone else says will never work," Godin told business writer Rex Huppke. "If you look at the people who get private parking spaces, people that the boss caters to, they didn't get it because they followed instructions better than you. They got it because they were viewed as being indispensable at what they did. They got it because they did it with passion and skill."

According to Seth, we live in changing times. The Internet has connected people in new ways, and those who once saw their weirdness as a lonely island in society are now finding that they are not alone. The quirky hobby that you thought made you an oddball now has an online community numbering in the millions. Yes, you are weird; but so, we are learning, is everyone else. You don't have to suppress your weirdness to fit in. You just have to find other people who share the same weirdness that you have. That's incredibly empowering, and it has brought weird charging directly into the mainstream. In fact, according to Seth, in today's world "the weird are the many."

Maybe that's why some of the greatest business success stories of our time are companies that embrace weirdness. I witnessed this firsthand a few years ago when a friend from high school landed a dream job at DreamWorks Animation in Redwood City, California. He offered to take my son and me on a behind-the-scenes tour of DreamWorks, from the rendering room to the staff cafeteria. In every section of every building, we saw that weirdness ruled. Cubicles were decorated and personalized, and not just with Dilbert cartoons or plush toys. At DreamWorks, weirdness is taken seriously. In one corner, several people had jointly decorated their cubicles and turned their section of the office into a Jimmy Buffett–like Tiki bar. Another area featured several Canadian ex-pats who used hockey sticks to create a tribute to their favorite game within their workspace. Weird rocked at DreamWorks! Is it just a coincidence that DreamWorks Animation has managed to put four of their films into the top fifty grossing movies of all time? With an average gross of $430 million, DreamWorks Animation makes the most profitable movies in the world. Embracing weirdness has created a culture of creativity that has allowed DreamWorks Animation to earn $10 billion worldwide.

"I want to work in a place like that," said my then-thirteen-year-old son as we left the park-like setting of DreamWorks. Beyond all of the financial success and the Academy Awards, that could very well be the most rewarding part of DreamWorks' weirdness: it will attract a new generation of brilliant, creative minds who are equally weird. In a future where every company is clamoring to attract the brightest among us, I suspect that companies like DreamWorks will have a much easier time recruiting.

CAN WEIRD WORK IN
THE REAL WORLD?

It would be easy to write off DreamWorks Animation's weirdness as another quirky aspect of the entertainment industry. After all, making movies is hardly dissimilar to making rock 'n' roll music. It is easy to be weird when your mission is to stand out from the crowd, especially when you live in California. Could this kind of weirdness possibly work in the real business world?

Less than ten years after their founding, in 2008 one of the weirdest businesses in the world accomplished two of its major goals: It cracked $1 billion in sales and it made the *Fortune* magazine list of "The Top 100 Companies to Work For." That company is Zappos.

Zappos was founded in 1999 as the world's first online shoe store. The company was built on two pillars: it existed only online, with no brick-and-mortar locations, and it provided exceptional service. Plenty of people thought the Zappos model was ludicrous. An online-only shoe store that boasted about customer service seemed like a long shot, yet year after year the company grew. They were so tremendously successful that in 2009 Zappos was acquired by Amazon for $1.2 billion.

The success that Zappos has experienced is largely attributable to the company's corporate culture, starting with CEO Tony Hsieh and his conviction that "if we get the culture right, then everything else, including the customer service, will fall into place." Hsieh oversaw the development of a 480-page "culture guide" to help new employees adjust to the weirdness of Zappos.

Just how weird is Zappos?

There is a company nap room, and you are encouraged to use it when you are tired. As at DreamWorks Animation, employees decorate their own workspaces in equally funky and unusual ways that go far beyond what any workplace would consider "normal." Managers are required (not encouraged, *required*) to spend up to 20 percent of their *working* hours goofing off with other team members away from the office. And at lunch, there's no need to bring any cash. Lunch is free, as are the company vending machines that won't accept your money.

In the ultimate sign of corporate weirdness, new recruits are taken through a rigorous training program . . . and then they are offered a $2,000 bonus to quit! Seriously. In order to weed out employees who aren't suited for the company and would likely jump ship anyway, Zappos offers $2,000 to anyone who quits after the training program. Astonishingly, 97 percent turn down the offer.

If you think that is weird, wait until you open up that 480-page culture book. "Weird" is one of the ten core values that define the brand! "Create Fun and a Little Weirdness" is a Zappos core value! If you aren't weird enough, you aren't getting a job at Zappos. In fact, weird is given such high priority at Zappos that it isn't just a core value . . . it is the very first word that appears on the cover, above words like "honest," "growth," "team," and "create." That's sending a powerful message about weirdness, isn't it?

THE MISSION TO REMAIN AMERICA'S WEIRDEST CITY

Weirdness has made its way into the cultural fabric of one of America's fastest-growing, and arguably coolest, cities. Austin, Texas, has the unofficial motto, "Keep Austin Weird." That weirdness has done wonders for the state capital of Texas! Though most of the nation experienced a sluggish real estate market in 2011, Austin was booming with home building and growth. Austin had the second-healthiest home building index in America in 2011, and with so much land surrounding this beautiful city, there is plenty of room to grow. But it isn't just the cheap land or the climate the draws people to Austin; it's the vibe.

With one of the most educated populations in the country, Austin attracts thought leaders, authors, professors, and researchers. With a thriving arts scene and the legendary annual South By Southwest festival, the city draws in musicians, filmmakers, animators, graphic artists, and screenwriters. Austin is also home to the Austin Film Festival, the live music TV show *Austin City Limits*, and countless regular celebrations, parties, and parades along the Sixth Street strip.

Austin's intrinsic weirdness attracts weird companies. Making their home here is grocery store chain Whole Foods Market, a company consistently ranked as one of the most socially responsible corporate entities in America. Whole Foods, by most standards, is weird. They place tremendous importance on green energy, sustainable farming, and organic foods. They forego easy profits and hold their food to higher standards than most grocery stores. In their corporate mission statement, the company clearly has a different—maybe even weird—set of priorities:

> *The deepest core of Whole Foods, the heartbeat, if you will, is this mission, this stakeholder philosophy: customers first, then team members, balanced with what's good for other stakeholders, such as shareholders, vendors, the community, and the environment. If I put our mission in simple terms, it would be, No. 1, to change the way the world eats, and No. 2, to create a workplace based on love and respect. We believe business should meet the needs of all the stakeholders, as opposed to operating it for shareholders.*

That's weird. Where's all the talk of increasing shareholder value and maximizing returns on investment? Isn't that what business is all about? Not at weird Whole Foods, located in weird Austin, Texas.

One of my mentors and friends, author and advertising consultant Roy Williams, makes his home in Austin. Roy has found other people who are his "brand of crazy," and together they have created Wizard Academy, a self-defined, nontraditional business school. Teaching business from an ancient-looking tower that rises above the hills and looks north toward the Austin skyline, Roy and various guest lecturers teach weird lessons on communications, marketing, and business. You won't find a business school like this anywhere else. I must be weird, because I keep coming back to commune with my fellow weirdos. It wouldn't surprise me if Joe Walsh walked in one day.

Even Greenleaf Book Group, the publisher behind this book and my first title, *Brand Like a Rock Star*, is also head-quartered in weird little Austin. It is no coincidence that we found each other!

SELLING WEIRDNESS

Paige Nienaber makes a living adding weirdness to businesses, in particular to radio stations. Paige consults radio stations all over the world on how to create more compelling promotions and marketing campaigns that get listeners talking. He's big on creating "buzz" about a radio station in a city, and he's very, very good at his job. Radio stations that Paige works with have hosted nude weddings, given away in-vitro fertilization, awarded a listener Justin Bieber's used and unwashed hotel bed sheets, and auctioned off Britney Spears's positive pregnancy test. He is well known for his ability to use weird and unusual tactics in order to get noticed, and radio stations pay him very well for it.

Starting with his unusual and memorable name, Paige has built weirdness into his personal brand. As Paige notes, "Weird is really about being different from everyone else. Why would you want to get lost in the crowd and be a conformist? Successful brands get noticed and they stand out, and they do that by doing the opposite of what everyone else is doing."

On a personal branding level, weird has worked for Paige,

who has made it part of his career mission to never be the "guy with the PowerPoint" when he visits his clients. And while his clients have been tremendously successful, that isn't what Paige is most noted for. Instead of his track record helping radio stations grow audience and profit, he says people remember the weird stuff. "People will recall, unsolicited, the time I set my wallet on fire on stage at a conference or the time in Minneapolis when I filled the manager's office with inflatable love dolls. I'll gladly take that any day."

What makes weird work for Paige isn't just memorability, it is also the levity it communicates. "Weird usually translates to fun," he observes. Fun resonates with people. Some of the most successful marketing campaigns are the weird ones, like the Old Spice "Man Your Man Could Smell Like" series. When people associate your brand, or your personal brand, with fun, that's almost universally a good thing.

According to Paige, being just a little weird and fun can set you apart when you are applying for jobs, when you are one of eight thousand resumes in a pile. "My friend Meredith Teplitz, who is outstanding, did her resume packaged in a customized *Sex and the City* DVD box, titled 'Meredith And The City.'"

Paige himself has used similar tactics when he was applying for jobs early in his career. He recalls sending prospective employers an overhead shot of his desk, with "betting stubs from the race track, a half eaten slice of pizza, a phone message from a drug dealer demanding payment, and a *Thor* comic book. When you opened it up it said 'Hire This

Desk And We'll Throw In A Promotion Director.'" Paige got plenty of jobs with that unorthodox approach.

Continuing his streak of embracing weird in all of its fantastic forms, Paige sent me this photo a few months ago as he was boarding a flight to Dallas. The subject of his email was "God bless the silly people." Yes, even in the cockpit of a commercial jet passenger jet, the most serious of all workplace environments, it is important to be a little bit weird. The pilot who brought the Staples "easy button" to work definitely gets an A+ in weirdness.

The Rock Star Playlist: Five Classic, Quirky Joe Walsh Tunes

1. **"Life's Been Good."** This classic tale of rock 'n' roll excess chronicles the real-life and imaginary experiences of a rock star. With stories about driving too fast, trashing hotel rooms, all-night parties, and plenty of drugs and booze, Joe Walsh's most memorable solo hit is the ultimate statement on rock 'n' roll self-indulgence.

2. **"Life Of Illusion."** Always a fantastic song on its own, "Life of Illusion" was given new life by the Steve Carell comedy *The Forty Year Old Virgin*, as it plays in the background while the nerdy Carell rode his bicycle home from work in the movie's memorable opening scene.

3. **"I.L.B.T's."** From his 1983 album *You Bought It—You Name It*, this song is a simple love song to large female breasts. The title is an acronym for "I Like Big Tits," which is essentially the only real lyric in the three-minute song.

4. **"Rocky Mountain Way."** Although hardly silly and not particularly funny, "Rocky Mountain Way" has a sense of optimism that came to Walsh while mowing his lawn in Colorado. According to a story he told on *The Howard Stern Show*, the lyrics came to him so quickly that he left the lawnmower running. As he wrote the song, the mower proceeded to eat the neighbor's garden, making "Rocky Mountain Way" an expensive song to write.

5. **"A Flock Of Wah Wahs."** Although not officially listed as a song on the album *But Seriously, Folks . . .*, this song appears after ten seconds of silence at the end of the LP. It is basically a minute of gibberish as people make sounds that somewhat resemble the sound of ducks or geese.

▼

PART THREE:

PASSION

▼

CHAPTER TWELVE

EMBRACE THE CHAOS: TURNING ABSOLUTE INSANITY INTO AWESOME OPPORTUNITY

Think of your typical day and all of the things that can influence you that you have no control over. You can't control the weather when you wake up; it could be stormy and nasty, making your commute a long and stressful trek. You can't control the idiot who cuts you off in traffic or the construction crew who decides that a road repair in morning rush hour is a bright idea. You have no control over the fight your boss had with her husband before work, putting her in a rotten mood when you walk in the door twenty minutes late. We all have situations just like these on a daily basis, resulting in stress, tension, and lost productivity. These situations create incredible frustration, yet we have essentially no control over any of it! Why do we let it drive us so crazy?

You can't influence the weather, the traffic, or the people around you. In reality, you can't control the vast majority of factors at play in your world. There is only one thing you have absolute control over: your reaction.

How we handle adversity is quite defining. Do you let adversity, stress, and challenge bring you down? Or do you use it as the inspiration and motivation to do great things? Og Mandino, author of the wildly successful and bashfully titled sales book *The Greatest Salesman in the World*, once said, "Always seek out the seed of triumph in every adversity." That certainly is a trait of rock stars in any field; they find a way to turn the challenges they encounter into opportunities to capitalize on.

FLEETWOOD MAC AND THE ART OF AIKIDO

The Japanese martial art aikido is rooted in the concept of harnessing the forces working against you to work in your favor. Instead of fighting an attacker head-on or attempting to block his attack, practitioners of aikido lead with the attacker's momentum, attempting to redirect the force. Aikido aims to protect oneself while also preventing injury to one's attacker.

One of the greatest albums in rock 'n' roll history is a perfect example of aikido-like forces at work. This legendary record was recorded amid the kind of chaos most of us can only imagine in our worst nightmares, yet the band in question was able to harness those powerful forces and redirect them into the creative process.

Imagine that you are in a band with your wife, and just as your band is taking off and experiencing phenomenal success for the first time, your relationship falls apart. You are scheduled to go into the studio to record a highly anticipated album together, and at the same time you are scheduling lawyers to negotiate a bitter divorce. Meanwhile, another couple in the band is going through the exact same thing, and the two of them have decided to express their deepest emotions and bitterness by writing powerful songs about each other. Finally, partway through the recording, your drummer and founder discovers that his wife is having an affair with his best friend, adding an entirely new layer of stress and chaos to the recording process.

Those were the exact circumstances that Fleetwood Mac faced as they entered the studio to record the album *Rumours*. John and Christine MacVie were getting divorced, and both had just started the awkward, difficult, and emotionally volatile process of dating other people. Songwriters Stevie Nicks and Lindsey Buckingham had also split up, inspiring each of them to write deeply personal songs that tore at each other's hearts. Meanwhile, drummer, bandleader, and father figure Mick Fleetwood was stung by the news of his wife's affair with his best friend, midway through the recording sessions. As all of this was transpiring, the band—like so many other bands in the 1970s—was more than casually experimenting with drugs.

Despite it all, the band created an album that went on to become one of the rock era's best-selling and most memorable recordings. Every single song on the album was played on the radio, not just a few select singles. *Rumours* gave us major Top 40 hits like "Dreams," "Go Your Own Way," "Don't Stop," and "You Make Lovin' Fun." Other gems from the album were "Gold Dust Woman," "Second Hand News," and "Never Going Back Again." With over forty million copies sold, *Rumours* currently ranks as the eighth best-selling album of all time, worldwide. It also won a Grammy Award for Album of the Year. And to top it off, the album influenced an entire generation of musicians from all genres.

TURNING FORCES IN HIS FAVOR

Rumours co-producer Ken Caillat wrote extensively about the creation of the band's defining album in his fantastic book *Making Rumours*, a deeply personal account of the making of a legendary album. It chronicles the good, bad, and ugly behind the record and the characters who created it, and it is a must-read for any Fleetwood Mac fan. Throughout, Caillat documents the incredible chaos surrounding the band and repeatedly illustrates how he, co-producer Richard Dashut, and the band were forced to embrace it instead of fight it.

For example, Caillat tuned in quickly to a sort of "twelve-hour rule." Essentially, he learned in very short order that no matter what time the band was scheduled to start recording, they would not show up in the studio until at least twelve hours after they last left the studio. This meant that on days when the band jammed until three o'clock a.m., Caillat would not expect to see the band until at least three o'clock p.m. the following day . . . even if they were scheduled to start recording at noon. Caillat, at first tempted to retain order and keep things on schedule, found a way to embrace the chaos of the twelve-hour rule and use it to his advantage. On days like that, he would use the extra time alone in the studio to refine the work they had already done and to conceive new ways to improve the songs. When the band finally wandered in, Caillat had already accomplished plenty.

While at the time it may have been hard to see the connection between the chaos and the creativity, in hindsight the members of the band are well aware that they created a better product, in part thanks to the insanity surrounding them. On songs like "Go Your Own Way" and "Second Hand News," Lindsey Buckingham expressed his raw emotions toward ex-girlfriend Stevie Nicks, who responded with her own optimistic breakup song, "Dreams," the biggest hit from the album. The songs, although painful for each to hear at the time, inspired both of them. Buckingham told *Blender* magazine about the process, saying, "We had to go through this elaborate exercise of denial, keeping our personal feelings in one corner of the room while trying to be professional in the other." So instead of fighting in the studio, they communicated their feelings in songs. Those songs captured intense honesty and emotions as few songs ever do, bonding with fans in a special way. Rather than letting the chaos of their breakup work against them, Stevie Nicks and Lindsey Buckingham, perhaps entirely subconsciously, found a way to harness those chaotic forces for good.

Even the album's title, *Rumours*, was a nod to the stresses and challenges of the recording process. Word of the band's breakups and affairs had leaked to the press, and there was plenty of speculation that Fleetwood Mac was on the verge of breaking up. As the recording sessions dragged on longer than planned, the rumors gained strength. When it was time to name their work, the band chose the British spelling with the extra "u" in honor (perhaps that should that be "honour"?) of the chatter and conjecture.

The circumstances at play during Fleetwood Mac's mid-'70s surge of creative brilliance were far beyond the kind of chaos most of us will ever have to deal with in everyday life, but our chaos is just as real and can impact our lives in the same way. On any given day, factors you have no control over will force you to alter your goals, change your approach, delay your project, or even completely take your plans off the rails.

BRILLIANCE BORN IN ADVERSITY

Tom Cochrane had a massive, worldwide #1 hit in 1991 called "Life is a Highway." For a few months, you couldn't go anywhere without hearing that song. Twenty years later, Rascal Flatts recorded a country version that also became a #1 hit. That song is Tom's claim to fame. But the years that preceded "Life Is a Highway" weren't always paved; there were plenty of bumps and potholes leading up to that break-through song.

As Tom and his band Red Rider were doing very well in the early 1980s, his relationship with manager Bruce Allen was falling apart. They had a rather acrimonious split in 1985, leaving Tom bitter and angry. That experience ignited a creative spark in Tom, and he entered into one of his most prolific periods.

Over the subsequent six years, Tom Cochrane recorded four albums, including his most successful album, *Mad Mad World*, featuring "Life is a Highway." His career owes a lot to the traumatic period after that bitter breakup, and Tom knows it. "Often out of adversity . . . that's when the best work comes," he told www.melodicrock.com. "You are always struggling to find something that makes sense. What defines us as a human being is struggling to do that."

We all have moments of adversity, where the stresses of the world seem to collapse upon us. In those moments we are presented with the choice to either fight head on or use Fleetwood Mac–like aikido to turn the stresses in our favor.

Sometimes those who choose to fight head on come out winners, often at a high cost. After all, every battlefield victory has its casualties. On the other hand, there is the option to accept a certain level of chaos and stress and use it as a catalyst to great things. Those who choose to embrace the chaos can accomplish just as much or more without the intense stress and struggle of fighting things head on.

TURNING THE RECESSION INTO A RESORT

When the economy suddenly stalled and then tanked in 2008, plenty of people with absolutely no control over it were left in total chaos. The recession impacted those at both ends of the economic spectrum, leaving many ordinary people out of work and slashing the fortunes and life savings of many wealthy people. During this turmoil, Ottawa-based investment adviser Peter Nicholson suggested to his clients that they do what they could to embrace the chaos. Since they obviously couldn't turn the economy around, his advice was to make the best of it and to see the glass as potentially half-full instead of definitely half-empty. Peter directed his clients to look for opportunities to invest wisely where they could afford to, knowing their ability to do so might be inhibited by the economy. Those investments, large and small, started to pay off when the recovery came. But, as Peter notes, once the recovery comes, it is often too late to get into the game. His clients were buying when prices were low, getting in before the recovery.

Peter himself seized an opportunity at the height of the collapse. A few years earlier a good friend had introduced him to the tiny Bahamian island of Great Exuma, and he immediately fell in love with the place. While destinations in the Bahamas like Nassau and Paradise Island are busy and active places, Great Exuma is the total opposite; it is a perfect slice of white powder sand with only a few thousand laid-back residents on the entire thirty-eight-mile-long island.

The *Washington Post* called Great Exuma one of the ten most desirable international locations for its aquamarine water, friendly people, sunny weather, and idyllic pace of life. The international airport is a tiny wooden building, there are no traffic lights, and around every corner are untouched white sand beaches that you can have all to yourself.

At the height of the recession, Peter learned that the developer of a new resort project in Great Exuma was running into financial challenges. Peter was able to gather together a network of investors to save the project and turn it into a five-star getaway retreat that now ranks as one of the ten best luxury resorts in the Caribbean. The beautiful villas of Grand Isle Resort sit on a peninsula adjacent to Emerald Bay, one of the island's stellar beaches. Wrapping around the grounds are the eighteen spectacular holes of the Greg Norman–designed Emerald Reef Golf Course. Yet for a period during the recession, the golf course was overgrown with weeds and the unfinished villas were boarded up. For Peter and his investors, the opportunity to create a spectacular place like Grand Isle Resort was made feasible entirely because of the economic downturn. Now, as the economy slowly recovers, the resort is paying dividends for the local employees, their families, the island economy, and the project's investors and shareholders.

FINDING UPSIDE IN THE DOWNTURN

Clearly not all of us have the means, wealth, or personal networks to invest in luxury Caribbean properties, but the lesson is the same no matter what income bracket you fall into. Recessions can present opportunities to the average person that otherwise would not exist, and if you retain Peter's perspective you can seize them.

Real estate price drops and foreclosures in recessions make ownership possible for many first-time homebuyers who otherwise might not be able to afford it. While accessing the credit to get a mortgage might be tougher, for those who do qualify the ownership opportunities are more affordable in an economic down cycle.

For existing homeowners, students in need of loans, or entrepreneurs starting new businesses, recessions generally bring about lower interest rates. When the cost of borrowing money comes down, small business growth often increases. Slower economic times can bring about day-to-day consumer bargains as manufacturers and retailers fight for your business. Big-purchase items like furniture and cars are often available at zero interest, and coupons and discounts abound.

From a career perspective, many people would look at an economic downturn as a glass-half-empty situation, and that would be easy to do so. As companies downsize and cut costs, many qualified and hardworking people are laid off and end up unexpectedly looking for work. While this is obviously not the ideal situation, it often presents career growth opportunities for those who remain employed. With fewer people on the payroll, companies tend to work harder to retain their key people through a recession. Helping a company successfully work through an economic downturn can also mean good things on the other side, when the economy recovers and the company is able to reward their best and brightest with promotions or raises.

Even for those left unemployed or underemployed in a recession, having a glass-half-full perspective is vital. Employers are looking for people who possess a positive outlook and can be an upbeat influence in the workplace. Becoming focused on the negatives is easy to do but terribly destructive to your future.

You can't control the economy, decisions made at the corporate level, agendas set by others, traffic on your commute, or your coworker who is having a bad day. You can't control the incompetence of others, the weather, the reliability of the mail, or the passing of time. So why fight those obstacles head-on? Doesn't it make more sense to use the aikido that Fleetwood Mac so brilliantly used on *Rumours*?

The Rock Star Playlist: Five Brilliant Results of the Fleetwood Mac Chaos

1. **"Monday Morning."** The first album to feature Lindsey Buckingham and Stevie Nicks was Fleetwood Mac in 1975, and it served to reintroduce the new incarnation of blues band Fleetwood Mac to their fans. "Monday Morning" was the opening song on side one of the album. In a short two minutes and forty-eight seconds, the tone was set for a much more accessible pop band with fantastic harmonies and insightful lyrics.

continued on following page

2. **"Rhiannon."** The first Stevie Nicks song to become a hit for Fleetwood Mac was "Rhiannon" in 1976. Stevie introduces the song on stage as the story of a Welsh witch, and in the late '70s Mick Fleetwood compared her powerful and theatrical performance of the song to an exorcism.

3. **"Second Hand News."** "Second Hand News" opens up the famous *Rumours* album, an album that many critics place among the all-time best of the rock era. The song's upbeat nature masked Lindsey Buckingham's appeal for personal space in the wake of a failing relationship.

4. **"Go Your Own Way."** Core to the success of *Rumours* were songs influenced by the personal struggles that each member of the band was going through. For Lindsey Buckingham, that was his breakup with Stevie Nicks. He chronicled some of those emotions in "Go Your Own Way," a song that Nicks sings harmony on. Knowing the personal angst between them at the time, the beautiful harmony they created puts an ironic twist on the classic song.

5. **"The Chain."** "The Chain" is a unique song in that it is the only one with writing credits to all five members of the band. John McVie and Mick Fleetwood had written the bass part but didn't have lyrics. Stevie Nicks had lyrics that fit the bass parts but needed help from Christine McVie to perfect them. Lindsey Buckingham came to the table with a song he had written a few years earlier that became the song's opening. Putting all of these disparate parts together, the band created the aptly titled song "The Chain."

▼

CHAPTER 13

FINDING PERFECT HARMONY: HOW DAVID CROSBY MADE HIMSELF AND OTHERS BETTER

O n a warm July night in 1968, David Crosby and Stephen Stills, as the story goes, were both at the same San Francisco party being thrown by Cass Elliot of The Mamas & The Papas. She was a magnanimous creature, and her home was often filled with good friends and the laughter they naturally bring. The two knew each other, and it wasn't unusual for them to pick up a guitar and sing together when they met up, as musicians often do. As they sang together in Mama Cass's living room, Graham Nash of The Hollies listened and found himself mesmerized by what he heard. It was a new song that Stephen Stills had written called "You Don't Have To Cry." When the song ended, Graham spoke up.

"Do that again," he said. So they did, from start to finish. Nash still hadn't heard enough. "Okay, one more time," demanded the Hollies singer.

Crosby and Stills looked at each other and decided no harm could come from playing the song a third time. This time, Graham Nash did more than just listen intently; he added a top harmony vocal to the song, and according to David Crosby, "at that moment, we knew pretty much what we were going to be doing for a long time."

They were right. Crosby, Stills, and Nash (and later, Neil Young), gave the world harmony vocals unlike any heard before, and forty-plus years later they continue to do it. While in hindsight it feels like the late 1960s were a fertile time for acoustic music, it really wasn't prime time for folkies.

The biggest acts in 1969 were guitar bands, not acoustic/folk/harmony trios. The Rolling Stones had massive hard-rock hits that year with "Gimme Shelter" and "Honky Tonk Women." Jimi Hendrix was huge. Led Zeppelin was shaking the planet with *Zeppelin II* and songs like "Whole Lotta Love," "Thank You," and "Ramble On." And then along came Crosby, Stills, and Nash with soft guitars and smooth harmonies, and everyone paid attention. CSN and their mesmerizing harmonies were a whisper that came along at a time when everyone was screaming.

Crosby, Stills, and Nash arrived with the benefit of instant credibility. All three of them had already achieved success in other bands, so the industry slapped a "super group" label on them. As such, they didn't need to pay their dues playing small venues. Their second-ever paying gig was on August 17, 1969, at a festival show in a New York town they had never heard of but would help make permanently famous.

By the time they got to Woodstock, the schedule was already way off track. Joe Cocker had opened the day on time, but an afternoon thunderstorm had delayed things for a few hours. So instead of a Sunday evening set, Crosby, Stills, and Nash hit the stage at three o'clock a.m. on Monday morning, opening their set by saying, "This is only the second time we've performed in front of people. We're scared shitless."

You couldn't tell. They opened with "Suite: Judy Blue Eyes" and then proceeded to captivate several hundred thousand people into rapt silence with a harmonic version of the Beatles' "Blackbird." It was clear from that moment on that the harmonies that Crosby, Stills, and Nash were creating were not only entirely unique, but also very, very special.

The beauty of harmony—vocals layered upon each other—first struck a young David Crosby when his mother took him to see a symphony orchestra when he was just six years old. They took folding chairs to the park and got there early enough to sit in the front row. When the music started, Crosby was blown away.

"It was like a wave crashed on me, and I was entranced with it," he told filmmaker Andrew Zuckerman for the 2010 movie *Music*. The way the orchestra created something greater than each of the individual instruments helped set David

Crosby on his musical journey with his mind focused on collaboration. He wanted to sing, but he didn't see himself as a solo performer or even a lead singer. "I always wanted to play with other people. I think it had something to do with that moment with the orchestra, because it was so powerful."

David's ability to create magical harmonies first burst through the speakers of your AM radio in the spring of 1965 when The Byrds scored a hit with "Mr. Tambourine Man." They followed that with a string of harmony-driven classics like "All I Really Want To Do," "Turn, Turn, Turn," and "Eight Miles High." Their jangly guitars and rich harmonies turned them into an extremely influential 1960s band, and their impact on music was immediate. Even leading bands like the Beatles found themselves incorporating elements of The Byrds' sound into their music. With The Byrds, the vocal collaboration was so pronounced that there really was no de facto lead singer. On any given song, Roger McGuinn, Gene Clark, Chris Hillman, or David Crosby could take the lead, accompanied in harmony by the rest of the band. Unfortunately, the sweet-sounding harmony masked a disharmonious chord within the group. Tensions rose quickly, and David Crosby left the band in 1967.

The harmonic partnership he found with Stephen Stills and Graham Nash a few years later has also faced its fair share of discord. Over the course of four decades, the trio has had numerous falling outs and reunions. They have expanded to a quartet with the addition of Neil Young, and then contracted back to a trio. They've been billed as a duo, with both Crosby/ Nash and Stills/Young recording albums and touring together.

In addition, all four members have had successful solo careers. They are, however, at their very best when they come together and, as Crosby himself has said, "give to a whole that is greater than the sum of the parts."

Harmony has been an essential part of rock 'n' roll from the very beginning. Crosby, Stills, and Nash, while among the most obvious examples, were not the only artists to use harmony as a key aspect of their music. The Eagles used smooth vocal harmonies to create their most memorable songs such as "Take It Easy," "Peaceful Easy Feeling," and "Hotel California." It was actually their harmonies, not their songwriting or musicianship, that resulted in legendary producer Glyn Johns working on their debut album. Johns wasn't keen on the band after hearing them, and with a track record of producing music by Led Zeppelin and The Who, he didn't need to take a risk on an unknown country-rock band from California. It was only during a break, when the band members used the song "Seven Bridges Road" to warm up their vocal chords, that Glyn Johns heard the magical harmonies of The Eagles. He immediately changed his mind and produced the band's first two albums, both of which became incredibly successful.

There are so many other examples. James Taylor was famous for his harmonious songs, and even had his good friends David Crosby and Graham Nash to sing together on his hit song "Mexico." Simon and Garfunkel are another example of prominent harmony in rock 'n' roll. Harmony isn't restricted to acoustic artists; it is everywhere in rock music. You'll hear fantastic over-the-top harmony in classic rock bands like Queen. Even '80s hair-metal bands liberally applied the technique, creating rising harmonic choruses to their slickly produced songs. Think Def Leppard's "Animal" or Whitesnake's "Here I Go Again," and you get the picture. Similar harmonic choruses are prominent today in country music.

The fine art of harmony has resurfaced with the recent rise of popular acoustic bands like Mumford & Sons, a UK group who are riding a resurgence of folk-pop. Keyboardist Ben Lovett remembers the day that the group first sang together in the studio, and much like Crosby, Stills, and Nash, they instantly knew something good was happening. "We sang in harmony in that studio and it clicked," he told *The National* newspaper in Dubai. "Four felt like a family." Mumford & Sons have become one of the top bands on the planet in a short six years since forming, and they have helped set the stage for a revival of acoustic harmonies. Bands like The Lumineers and Of Monsters and Men have kept the revival going, demonstrating that the best music is created when the entire group collaborates, which is exactly what a symphony orchestra playing in the park did for David Crosby many years ago.

CREATING HARMONY THROUGH DIFFERENCES

The reality is that no matter what era or style of popular music you are listening to, from hip-hop to country, you are probably hearing harmony. Finding harmony isn't difficult, but finding someone to create that illusive perfect harmony with is. Two people with wonderful voices on their own can sing together and have terrible harmony. In other cases, two voices sound fine harmonizing together but fail to capture that magic that artists like Crosby, Stills, and Nash had. One of the reasons CSN created such perfect harmony goes beyond music and strikes to the heart of the unique relationship between the three men. Each member of the band brought a different set of skills and experiences to the table. With the success each of them had prior to teaming up, they all had the chance to develop into seasoned artists. David Crosby had spent time in The Byrds. Stephen Stills was a key part of Buffalo Springfield, a short-lived but extremely influential band. And Graham Nash was a pop star with The Hollies before becoming disillusioned with their musical direction. Crosby was born and raised in Southern California and brought with him all of the musical influences of the west coast. Stephen Stills had a nomadic childhood on American military bases in Florida, Panama, Costa Rica, and El Salvador, and he was heavily influenced by Latin music. Meanwhile, Graham Nash was from the northwest corner of England, raised in the city of Blackpool in Lancashire. The result was three very different men who all contributed in unique ways to the greater group.

THE APPLE HARMONY

We've all experienced those types of relationships, where, despite very different backgrounds and experiences, two people seem to complement each other almost intuitively. Sometimes one person is the missing piece to the other person's puzzle, as Apple cofounder Steve Wozniak was to Steve Jobs. While both were into computers, Jobs was passionate about the design, feel, user interface, and marketing. Wozniak was an under-the-hood guy, deeply involved in how the products were assembled and how they worked. In 1976, Wozniak created the first Apple computer. It was, like most small computers of the day, a "homebrew" model, meaning that when you purchased the computer you essentially bought the guts—the ingredients and the instructions—and you put it together yourself. That was how personal computers were built in the days of massive mainframe computers. The idea of a fully assembled complete home computing package hadn't struck anyone yet, except for Steve Jobs.

Jobs had the puzzle piece that Steve Wozniak was missing. He was the person who believed that they could change the game by selling a completely assembled computer. Instead of selling parts and instructions, Apple started selling the entire computer, completely assembled with keyboard and monitor. While it may seem like a small point in hindsight, there's no question that this was a pivotal move in home computing. By selling a completely assembled product, Apple was taking the computer out of the hands of computer geeks and university professors and putting it into the homes and financial reach of average, everyday people. Steve Jobs went on to be the charismatic and engaging face of a product inspired by Steve Wozniak's technical brilliance. Although in time their relationship had more than its fair share of unharmonious moments, the work of Jobs and Woz changed the world, because each of them brought a different piece to each other's personal puzzle.

WITH GOD AS MY BLOODY WITNESS

Modern career harmony doesn't even need to happen in person. Thanks to technology, harmonies are being created across time zones and continents. Elaine Joli and her business partner Tim Forrest have never actually met in person, but together they are creating an online business that allows entrepreneurs to do exactly what they are doing: network across great distances. Their site, www.indie.bz, allows entrepreneurs and small business people to connect, share ideas, and learn from each other. Tim and Elaine haven't met in person, because Tim lives in Australia and Elaine calls Arizona home. Despite an eighteen-hour time difference, Elaine and Tim thrive together. After all, as a team they are on the job essentially twenty-four hours a day, thanks to the time zones, so work is always moving forward. Like most great business partnerships, the two bring different qualities. In this case, Elaine brings her marketing savvy to the team, while Tim is an expert in the tech side of the business. But their relationship goes much deeper, and over the course of two-and-a-half years together, Elaine has come to refer to Tim as "the salt to my pepper."

Like nearly every start-up, life at indie.bz isn't easy. Success seldom happens overnight and almost never happens without pain, suffering, and second-guessing. There are always moments in launching a new venture when you feel like it is pointless to continue, and Elaine is no exception. At precisely one of those pack-it-in-moments, Elaine and Tim connected on Skype. They talked through their next set of challenges and the next steps each would take to get their project off the ground. Elaine tried to keep her mood out of the equation and focus on the project, but evidently Tim could hear how discouraged she was.

Moments after the call ended, Elaine's email buzzed. It was a message from Tim with the subject, "With God as my witness." There was no message from Tim in the email, only an excerpt from an interview that Elon Musk did with Wired.com. Elon is the founder of SpaceX, PayPal, and Tesla Motors. Although he is an incredible success today, many of his previous ventures have failed miserably. At the time of the interview, SpaceX had yet to achieve orbit with its spacecraft, and Wired.com was focused on the lack of success the company was having.

> **Wired.com:** *At the end of the day you're still zero for three, you have failed to out a rocket into orbit.*

> **Elon Musk:** *We haven't gotten into orbit, that's true. But we've made considerable progress. If it's an all-or-nothing proposition, then we've failed. But it's not all-or-nothing. We must get to orbit eventually, and we will. It might take us one, two, or three more tries, but we will. We will make it work.*

> **Wired.com:** *How do you maintain your optimism?*

> **Elon Musk:** *Do I sound optimistic?*

Wired.com: *Yeah, you always do.*

Elon Musk: *Optimism, pessimism, fuck that. We're going to make it happen. With God as my bloody witness, I'm hell-bent on making it work.*

It was exactly the encouragement that Elaine needed to burst out of her trap of disappointment and tackle the work ahead. Despite having never met her in person, Tim knew the perfect remedy for his business partner. He provided the harmony she needed to wake up the next day and forge ahead, "hell-bent on making it work." Today Elaine and Tim continue to work on their indie.bz project, determined to make the world a better place for new business ventures and the brave entrepreneurs who turn them into realities. And whether or not indie.bz takes off, the two intend to continue to collaborate, recognizing that they have a certain creative business harmony that is difficult to find and capture.

Interestingly, Elaine and Tim only use the audio version of Skype, not the video version. Not only have they never met in person, they've never even seen each other. They connect through voice, thought, and action. How's that for harmony?

The Rock Star Playlist: My Personal Favorite Rock 'n' Roll Harmonies

1. **"Suite: Judy Blue Eyes" by Crosby, Stills, and Nash.** This is the song the band recorded first and one of the few songs to be performed at both Woodstock in 1969 and Live Aid in 1985. It is a perfect example of the harmony created by this incredible trio.

2. **"The Sound of Silence" by Simon and Garfunkel.** When the song was first released, it was a flop, and Paul and Art went their separate ways. A year later, Columbia Records reissued the song, and it became a hit. They reunited and entered a prolific creative period that produced their greatest harmonic hits.

3. **"Seven Bridges Road" by The Eagles.** Two-part harmony is powerful enough, but five-part harmony is impressive. The Eagles made this 1969 Steve Young song famous when they recorded it live in 1980. For years, the band had used "Seven Bridges Road" as a backstage warm-up. They finally brought it to the front of the stage for their *Eagles Live* album.

4. **"Mr. Tambourine Man" by The Byrds.** Almost any Byrds song could qualify for this list, but "Mr. Tambourine Man" stands up as their lasting legacy. Written by Bob Dylan, it was The Byrds who made the song into a Top 40 hit with their layered harmony.

5. **"The Weight" by The Band.** Having backed up Bob Dylan on tour, The Band was a seasoned outfit when they struck out on their own. Recorded in 1968, "The Weight" featured Levon Helm singing lead and harmony vocal, Rick Danko singing harmony and taking the lead vocal in one verse, and Richard Manuel singing harmony. Frequent lead singer Robbie Robertson played acoustic guitar but didn't sing on the track, while Garth Hudson played piano.

▼

CHAPTER 14

GO WITH YOUR GUT: THE BEATLES PROVE THAT SOME THINGS CANNOT EASILY BE PREDICTED

"**G**uitar bands are on the way out. The Beatles have no future in show business."

That was the famous phrase that Decca Records used in their rejection letter to the Beatles in January 1961. Decca sent the Beatles and their out-of-style guitars packing and chose instead to sign a new beat band called the Tremeloes. Everybody knows the Tremeloes, right?

The trained ears that heard the Beatles audition at Decca and turned them down were among the best in the business. The legendary Dick Rowe was responsible for signing

UK bands like The Rolling Stones, Van Morrison, The Moody Blues, The Animals, The Zombies, and many others. Rowe's track record makes him one of the most important UK record executives and producers of his era, yet history remembers him best as the man who rejected the Beatles.

Did Decca Records have information that influenced their decision to reject a new guitar band? Probably. Clearly they believed that the type of music the Beatles were making was a passing fad. With access to sales statistics, research, customer feedback, and the brightest production minds in the music industry, the odds are pretty strong that they had solid numerical evidence to back their opinion that guitar bands were on the way out. There is a strong possibility that they had both a gut feeling and a wealth of numbers to support their decision to turn down the Beatles.

But they were wrong. And the Beatles changed the world.

That's how business works, for the most part. We have been conditioned to look to spreadsheets to help us make safe business decisions. When restaurant chains plan to introduce new menu items, they turn to test markets. For two months late in 2011, McDonald's test-marketed in Houston an English Pub Burger: a one-third pound Angus beef patty, hickory smoked bacon, white cheddar cheese, American cheese, grilled onions, steak sauce, and Dijon mustard on a thick bun. Houston isn't alone as a test market; companies look for cities that are demographically similar to the nation as a whole. Cities like Nashville, Rochester, Wichita, Birmingham, Peoria, and Albany are some of the cities in which you are most likely to encounter unusual menu items like the McDonald's English Pub Burger.

So how did the English Pub Burger fare? Apparently well enough to be expanded into other cities, but not with the same name. A few months after its Houston test, the burger was brought back for more test marketing in San Diego as the Clubhouse Angus. Through a combination of sales data, customer surveys, and in-depth research, McDonald's was able to determine that this new burger was worth pursuing further.

There's nothing wrong with data. But we live in a world awash with data. Unlike any time in the past, we can use online and social media resources to gauge consumer opinion, extremely quickly and efficiently. The problem with numbers, data, and research, however, is that it hardly ever leads you to the big, breakthrough idea. Data and numbers almost always point you down the safe road, and the safe road is no place to be if you intend to change the world.

While McDonald's used market testing and consumer data to determine the eventual fate of the English Pub/Clubhouse Angus burger, it is worth noting that they invented their most famous menu item, the Big Mac, without any data at all. The legendary sandwich was created by Pennsylvania franchisee Jim Delligatti at his McDonald's restaurant in Unionville, Pennsylvania. He started serving it in 1967 for forty-five cents. A year later, it was added to the national McDonald's menu. It has gone on to become their signature item worldwide. All of that success was achieved with essentially no market research.

On the other hand, the most famous branding blunder

in history came about entirely because of market research. Coke had been steadily losing ground to rival Pepsi throughout the 1970s and early 1980s, mainly because younger consumers preferred the sweeter taste of Pepsi. That was clearly evidenced by market research at the time. In response, Coke embarked on a top-secret mission to reformulate its iconic blend. The new product, a sweeter mixture, repeatedly topped both Coke and Pepsi in taste testing. Although there was negativity in focus groups about the concept of changing Coke's legendary formula, there was no doubt about the positive reaction that consumers were having to the new, sweeter mixture. Coke made the decision to discontinue their old formula and very publicly introduce "New Coke" on April 23, 1985.

On July 10, less than three months after New Coke was launched, Coca-Cola bowed to extreme pressure from their consumers and brought back the old formula under the banner "Coke Classic." What transpired in the span between the April launch and the July reversal is the stuff of business legend: consumers were outraged; protests were organized; contraband "old" Coke was smuggled in from European regions where it was still in production. The media was relentless in its coverage of the fiasco. Local bottlers of Coke even launched a lawsuit against Coca-Cola for messing with the brand.

The entire mess was brought about thanks to market research that *clearly* indicated that consumers preferred New Coke over both traditional Coke and Pepsi. It was, in effect, consumer research that instigated the disaster.

Legendary Apple CEO Steve Jobs was notorious for

relying very little on research and data crunching. Instead, Jobs considered himself to be the kind of innovator who shoots for the stars with fantastic, big ideas. Jobs believed he was the kind of visionary who could see what people wanted *before they knew they even wanted it.* And to a large degree, history has proven him to be exactly that.

Jobs was always a contrarian when it came to research. When Apple launched the revolutionary Mac decades ago, Jobs fielded the question about how much research they did with a witty retort: "Did Alexander Graham Bell do any market research before he invented the telephone?"

Years later, when asked about what market research Apple did to design the iPad, Steve was equally clear in his reply. "None," he answered. "It's not the consumers' job to know what they want. We figure out what we want."

Steve continued, "It's hard for consumers to tell you what they want when they've never seen anything remotely like it. Take desktop video editing. I never got one request from someone who wanted to edit movies on his computer. Yet now that people see it, they say, 'Oh my God, that's great!'"

When you want to change the world, you won't be able to rely on market research to guide you. There won't be numbers and spreadsheets and roadmaps. If that were the case, everyone would change the world.

Now, before you go crazy and abandon every ounce of research in your decision-making process, step back and remember that Steve Jobs was prone to grandiose sweeping statements like that. No doubt Apple did conduct some form of research and continues to use research to this day. But what sets Apple and Steve Jobs apart from the bulk of the business world is their willingness to put research aside and boldly go where no man has gone before. Steve Jobs and his team were among the best at realizing that consumer research can only predict so much and that attempting to use it to predict future behavior is nearly impossible. Instead of giving consumers what they said they wanted, Apple famously created things people didn't even know they could want.

In rock 'n' roll and in business, plenty of evidence suggests that there is considerable merit in the Steve Jobs approach. Should it come as any surprise that Steve Jobs's all-time favorite rock band is the same one that Decca rejected because of their research that told them "guitar bands are on the way out"?

No one could have researched the comic book personas and stage-destroying pyrotechnics of Kiss. That's because no one had ever seen such a spectacle before Kiss came along. You can't research something when, as Jobs noted, "They've never seen anything remotely like it." Kiss rocked the world because they did something boldly different and showed the world something it had never seen before. That's when the world decided that it wanted what Kiss had to offer.

Likewise, it would have been impossible to research Jimi Hendrix and his guitar burning. No record label had ever seen research indicating that music lovers were looking for a black blues-rock singer who exuded sex appeal, played guitar better than anyone else, and ritualistically burned his guitar on the altar that was his stage. Jimi just did it and showed the world what he believed they wanted.

On the other hand, the music industry is littered with the carcasses of copycat acts that attempted to give the world exactly what it said it wanted. The late 1980s explosion of New Kids on the Block was just such an event. Witnessing the mass hysteria that the Boston boy band created, producers clamored to find the next boy band, created in the New Kids image. In the UK, Take That was formed, along with "rival" boy band East 17. That led to a rush of copycats including Boyzone, MN8, 911, and Damage. Within a few years, all of them had broken up. Twenty years later, only Take That and New Kids on the Block have managed to put together a reunion of any notable success. The copycat boy bands all failed, even though the available evidence indicated that the world loved boy bands.

Nearly a decade later it happened again. The Backstreet Boys reignited the boy band phenomenon, and they were quickly joined by *NSYNC, O-Town, LFO, 98 Degrees, Dream Street, and McFly. Most failed in the long run, even though they emulated exactly what millions of music fans wanted.

All this leads to the inevitable question: What will happen now that UK boy band One Direction is riding worldwide fame and fortune? Past history tells us that within a few years there will be a glut of similar bands all trying to replicate the One Direction formula, and most will fail miserably.

In your personal branding quest and career development path, it is vital to throw away conventional wisdom now and then and give the world something it doesn't yet know that it wants.

Steve Andrews, the vice president of marketing for a nationwide furniture chain, recently interviewed candidates for a senior regional marketing position in the southwest. Working under Steve's direction, this person would be responsible for the local execution of national campaigns as well as the conception and execution of various local marketing campaigns. The company was engaged in an extremely competitive battle with another furniture chain, especially in the southwest region. Every great marketing and promotional move they came up with was mirrored by the new upstart, making it difficult for the company to retain market share. With so much on the line, Steve was determined to find the perfect candidate.

"I eliminated nearly everyone with just a passing glance at their résumé," he told me. "Spelling mistakes, awkward phrases, and amateur mistakes took care of 90 percent of the applicants." Then it got serious. Steve narrowed it down to five potential candidates and began to conduct interviews in person. Surprisingly, the same thing happened. "I found that within a minute or two of meeting, I had a gut reaction about each candidate, and I was able to eliminate three of the five of them within a minute or two of starting the interview." Steve continued, "I completed the interviews and did my due diligence, and in all three cases I found things that supported my initial gut reaction. It was amazing."

Finally, Steve's search was down to two finalists, and additional interviews were scheduled. One candidate had the perfect résumé: he had done the job before, working with a different company in a very similar role; he knew the region

well, having lived and worked there previously. "His experience level was deep, and he had the depth of knowledge to
really make a difference in our company," said Steve. "But
he was too perfect. He answered every question with the
answer I wanted to hear. It was like he was reading from a
script. There was not a hair out of place on the guy."

The second candidate was experienced but not at the
same level as the first candidate. He hadn't done the same
job for a different company in the same field, but instead
gained his experience in an entirely different field. He would
be learning a new industry in a new region. The second candidate came with plenty of risk.

"What set him apart was the interview. He surprised me
with his answers," noted Steve. "Instead of the go-to answer
you would expect, this guy went in entirely different directions. He actually came to the table with ideas that chal-
lenged our way of thinking."

After conducting the interviews, Steve and his three-
person recruiting team debated which candidate should get
the job. At first, Steve was the only one leaning toward the
less-experienced candidate. "I felt that the first guy would
give us more of the same. He would do a great job, no question. But would he change the game?"

The debate and discussion was intense, but in the end the
second candidate, the less-experienced one with liabilities
and imperfections, got the job. When all of the options were
considered, the consensus was that the second candidate
delivered a potential upside that could not be ignored. "He
seemed like the kind of person that our competitor would

hire in order to kick our ass. Even though the first candidate brought all the goods to the table, this guy brought something intangible that we needed on our team."

The lesson that Andrews learned in this hiring process is the same one that inspired Steve Jobs to invoke Alexander Graham Bell when asked about the market research that led to the launch of the Mac: If you plan to change the world, there is no blueprint. It is nearly impossible to research game-changing moves.

By the way, after the executives at Decca Records were thoroughly embarrassed by passing on the Beatles, they approached another guitar band and offered them a record deal. That band's manager knew that Decca was under tremendous pressure to make up for missing out on the Beatles, so he negotiated an extremely favorable deal for his band, giving them three times the royalty payments a new band would normally receive. And that's how the Rolling Stones got their first recording contract.

The Rock Star Playlist: Five Songs That Defied the Critics

1. **"Money (That's What I Want)" by the Beatles.** This was the second of fifteen songs that the Beatles recorded on January 1, 1962, when they auditioned for Decca Records. The audition became famous when the band went on to become the biggest rock 'n' roll band in history, leaving Decca Records forever regretting their decision.

2. **"Love Me Do" by the Beatles.** After being rejected by Decca, the Beatles entered the studio to audition for EMI Music on June 6, 1962. That evening, "Love Me Do" was one of four songs the band recorded. Pete Best was still the drummer, although his days were numbered. He was replaced by Ringo Star just two months later.

3. **"Please Don't Go Girl" by New Kids on the Block.** This debut song was almost a forgotten track. When it was released to radio in spring 1988, nobody seemed to care. Just as the record label was about to give up on it, a radio station in Florida started playing it and reported fantastic listener feedback. Other stations began to play it, and the song began to climb the charts. It peaked at number ten and became the band's first hit single.

4. **"I Was Made For Lovin' You" by Kiss.** It would have been impossible to use audience research to measure the success of Kiss. The entire concept—glam rock, makeup, pyrotechnics, comic book imagery—would have been far too difficult to explain. Kiss was just that different. They did hit the mainstream pretty hard with this song, the disco-infused, love-it-or-hate-it classic, "I Was Made For Lovin' You." Although core fans declare it a sellout, the song remains a staple of the band's live show.

5. **"All Along The Watchtower" by Jimi Hendrix.** Like Kiss, what Jimi Hendrix did was so out-there that it would have been impossible to quantifiably research. But the sounds that Hendrix made went straight to the gut and the heart. His most enduring song is this version of a Bob Dylan composition.

▼

CHAPTER 15

THERE IS NO PLAN B: FAILURE IS NOT AN OPTION

My parents meant well; so did my high school guidance counselor. When I decided to make a career out of the music business, they all smiled supportively. They listened patiently as I explained how I would make a living as a DJ on the radio and how I would eventually work with some of the biggest rock stars and music executives on the planet to share their music with fans. And then they replied in soft tones to explain that while my career aspirations were exciting, it would be very wise to have a backup plan. After all, they told me, the music industry was a notoriously vicious field where success was a long shot at best. They correctly asserted that I would have to be extremely fortunate to make even a reasonable living in my field of choice. They noted that while my plan to leave high school and dive headfirst into music, media, and broadcasting sounded fun and exciting, it was very likely to leave me without a job and without a decent education before my thirtieth birthday. A "plan B," they explained, would be a solid college or university degree that would allow me to have more options when (not if) my dream of fame and fortune in the music biz fell apart.

I was having no part in their "isn't that nice" approach to my career dreams. In my heart I believed that I would be successful. My plan B *was* my plan A. To borrow from screenwriter Bill Broyles in *Apollo 13*, failure was not an option. There were plenty of options, forks in the road, obstacles in the way, and potential ways to screw it up. But failure was never an option, because I didn't have a safety net to catch me. I couldn't give up on my dream and fall back on something safe when the times got tough. In hindsight, I think that the need to succeed because of a lack of other options played a major role in my career.

THE LONDON SCHOOL OF ROCKENOMICS

The list of graduates from the London School of Economics is long and illustrious, including nineteen Nobel Prize winners, thirty-four heads of state, and numerous Pulitzer Prize winners. Mick Jagger is not on its list of famous graduates that includes the likes of John F. Kennedy and George

Bernard Shaw. Mick, known then as Michael, was debating between a career in politics or journalism, so he was enrolled in the perfect school. The London School of Economics seems to breed world leaders and big thinkers. But Mick dropped out in the fall of 1963 so that he could focus on his musical career with the Rolling Stones. "My father was furious with me," Jagger told author Gavin Edwards in 2006. "But I really didn't like being at college."

His father, like any good father, wanted his son to finish his studies at the prestigious school. After all, a degree from the London School of Economics would virtually guarantee his son plenty of good career options. As Jagger embarked on a risky career making music, his father figured that a degree from LSE would be a fantastic backup plan. But Mick Jagger wasn't interested in plan B. He was focused on being a rock star, and an economics degree on the side was only going to get in the way.

A PRINCE WITH A PLAN

Will Smith felt the same way as Mick Jagger when it came to having a plan B. Like Mick, Will was a smart kid. Growing up in Philadelphia, he had the marks to get into a great school like MIT, but in reality Smith says he never had any intention of going to college. He was too focused on music and didn't figure a backup plan was going to be necessary. In his mind, he would be world famous soon enough without one.

Will Smith first rose to fame as the "Fresh Prince" half of the rap duo DJ Jazzy Jeff & The Fresh Prince. Together Jeff and Will scored plenty of hits on the radio, and in 1988 they even won the first-ever Grammy awarded in the rap category. Smith then evolved from music into TV, starring in *The Fresh Prince of Bel-Air* in 1990 and then moving into lead roles in hit movies like *Six Degrees of Separation*, *Men in Black*, *The Pursuit of Happyness*, and *I Am Legend*. Even US president Barack Obama became a fan, suggesting that if they make a movie about his own life he would like Will Smith to play him.

Will Smith has always gone all-in; there has never been a plan B. Despite great marks in school, he dove headfirst into music. A few years later, nearly bankrupt from mismanaging his musical fortune, he went full-bore into TV. And when he decided to become a movie star, he did so with absolute focus and dedication. He started by studying the biggest box office hits of all time, looking for common threads that he could learn from in his pursuit of success. Will's plan A for his movie career has always been clear: he wants to be the biggest movie star in the world.

"There's no reason to have a plan B, because it distracts you from plan A," said Smith. Even if you have ambitious dreams that seem over-the-top to others, Will advocates following through on them, no matter how unrealistic they may seem. If you don't, you'll never achieve the great things you aspire to. "Being realistic," says Will, "is the most commonly traveled road to mediocrity."

A PROLIFIC PRISON BREAK

After eleven-and-a-half years working in various positions as she climbed the corporate ladder at Cisco, Farnoosh Brock had a revelation: she was in a prison. She loved the money but hated the job. Going to work wasn't fun, and it was draining her spirit on a daily basis. Despite a comfortable six-figure salary, she couldn't bear another day chasing after a corporate dream that had long since disappeared. In April 2011, Farnoosh walked away from Cisco and turned her experience into the foundations of a new career, launching an online company called Prolific Living that helps others take the leap from the corporate world into entrepreneurship.

"I've never been so terrified and so excited at the same time," Farnoosh explained. "Everything was scary at first. The only thing I knew how to do was be a good old employee." But the freedom that Farnoosh felt overwhelmed the fear, and without any other options, she pursued her dream relentlessly. Despite having no formal training as a writer, she found herself writing endlessly on her own blog and others, fueled by the passion she felt toward her new project. "Be inspired by what you can do in a short time when you are focused and doing what you love!"

Today Farnoosh Brock coaches others on how to achieve freedom from the corporate world, and just like Will Smith, she believes that having a backup plan does nothing except get in the way of the big dream. "Plan B generally means, 'If I fail then I can escape into this other thing which is slightly better than my last prison, but it's still not that great,' and we do not need such a plan," she says. "I teach people to figure out what they want, to get clarity around it, and to stop being wishy–washy. That's where the plan B comes into play. If you are not determined and have an intense desire for what you want, then any plan looks good as long as it allows you to escape from the current condition." Farnoosh encourages her clients to come up with a clear and concise plan A and forget that any other options even exist.

SCREENPLAYS AND SKIN CREAMS

For filmmaker Jeff Bollow, having no plan B meant creating an entire business to help follow through on his plan A. In his mid-twenties, stricken with a case of wanderlust, the former child actor left Los Angeles and ventured off to Australia with a plan to see the world and gain the perspective he would need to start his own independent film studio. He planned only to visit, but Jeff never left Australia, instead discovering that there was a tremendous untapped creative energy outside of Hollywood. Unfortunately, tapping into it wasn't that easy. Despite the creative energy, there was a lack of viable screenplays for Jeff to turn into movies. After looking at thousands of scripts, Jeff couldn't find any that were good enough to turn into movies for his independent studio. The rare gems he did find were already optioned off to bigger studios by the time he read them. Jeff knew that without great screenplays, he could never build an independent studio. With no plan B, Jeff decided to build a system to develop the screenplays his studio needed. He started teaching writers how to write screenplays that producers could really use, eventually creating a complete online screenplay development system so that writers around the world could tap into his knowledge and experience and turn their idea into a viable screenplay. Jeff believes that FAST Screenplay (www.fastscreenplay.com) will not only help him with his long-term plan A of creating a great independent film studio, but it will also help develop a wealth of new moviemaking talent worldwide.

Had Jeff Bollow had a safety net to fall back on, FAST Screenplay wouldn't exist today. "I never would have built what I did if I had a plan B," says Jeff. "Having no plan B forces you to keep pushing, even in the face of impossible obstacles. If you have a plan B, you don't ever solve your problem. You just sidestep it or retreat."

Will FAST Screenplay turn out to be the catalyst for creativity that Jeff hopes it will be? That chapter to the story hasn't been written yet. But what is evident is that the lack of easy and safe options forced Jeff to come up with an innovative solution that has the potential to not only help him, but also to help many others in similar situations. Thanks to no backup plan, Jeff could change the world.

Unlike Jeff Bollow, Charlotte Mills didn't have experience in the field in which she decided to take a leap of faith. After a trip to South Korea, Charlotte discovered a skin care secret that took her from a career in agricultural insurance to owning her own line of skin care products. Nephria Skin Care was born with no plan B, a reality that Charlotte believes helped get the ball rolling. "I think having no other option makes you work harder and it makes you hungry for success," she claims.

It also focused her energy. She thought about the business from morning until sleepless night. She talked endlessly with her husband about the business and their plans for it. It was their entire existence, as her husband had recently left the navy. Without a backup plan or secondary source of income, Charlotte spent many, many hours worried about the outcome, scared that things might not work out as planned. She channeled that fear into a positive energy, constantly visualizing her eventual success. After a lot of hard work, Nephria started to take off. Through home shopping channels on TV, the product was able to successfully launch in the UK and Germany and has now reached high-end boutiques in Santa Monica, Knightsbridge in London, and St. Moritz in Switzerland. While Nephria is still a young and growing brand, Charlotte and her husband have been able to breathe a little easier these days, knowing that their hard work is finally paying off.

NOT FOR EVERYONE

However, not everyone is cut from the same cloth. For every brave Charlotte, Jeff, and Farnoosh, hundreds of people are paralyzed by the fear of going out on a limb and risking everything on a new venture. Their ideas may be just as good, but without the courage to roll the dice, the world may never see the greatness they have to offer. Rebecca Tracey is a Life-Switch coach who specializes in helping these people realize their potential, and for her clients, sometimes a plan B is exactly what they need to achieve the dreams.

"Fear tends to be the number one thing holding people back from making bold career moves or starting their own businesses," she explains. "So I ask them to create backup plans based on the worst-case scenario." Sometimes her clients create a plan B. Some create a plan C. Some even go for a plan D. For these people, understanding that there are options, even in the face of absolute failure, is the security blanket that they need to make their bold move seem much more doable.

So do you need a plan B? It really depends on the type of person you are, says Rebecca. "The seasoned businesspeople who have been there and done that before have probably already survived a worst-case scenario, so they know that everything will be okay even if it all goes to shit."

According to Rebecca, the creation of a plan B is really more of a mental exercise than a true plan. The goal is to make risk-averse people aware that most of the time, the worst outcome really isn't as bad as they think it might be, thereby giving them the mental freedom to take the leap they dream of taking. "The good news," says Rebecca, "is that they seldom ever have to use their backup plans."

The Rock Star Playlist: My Five Favorite Rolling Stones Songs of All Time

1. **"Gimme Shelter."** The opening notes are haunting and sinister, and the background vocals by Mary Clayton are simply breathtaking. The song was a fitting close to the 1960s, as the Woodstock peace-and-love spirit gave way to the tumultuous 1970s.

2. **"Sympathy for the Devil."** What makes this song so intriguing is the display of lyrical depth. For six minutes, Mick Jagger takes you on a history lesson through the eyes of the devil himself.

3. **"Start Me Up."** Is there a better opening guitar riff in rock 'n' roll history? "Start Me Up" is one of the rare post-1970s Stones classics.

4. **"Mixed Emotions."** While most Stones experts don't rank this song near the top, it remains a classic for me. As a teenager in the 1980s, I didn't think I would ever get to see the Rolling Stones play live; there was too much tension between Mick and Keith. Then, in 1989, they overcame "Mick's Emotions" with this song. Since then, I've seen them live several times.

5. **"Jumpin' Jack Flash."** The opening guitar riff is Keith Richards at his simple best. It grabs your attention instantly and makes you want to play air guitar at the highest volume possible.

▼

CHAPTER 16

MAKING EVERY PERSON COUNT: HOW THE BOSS TREATS HIS CUSTOMERS AND EMPLOYEES

One of the magical things about a great song or a great concert is that sense that the singer is speaking directly to you. Music can do that. I remember being a brokenhearted seventeen-year-old and thinking that Def Leppard totally understood what I was going through when they sang "Love Bites." Music has a way of speaking to you one-on-one in a special and extremely powerful way . . . even hair band music, apparently.

I'm sure you've had a negative customer service experience—probably many. You've likely had a run-in with an uncooperative coworker or a person enforcing a policy that made no sense. These days, unfortunately, it feels like most of our interactions with other people go this way. Many people simply do their jobs to the letter, never striving to go above and beyond or to turn their actions into something special and memorable.

It is too easy to forget how personal our interactions are. We serve so many customers, talk to so many coworkers, and deal with so many pressing issues that we often forget just what kind of impact our actions can have on others. We forget that every interaction has the ability to change lives.

George Travis never forgets that. He has a reputation as one of the best tour directors in rock 'n' roll, and for more than three decades he was worked alongside Bruce Springsteen. In those many years spent on the road, he has developed an ability to keep even the craziest rock show rolling through ridiculously difficult circumstances without losing his mind. Working for Springsteen, one of rock's most famously customer-centric performers, George Travis has gained a unique perspective on how each concert impacts the fans in the seats.

In the Springsteen biography *Bruce* by Peter Ames Carlin (Touchstone, 2012), George's backstage ritual serves as a reminder to even the most jaded customer service representative. When a new person joins the backstage crew for a Springsteen tour or when a veteran gets down in the dumps, George has a routine that inevitably shakes them up. He takes them to the back of the arena in the middle of a Springsteen show. Together they gaze out at the fans, and he reminds them that for some of these people, this night will be life changing. For many of these fans, tonight's concert will stay with them for their entire life.

"It could be buddies who experience something together," he says. "It could be the guy who chose this night to propose to his girlfriend. Being a part of this with Bruce makes you a part of what made that happen, and I want all the guys who work with me to take that into account. That's what makes their job, no matter what it is, important."

Wow. That's the perspective of a relatively invisible man who works behind the scenes, never playing a single note of music. He isn't on stage with the band; he doesn't get asked for his autograph or get swarmed by groupies after the concert. He's the guy who makes sure the coffee is hot, the beer is cold, and the food arrives on time. He's the tour director, not the rock star. But George Travis is a rock star in his own right, because he treats his job like that of a rock star.

It is fitting that George has a rock-star mentality, considering the mentality of the man George, and the rest of us, call "The Boss." Bruce Springsteen takes the exact same approach, night after night, doing everything in his power—and then some—to make each moment special for his fans. When speaking with *Bruce* author Carlin on the opening night of the Wrecking Ball tour in 2012, Bruce acknowledged the immense responsibility he felt toward the people who bought tickets to his concert. "Tonight I'm the custodian of all those people's feelings and memories," he told Carlin. "That's my responsibility. The E Street Band is a purpose-based organization."

I've been to many Bruce Springsteen shows, including the ones without the famous E Street Band in the 1990s, the post-9/11 "Rising" tour, and the more recent "Magic" and "Wrecking Ball" tours. Every show was presented with purpose, always reflecting, impacting, moving, changing, inspiring, and entertaining people through music. There are countless rock stars, but few who take customer service so seriously. Bruce Springsteen knows that on any given night, thousands of people will see him for the first and possibly only time in their lives. He has one chance to move them, one chance to touch their hearts, and one chance to thank them for spending their hard-earned cash on a night with Bruce and his band. When you take customer satisfaction that seriously, you never take a night off; you never settle for good enough.

Just like Bruce Springsteen stepping out on stage, every interaction you have has the power to stay with someone for life. How cool (and scary) is that? The way you treat someone can alter her life from that point forward. And while that may seem very *Butterfly Effect*, it really isn't that far-fetched.

You are changing lives every day, with every customer, friend, family member, total stranger, and coworker you interact with. You simply never know what positive, or possibly negative, impact you can have on someone through your actions. You can change lives for the better or for worse, but in every human interaction you, in some big or small way, can change a life.

CHANGING LIVES ON THE JOB

I experienced exactly that in August of 2012. Someone who wanted to do her job with purpose, passion, and lasting impact quite literally changed my life. I was booked to speak at a business luncheon in Honolulu, Hawaii. Since our kids were off on summer break, we booked a family trip to Hawaii around my speaking engagement. With my airfare and accommodations looked after, it was a no-brainer to bring the entire family along and turn this into a working holiday. Because of other work and life commitments, it would have to be a short trip, but a family vacation to Hawaii, no matter how short, is too good to pass up.

On the day we were to leave, everything went wrong. Bad weather moved in, and the heavy rain and dense fog prevented flights from leaving. The airline cancelled our flight, rebooking us to leave three days later! I called their customer service line and gently tried to explain that our already-short five-day vacation couldn't be cut short by three days. I had no luck. The so-called customer service agent was unable to help us at all. Because we were a family of four traveling together, the only option he could offer me was a flight three days later—take it or leave it. All of the other airlines were cancelled, overbooked, or ridiculously overpriced for a last-minute Hawaii round-trip ticket for four people.

I hung up with the customer service agent to talk the situation over with my wife, and we decided the only sane option was to cancel our family trip. I could buy a single return ticket to Hawaii and live up to my speaking engagement, but it wouldn't be the family vacation we were so excited about taking.

When I called the airline back to cancel the ticket, a different agent answered. She had a pleasant tone and calming demeanor. I told her I was calling to cancel our trip to Hawaii.

"I'm so sorry to hear that. Why on earth would you cancel a family vacation to Hawaii?" she asked. I explained the situation about the canceled flights, the rebooking for three days later, and the total lack of options I was presented with. "That's not good enough," she said. "We can do better than that."

For the next forty minutes she examined every possible option, sought the advice of her manager several times, and finally was able to get my family on a flight the next day and extend our trip by one day. Thanks to her, we were going to Hawaii after all. When we hung up, she sounded as excited as I was!

We spent five days swimming and walking Waikiki beach, surfing on the North Shore, and dining together at some fantastic beachside restaurants. It was a great trip, and it did change our lives. When you have teenaged kids, finding time to be alone and connect with them is rare. You know that in only a few short years they'll be grown up. This trip gave us that opportunity to spend time together as a family. Because one airline agent was determined to make her customer happy, our lives were changed.

That agent, by the way, was Simone. She was working her shift on the reservation line at US Airways when our lives intersected. I should have asked for her last name, but I was too excited and I forgot. So, to Simone at US Airways: please accept this sincere thank you from me, my wife Sue, and Isaac and Matthew, our two boys. We had a great trip, thanks to you.

Do you take your job with the degree of solemn seriousness that Simone does? Simone has the same commitment to creating an experience for her customers that George Travis has for Springsteen fans. Playing in different cities, night after night, is surely a grind on the band and the tour staff that George oversees. So he takes the time to remind himself why his job matters so much. He does what he needs to do to make sure he never loses sight of why he does what he does. He changes lives!

NEVER LOSE SIGHT

When I took my first job managing a big radio station in a major city, it was a huge accomplishment for me. You see, in the radio business, the larger the city (or "market" as they call it), the more lucrative the pay and influential the position. If you work in a "top 100" market, meaning one of the one hundred biggest media markets in the USA, you are on the radar. A top 20 market is better on your resume, for sure. But if you work in a top 10 market, you are gold. You are considered among the best of the best. So when, in July of 2005, I started managing WMKK-FM in Boston, I felt that I had made it to the big leagues. I was running a radio station in a top 10 market! In my career, this was a pretty big deal.

The building that was home to WMKK-FM, known

then as 93.7 MIKE-FM, is the New Balance building overlooking the Massachusetts Turnpike as it snakes into downtown Boston. On the top floor are the offices of New Balance shoes. We were on the lowly third floor, but thanks to our location and elevation, even the view from the third floor was pretty damned impressive. Looking east from my office I could see the Prudential Center tower, the Hancock Tower, and the edge of Fenway Park. To the north I could see the Harvard Campus, MIT, and parts of Boston University. Directly below me was Interstate 90, the longest stretch of interstate highway in America. Depending on your perspective, my office overlooked either the very first or very last miles of a 3,101-mile strip of pavement that runs from Seattle, Washington, over the continental divide in Montana, across the northern great plains of Wyoming and Minnesota, into Chicago, on through Detroit, Buffalo, Albany, and straight into downtown Boston. It was a pretty impressive view for a kid from a small town in northern Canada.

On one of my first days working there, I commented on the spectacular skyline view to a grizzled veteran who had worked in the office for years. He was far less excited about the view. He rolled his eyes at me. "You'll get tired of it soon enough," he said. "And soon you'll stop noticing altogether."

That thought saddened me. In my newbie and naïve mind, that vista of the Boston skyline represented every single listener who turned on a radio that day to be entertained, engaged, and connected with. It represented all of my career accomplishments to that point. When I looked at those office towers, freeways, airplanes coming and going from Logan, and millions upon millions of people, I was looking at all that mattered to me professionally. That view was what it was all about! Apparently not everyone felt the same way. On that day, I promised to never let myself get sick of the view.

I made a point of savoring it every chance I got. I let that skyline and my unhappy coworker's fatigue of it inspire me to take every listener into account. What could we do to connect with them on a deeper level? How could we impact their life more profoundly? What experience could we deliver to their ears that might change their commute, their day, or even their life for the better?

Like George Travis finding the inspiration to be great by looking out over a sea of twenty thousand Springsteen disciples, I found my inspiration for greatness by looking out at four million listeners in the gleaming office towers of the Pru, classic old brick walk-ups along the back bay, New England saltboxes of the suburbs, and apartments and homes in places like Dorchester, Quincy, Newton, Medford, and Marlborough. What a powerful reminder of my mission!

Today, many years later, I am long removed from living in the great city of Boston, although I visit every chance I get. MIKE-FM doesn't even exist anymore, replaced a few years ago at 93.7-FM by WEEI, an all-sports radio station that serves fans of the Sox, Pats, Bruins, and Celtics very well. Yet every time I look out over at the Boston skyline or even just see a picture of it, I inevitably think about all of those people listening to the radio, reaching out for a connection from the songs and voices coming through their speakers. The Boston skyline will forever remind me that my actions can impact others in profoundly powerful, and, I hope, positive ways. I'm proud to say that I lived up to my promise to never get tired of that view.

Never lose your desire to make every fan supremely happy. When you find yourself disillusioned or discouraged, do what George Travis did and look at what you do from the point of view of your fans and customers. See what they see, and realize how much you can impact their world when you act with purpose and passion on their behalf.

The Rock Star Playlist: The Fans' Choice Top Five Springsteen Classics

Mark James and Mike De Souza, two Springsteen fans from the UK, decided to survey Bruce Springsteen fans worldwide for their favorite all-time Boss tracks. Here is their top five.

1. **"Thunder Road."** This song has been a fan favorite for many years. It was the opening track on his breakthrough album *Born To Run*. Originally given the working title "Wings For Wheels," the song evolved into the epic we know and love today.

2. **"Jungleland."** Another epic from *Born To Run*, "Jungleland" comes in at almost ten minutes in length and features one of the greatest Clarence Clemons saxophone solos of all time.

3. **"Backstreets."** A third lengthy *Born To Run* track ranks third. "Backstreets" closes out side one of the album and is famous for its lengthy piano and organ opening, masterfully played by Roy Bittan.

4. **"Born To Run."** The title cut from the breakthrough album ranks fourth on the fan list. "Born To Run" was Bruce's last-ditch attempt to make it big. After years of trying to succeed, Bruce was at the end of his rope. That desperation oozes through in the song's lyrics and music.

5. **"Incident on 57th Street."** *The Wild, The Innocent, and The E Street Shuffle* is, in hindsight, ranked as one of the greatest rock albums ever. But when it came out, the album did not live up to sales expectations. Critics loved it, but fans didn't seem to notice much. Years later, songs like "Incident," the album's fifth track, stand out as Springsteen classics.

▼

CHAPTER 17

DIVERSIFY YOURSELF: HOW NIKKI SIXX BUILT A PERSONAL BRAND THAT ROCKS

On the night of December 23, 1987, Nikki Sixx died. The bass player, founding member, and creative force behind Mötley Crüe, his heart burdened by yet another heroin binge, experienced cardiac arrest. Nikki Sixx was dead.

Today Nikki Sixx is alive and very, very well. Best known for his role in the Crüe, the Sixx of today is a respected fashion designer, best-selling author, photographer, philanthropist, and the host of a syndicated radio show heard around the world. And yes, in his spare time he continues to write, record, and rock out with Mötley Crüe and his own band, Sixx:A.M.

None of this success could have been predicted on that wild night in 1987 when Sixx's heart stopped. He recounts the night in his book, *The Heroin Diaries: A Year in the Life of a Shattered Rock Star* (MTV Books, 2008). Finding him unresponsive, his friends frantically called 911. According to Sixx, one of the paramedics who arrived was a Mötley Crüe fan, and he refused to let his idol die. En route to the hospital, the paramedic administered two adrenaline shots to the heart, and Nikki Sixx was revived from the dead. His experience was the inspiration for a hit Crüe song, "Kickstart My Heart."

Unbelievably, that near-death night didn't stop the heavily addicted rock star from his downward spiral. He spent plenty of time in rehab in the ensuing years, finally declaring himself completely sober in 2004. But this isn't a story about recovering from addictions, as noble and inspirational as that story might be. This is a story about diversifying your personal brand and exploring your many passions, and Nikki Sixx, in his post-addiction days, is a rock 'n' roll role model for having a strategically diverse personal brand.

Nikki Sixx always had a unique sense of fashion. Even as a high school student, he would fuse together his own individual styles, blending punk, goth, and glam-rock. He took that with him to the stage, and when Mötley Crüe made it big, people began to notice Nikki Sixx's unique look. Despite the passionate interest in fashion, Nikki didn't share his style with the world until a chance meeting backstage at a Crüe concert set in motion what would eventually become Royal Underground clothing.

Sixx was introduced to a young woman named Kelly Gray, whose family had started St. John Apparel years earlier. As a child, Kelly was surrounded by the fashion industry and actively engaged in every aspect of the company as she grew up. From receptionist to model and eventually CEO of St. John, Kelly lived fashion. Her industry smarts and fashion sense, combined with Sixx's creative spark and dark perspective, were a perfect combination.

Their company, Royal Underground, combines edgy rock 'n' roll looks with luxury, and it has spread to more than sixty upscale retail locations across America, including high-end stores like Nordstrom's, Saks Fifth Avenue, Neiman Marcus, and Bloomingdale's. Royal Underground has become the go-to look for countless celebrities and rock stars, including Steven Tyler, Fergie, and Chelsea Handler.

While Royal Underground fashions may be Nikki Sixx's most high profile non-musical creative outlet, his most personal one is likely photography. Next to his guitar, Sixx's perpetual companion for decades has been his camera, and as his band tours city to city, Sixx captures the world around him through his personal lens. Sixx told *Rolling Stone* magazine that his work is often dark, capturing the "old, decrepit, and deranged." He compiled his photographs into the 2011 book *This is Gonna Hurt: Photography and Life Through the Distorted Lens of Nikki Sixx* (William Morrow, 2013), which was accompanied by an album of the same name by Nikki's band, Sixx:A.M.

After boldly and personally sharing his raw stories of rock, recovery, and rehab through his book, Nikki turned his storytelling ability into a career in broadcasting, launching a radio show called *Sixx Sense*. Along with cohost Kerri Kasem, daughter of the legendary Casey, Nikki shares his view of the world with radio listeners around the world on a daily basis. The show explores life from the unique perspective of the veteran rock star, including stories from backstage and a wealth of rock music guests from Nikki's extensive network of friends.

DIVERSE SKILLS CREATE OPPORTUNITIES

Diversifying your personal brand is vital today. Every business is expected to do more with less, relying on employees who can accomplish tasks beyond the traditionally defined roles. Developing a strategically diverse personal brand allows you to acquire skills that make you a more desirable employee.

Perhaps more important are the connections you make when you diversify yourself. All of us develop a network of acquaintances around our jobs—our work friends. For many of us, they represent our largest network of friends. Unfortunately, while they may be great people, they really don't expand our horizons: they do a similar job to yours; they worry about the same things; they want to talk about the same things. In many ways, they make your world smaller, not larger.

When you diversify, you meet people you would have

otherwise never met. Your world expands. You become part of a wider network of people, opening you up to opportunities that would have gone undiscovered. Those networks result in job offers, partnerships, business ventures, and brainstorming breakthroughs.

ISN'T A STRONG PERSONAL BRAND SINGULAR IN FOCUS?

Being known for something—one thing—is vital to developing a strong personal brand. Just like branding a product, effectively branding yourself requires that you represent something definitive in the minds of others. When your employers, customers, fans, and friends identify you as an expert in something specific, you have a strong personal brand.

Logically, you might then ask, what is Nikki Sixx? Is he a bass player? Is he a photographer? Is he a fashion designer? Is he an author? Is he a broadcaster? Having such a diverse portfolio could be seen as negative when it comes to building a solid, consistent, and clearly defined personal brand. However, when you look deeper, you start to see a common thread running through all of Nikki's seemingly diverse ventures. His fashion designs, photographs, books, broadcasts, and songs all focus on his dark and edgy view of the world. All of them showcase and support his rock 'n' roll persona. Each venture serves to add additional profile to the one that came before it. His photography adds clarity to the type of fashions he creates, and they both complement the kind of music he writes. Nikki Sixx has brilliantly brought everything he does full circle. So what is Nikki Sixx? He is a dark and edgy rock 'n' roll veteran. He's been to hell and back and seen it all. He has a view unlike anyone else on the planet. Everything he does reinforces that personal brand.

On the other hand, if the fashion designs created by Royal Underground were wedding gowns, they would hinder his hard-rock personal brand. If his photographs were colorful portraits of kittens and babies, they would work against his hard-rock personal brand. If his radio show featured the newest hits by Lady Gaga and Katy Perry, it would backfire on his hard-rock personal brand. Nikki Sixx has woven his dark and edgy rock 'n' roll image into everything he has done.

STRATEGIC DIVERSIFICATION

Personal branding, like business branding, is best done with consistency and focus. The most successful brands in business are the brands that are focused, and their customers clearly understand what the brand stands for. Brands that are diverse are always weaker, failing to stand for any particular set of values.

Strategic diversification of your personal brand is done with a similar sense of purpose and consistency. Your goal should be to establish yourself as an expert in your field . . . a master of your craft. In the case of Nikki Sixx, each new adventure contributed to his core values as a dark, edgy, wild rock 'n' roll hooligan. The fashions, photography, books, and broadcasts all add to his image. Although they are diverse, they all contribute to his core values. They are strategic.

Other celebrities have done the same thing. Oprah Winfrey has invested in many diverse adventures, but as an individual she represents a very well-defined set of core values. Oprah represents warmth, humanity, caring, potential, and vision. Her TV network, magazine, movies, Sirius radio channel, and books all strategically feed into those core values. She would never attach her personal brand to a horror movie, because it goes against her core values.

NONSTRATEGIC DIVERSIFICATION

None of us are one-dimensional. Every individual has interests that are unusual, that our friends might be surprised to learn about. For example, in my book *Brand Like A Rock Star* I wrote about Brian Johnson, the lead singer of legendary hard-rock group AC/DC. You would never expect it from his public persona, but Brian Johnson is a massive fan of Broadway musicals, especially Rodgers and Hammerstein. His love for the genre goes so deep that he has helped to write a musical based on the myth of Helen of Troy.

There's nothing wrong with being interested in many diverse things! It is healthy and normal and makes you a better person. However, from a personal branding perspective, it is important to be known for *one specific thing*. For Brian Johnson, that specific thing is being the screaming voice behind hits like "You Shook Me All Night Long" and "Back in Black." It isn't for Broadway musicals.

That's why you'll likely never see Brian Johnson's name and picture prominently displayed on a marquee promoting a Helen of Troy musical. When AC/DC comes out with a new album, it won't make mention of the side project that Brian has been working on.

When you have interests that contradict what you are known for, explore them and enjoy them. But understand that if you promote those diverse interests they will likely work against you. Becoming famous as the carpenter who fixes your car doesn't help you become known as a better carpenter *or* a better mechanic.

▸ **Strategic diverse interests** are the pillars of your personal brand. They are passionate interests that contribute to your overall image. You should make them very visible and you should be very good at them. They are a part of your résumé and a key part of your image.

▸ **Nonstrategic diverse interests** are simply hobbies. They are fun, relaxing, and healthy. They are personally important but professionally dangerous. As they take away from your ability to develop a strong personal brand identity, you will not benefit from making them a part of your résumé. In fact, including them will likely take away from your personal branding mission.

THE BENEFITS OF STRATEGIC DIVERSIFICATION

With so many diverse interests, it would seem that Nikki Sixx has plenty of options in his life. If Mötley Crüe breaks up, he can lean on Royal Underground fashions. If photography doesn't work out, he can rely on his radio show. But wisely diversifying your personal brand isn't about replacing lost income, for Nikki or for anyone else. Nikki Sixx is more than wealthy enough to not have to worry about putting food on the table, and in order for you to build income from your personal brand you need to be known for something specific. So why should you put your eggs in so many different baskets?

▶ **You need to explore in order to grow.** Each interest allows Nikki Sixx to explore another creative outlet. Creativity is like a muscle—the more it is used, the stronger it tends to get. So with each new avenue explored, Nikki strengthens his creative abilities. His camera opens doors in the mind that result in groundbreaking new fashion concepts. Writing a book inspires ideas that turn into hit songs. Flexing his creative muscle over and over again makes Nikki Sixx a stronger creative force.

▶ **It helps you build your overall image.** Each interest serves to support the overall Nikki Sixx personal brand. Nikki the fashion designer creates clothing that reflects the music made by Nikki the musician, and so on. Every time a fan comes in contact with one aspect of Nikki Sixx, it reinforces the other aspects. All of the interests are pillars that support the overall "Nikki Sixx" brand.

▶ **All of your interests introduce you to different people.** Listeners who hear Nikki on the radio and enjoy his storytelling ability are more likely to enjoy his books, photos, fashions, and music. With a wide range of similarly themed brands in his portfolio, Nikki has a large funnel to attract new fans. Once he engages a new fan, he can use them to cross-pollinate his other brands.

Strategic vs. Nonstrategic Diversification

STRATEGIC DIVERSIFICATION	NONSTRATEGIC DIVERSIFICATION
A chef known for amazing Italian food opens a gelato café with his name on them.	A chef known for Italian food opens an upscale burger restaurant with his name on it.
A graphic artist writes a book about rock 'n' roll album covers.	A graphic artist writes a book about customer service.
An accountant highlights on his résumé that he has an interest in software development.	An accountant highlights on his résumé that he has an interest in skydiving and extreme sports.
A business book author, inspired by *50 Shades of Grey*, writes a book about how the famous erotic novel was marketed and promoted.	A business book author, inspired by *50 Shades of Grey*, writes a book of erotic fiction.

One final note on diversifying yourself: If you find yourself exploring something so cool and awesome that you want to turn it into something bigger, you may want to consider doing it under a different name. Authors commonly do that. A nonfiction author under one name may be a fiction author under a completely different name. It is also common in business, where a company like Honda, makers of affordable cars, can also own Acura, makers of high-end luxury cars. You can change your name, open a business with a different name, or create a brand with a fresh name. By doing so, you preserve what your original brand stands for and you give yourself the freedom to explore new ways to grow and potentially profit.

The Rock Star Playlist: Five Nikki Sixx Songs That Rocked the World

1. **"Live Wire" by Mötley Crüe.** From the debut Crüe album *Too Fast for Love*, this Nikki Sixx composition was the opening song on side one, the song that the band chose to introduce Mötley Crüe to the world. In the video, Sixx sets himself on fire. Although the album and the song didn't perform that well when they were initially released in 1982, they both went on to sell very well over time as the band's popularity rose.

2. **"Too Young To Fall In Love" by Mötley Crüe.** Another song composed by Nikki Sixx, "Too Young To Fall In Love," was the band's second hit single from the album *Shout at the Devil.* It followed "Looks That Kill" into the Top 20 on the rock charts in 1984, although it would take a cover version of "Smokin' in the Boys' Room" the following year before they would reach the Top 10.

3. **"Kickstart My Heart" by Mötley Crüe.** This is the autobiographical story of Nikki Sixx's near-death encounter after a

continued on following page

drug overdose. When the first adrenaline shot to the heart didn't work, the EMT—a passionate Mötley Crüe fan—decided to administer another adrenaline shot. That one worked, reviving the nearly dead Nikki Sixx. In the opening notes of the song, guitarist Mick Mars recreates the sound of a motorcycle revving on his guitar.

4. **"Life Is Beautiful" by Sixx:A.M.** When Sixx released his book *The Heroin Diaries*, he also released an album to accompany it. The album is credited to his new band, Sixx:A.M. "Life Is Beautiful" was the uplifting first single from the album, a song about his recovery from drug addiction and realization that he had plenty of good reasons to live.

5. **"Lies of the Beautiful People" by Sixx:A.M.** The second Sixx:A.M. album, *This Is Gonna Hurt*, was released in 2011, following a successful 2008 Mötley Crüe album, *Saints of Los Angeles*. Once again Nikki Sixx chose to combine a book and an album. The book, *This Is Gonna Hurt: Music, Photography, and Life through the Distorted Lens of Nikki Sixx*, is a collection of photographs and journal entries by Sixx that chronicle his tumultuous life.

CHAPTER 18

BREAKING OUT ON YOUR OWN: HOW TO FORGE YOUR OWN IDENTITY IN THE SHADOW OF GREATNESS

I am the oldest child in my family, so the challenge of following in someone else's footsteps never occurred to me. It did, however, cause my sister plenty of pain and suffering when she first started high school.

"Oh," teachers would say to her in that disappointed and condescending tone. "You're Stephen's little sister." Once those words were uttered, she knew she would have to work extra hard to break their impression of our family name. To be fair, I wasn't a delinquent. I didn't get arrested, kicked out of school, or anything too serious. Instead, my badge of honor was doing the bare minimum and treating the entire four-year process with an overwhelming sense of indifference. Teachers came to know me as a student who always performed below his ability and did just enough to get by.

In certain subjects I did very well, but those A-list marks came only in subjects that I loved to do. If I didn't enjoy it, I simply didn't do it. My proudest high school moment was in eleventh grade math. Math wasn't a subject I enjoyed. At all. I hated math, but I desperately needed to pass eleventh grade math. It was a mandatory course for any college or university. On the first day of school, the math teacher told us that he didn't give out 50 percent as a final grade. If any of us received a 50 percent grade on the final report card, he informed us, we would owe him a thank you. When a student actually got 50 percent, he always found a way to raise the mark up a few points, reserving the 50 percent mark for those who actually finished with a failing grade but were saved only by the gift of his heart. Needless to say, when my final report card was issued I stopped by his classroom to shake his hand and say thanks. It was only thanks to his generosity that I was granted admission into the university, where I promptly dropped out a few months later.

To this day, like many people, I just can't muster the urge to tackle any project that doesn't interest me. Unfortunately for my wife, that often means home improvement projects, housework, and tasks as simple as taking the garbage out, all of which get conveniently forgotten. I know I'm not alone here, right? Right?

So my sister had her work cut out for her in high school. The good news is that she is very smart and hardworking, and her studious nature quickly erased any memories that her teachers had of me. I guess I didn't leave nearly as deep an impression upon them as I could have!

We are inevitably measured against those who came before us, no matter what we do. If you take a new job and the person who held the position before you was perceived to be incompetent, you instantly have an easier task to gain the confidence of those around you; the bar was set pretty low before you walked in the door. Conversely, when you step into big shoes and expectations are lofty, you'll need to achieve a higher level of success before you will gain the same level of credibility. That's a simple fact. The only way we can measure the present is to compare it with the past.

When the past is seen as brilliant, wildly successful, and extremely profitable, you certainly have a challenge ahead of you. And when your last name perpetually reminds everyone of the past, the job gets even tougher.

THE DYLAN LEGACY

Bob Dylan's son Jakob discovered that while having a famous father was great, it wasn't all a blessing, especially when it came to his career in music. "I think the name itself worked against me," he said. "And I actually found some kind of power in that. I still do."

For many years, Jakob avoided talking publicly about his father, preferring to forge his own identity in the music business. His band, The Wallflowers, did all of the dues-paying that a young band is expected to do. They became successful on their own merit, selling four million copies of their 1996 album *Bringing Down the Horse*. All of their success came without any visible help from Bob Dylan. In time, Jakob found that his silence on the topic of his famous father actually led to more media speculation about their relationship. So instead of dodging the issue, he eventually chose to acknowledge the reality of growing up as the son of the legendary Bob Dylan. In a 2005 *New York Times* interview, Jakob opened up about Bob's affection, his presence at Little League baseball games, and their ongoing, close relationship. He disclosed things about his intensely private father that the elder Dylan might have preferred to keep quiet, but Jakob insisted on telling the truth. He needed to get beyond his last name so that people could instead pay attention to what really matters: the music.

THE MARLEY LEGACY

That's also the task that Ziggy Marley was faced with when he decided to pursue a career in music. His father, the legendary Bob Marley, was more than just a musician. Bob Marley was viewed by many as the high priest of reggae music, a cultural and religious icon who represented Jamaica to the world. As Bob's career grew with the 1970s rise of reggae music, his humble roots gave way to a status that very few musicians ever dream of reaching. People looked to Bob Marley and his music for political and moral guidance.

He became a religious figure. In fact, Marley is widely considered to be personally responsible for the spread of the Rastafarian religion in Jamaica and around the world.

When he was stricken with cancer in 1977, his fans were shocked. The melanoma was located under his toenail, and with a simple toe amputation, Bob Marley would likely have survived. But his religious beliefs would not allow an amputation, and Bob Marley sought alternative treatments in Germany. His condition worsened. Knowing he was near death in May 1981, he decided to return home to Jamaica. He never made it. En route from Germany to Kingston, his vital signs started to worsen. The plane landed in Miami. With his son Ziggy by his side, Bob Marley passed away. His last words, spoken to his eldest son, were, "Money can't buy life."

Bob Marley's death sparked incredible mourning across Jamaica. He was buried with a full state funeral, with the prime minister of Jamaica delivering the eulogy in which he praised Marley as more than a mere man, but rather "an experience . . . that cannot be erased from the mind. He is part of the collective consciousness of the nation."

Following in the footsteps of Bob Marley would not be easy. How could Ziggy Marley, one young man, possibly carry on such a legacy? Could he ever escape from a shadow so large? Being Bob's eldest, he was viewed as the leader of the Melody Makers, a band that Bob had put together featuring four of his children. The Melody Makers included Ziggy, younger brother Stephen, and sisters Cedella and Sharon. In 1979, while their father was still alive, they recorded their first song, a composition of their father's called "Children

Playing in the Streets." All of the royalties from the sale of the song went to the United Nations during the International Year of the Child.

Two years later, after performing at their own father's funeral, the Melody Makers were left to find their own way in the world. Their music wasn't a replica of their father's sound, instead including more pop influences with a heavy reggae backbeat, accompanied by more electronic instrumentation. While some critics loved the new sound, the Melody Makers dealt with plenty of scorn for not sounding more like Bob Marley. With the Marley name on it, many fans and critics felt that the Melody Makers should be more respectful of their father's musical traditions. Ziggy was caught between his own sound and the ghost of his father.

Ziggy Marley and the Melody Makers scored their biggest hit in 1988 when the song "Tomorrow People" reached the Top 40 charts, peaking at number 39. The album on which the song appeared, *Conscious Party*, won a Grammy Award in 1989 for Best Reggae Album. Unfortunately, the group would never achieve that level of commercial success again.

However, it was by no means the end of the road for Ziggy Marley and the offspring of the greatest reggae artist in history. It has taken more than thirty years, but the children of Bob Marley have finally found a balance between carrying the Marley torch and creating their own unique sound. Almost everyone in the family continues to make music. Ziggy Marley continues to tour and record. Stephen Marley, known as Raggamuffin, has won five Grammy Awards, including the one he won as a member of the Melody Makers. Stephen has also produced tracks for numerous artists, including younger brother Damian Marley, arguably the most successful of Bob's musical offspring. Damian is Bob's youngest and was only two years old when his father died. He has cultivated a unique blend of traditional reggae, modern dancehall reggae, and hip-hop. As a singer, rapper, and DJ, Damian Marley has pushed the limits of what fans expect from the Marley name. Along the way he has won three Grammy Awards. His biggest night was at the 2009 Grammy Awards, when he became the only Jamaican artist in history to win two Grammy Awards in one night, claiming Best Reggae Album and Best Urban/ Alternative Performance for his album *Welcome to Jamrock*.

Growing up mostly in Miami, Ky-Mani Marley was raised away from the spotlight of Jamaica. In his early days he seemed to lean more toward athletics than music, but eventually his love of sports lost out. He started as a rapper and DJ, later recording his own tracks and often collaborating with brothers Stephen, Damian, and Julian. Ky-Mani has since expanded his horizons and become a serious actor in Jamaica, all while continuing to make music. One of the lesser-known offspring, Julian Marley continues to perform and record from his home base in London, England.

Clearly the Marley DNA comes with immense musical talent. But the name also carries a curse. Bob Marley is simply so popular and powerful that his brand naturally extends to his children. Fans of Bob Marley expect his children to stay true to the Bob Marley sound and style, and they expect them to be successful. The fans have an expectation of Marley that they would never hold any other Jamaican musician to. While the Marley surname has opened countless doors for all of the children, it has also forced them to push hard to find their own identity against a flood of powerful Bob Marley memories and images that fans expect them to uphold.

ANOTHER FAMOUS JAMAICAN NAME

Your last name doesn't have to be as famous as Marley for people to have expectations of you. Another well-known Jamaican is faced with a similar challenge. Adam Stewart is the son of well-known island businessman Butch Stewart. Butch is a famous Jamaican homegrown success story. From his entrepreneurial start as a twelve-year-old boy running errands for the crew filming a James Bond movie in Ocho Rios, Butch created an island empire. He started by importing and selling air conditioning units, a natural way to earn money in the tropical Caribbean. In 1981 he took a major risk and purchased a pair of downtrodden Montego Bay hotels. Losing more money than he imagined possible, Butch turned the old hotels into luxury resorts, adding fine dining, swim-up bars, and hot tubs. His gamble paid off, and his two lowly hotels formed the foundation of the Sandals Resorts chain, a network of thirteen luxurious, all-inclusive resorts in Jamaica, St. Lucia, Antigua, and Bahamas. He also owns the trio of family-oriented Beaches Resorts, a pair of Grand Pineapple Resorts, and the Fowl Cay Resort, a private island retreat in the Exuma chain of islands in the Bahamas.

With more than ten thousand employees, Butch Stewart became one of Jamaica's most visible business personalities.

Taking over for him wouldn't be an easy task for anyone, and for his son it would bring the added hurdles of living up to the family name and winning over those who may have attributed his job title to his last name. Adam Stewart was well-prepared for those challenges. He was born the year his father opened the first resort, Sandals Montego Bay, so the younger Stewart grew up surrounded by the family business. He witnessed firsthand the happiness that it brought to his father, and he knew from an early age that he wanted to be involved as well. "My father often claims that he has never worked a day in his life, such is the enjoyment he takes from this company," Adam confided to me. "There was never a chance I was going to miss out on all the fun!"

Jumping into the CEO role at Sandals, Adam has quickly established himself as the public face of the company and earned the respect of his colleagues and industry peers, even the ones who may have doubted his credentials because of the legacy of his last name. "I am in this position on merit," he notes. "There's too much at stake to be in a job such as this purely because of who my father is. At the end of the day, I will be judged on results."

Adam may be young for a CEO, but he crammed a lot into his years, and he has learned his business from the bottom up. There isn't a job at Sandals that Adam hasn't done at some point, from PR to reservations, from incentives to technology. Adam has added a wealth of experience to his hospitality management degree from Florida International University. In his role as CEO, Adam brings the vision of a younger generation to the industry, embracing social media and digital technology to evolve the company. He believes his youthful perspective and his father's experience create a team with unique gifts. "The blend of new and old school works tremendously well for us."

The two generations of Stewarts don't always agree. Both men are passionate about the family business, and sometimes it can be hard to separate those two words, "family" and "business." Yet conflicts are rare, and Adam is grateful that by maintaining a clear path of communication and always putting their mutual love of what they do ahead of everything else, they have been able to work through any differences productively.

To a second-generation entrepreneur looking to forge their identity, build respect, and carry on the legacy of a family business, Adam provides some sage advice. "Remember, the company comes before everything. Try not to be hell-bent on putting your own stamp on the company without stopping to establish what will keep it successful," he says. "Be patient, humble, and always willing to learn from everyone, and the trust and respect will follow."

KEEPING NEW COMPANY

Creating your own identity doesn't always mean coming out from under the shadow of a legendary family name. It can be mean coming out of one high-profile company to take a leadership position with another, just as Marissa Mayer did in 2012 when she departed Google for Yahoo!. Mayer had built up a tremendous reputation as an industry thought leader while helping to grow Google into the search engine giant it is today. With her stock high, she abruptly left to take on the immense task of rebuilding Yahoo!, a once-glorious company struggling to find its way. The early results are positive, largely because Melissa has focused on the same thing Adam Stewart has focused on: doing the right thing for the business, regardless of the circumstances.

STAYING TRUE TO THE BAND

Forging your own identity, be it in the shadows of a legendary family name or in the shadows of a legendary group, can be a tremendously challenging task. Your work is likely to be both highly anticipated and highly scrutinized. You will be held to the standards of your previous incarnation as a member of a team or your family, yet your new project will come without the support network a team provides.

John Fogerty, the singer and creative force behind Creedence Clearwater Revival, took his time coming out from the shadows of CCR. The incredibly successful California band split apart after a string of massive early '70s hits. Instead of immediately striking out as a solo artist, Fogerty kept a low profile. It wasn't until nearly a decade later that he really started to shine as a solo artist, releasing the very successful *Centerfield*. That album gave us songs like "The Old Man Down the Road," the baseball anthem "Centerfield," and the hit "Rock and Roll Girls." Fans of CCR were, for the most part, ecstatic about the John Fogerty solo album, because it was fresh and new, yet it never strayed from the CCR sound.

Unfortunately, from a strictly legal view, it didn't stray far enough from the CCR sound. The problem was that back in the heyday of CCR, John Fogerty unwisely signed the rights to his songs over to his record company. That meant that the company, not John himself, effectively owned all of the songs that Fogerty wrote while with CCR. When he emerged a decade later as a solo act, the record label felt the new songs sounded eerily similar to the CCR songs that they owned, and they sued Fogerty. In a very unusual lawsuit, John Fogerty was found guilty of plagiarizing . . . himself.

There is a fine balance between creating compelling new work and copying the great work you did as the member of a legendary team.

The Rock Star Playlist: Five Great Songs by Members of the Marley Family

1. **"Redemption Song" by Bob Marley & the Wailers.** "Redemption Song" is such a powerful and personal song, especially considering that Bob wrote and recorded the song while suffering greatly from cancer. As the final song on the last album released in his lifetime, "Redemption Song" serves as an epitaph for a legend.

2. **"No Woman, No Cry" by Bob Marley & the Wailers.** One of Bob Marley's most well-known songs, "No Woman, No Cry," is about growing up in the ghetto of Trenchtown, Jamaica. Bob wrote the song but attributed part of the songwriting credit to Vincent Ford, a friend of Marley's who ran a soup kitchen in Trenchtown. Thanks to the royalty checks from the song, Ford was able to continue to operate the soup kitchen for years.

3. **"Stir It Up" by Bob Marley & the Wailers.** Bob wrote "Stir It Up" for his wife Rita in 1967. The song was included on Marley's first international album, *Catch A Fire*, in 1972. It was recorded by American Johnny Nash and made famous as a pop hit. Nash was one of the first non-Jamaican artists to discover and record reggae music in Jamaica.

4. **"Welcome to Jamrock" by Damian Marley.** When Damian Marley released this song in 2005, it was clear that despite differing musical styles, he held true to the values of his father. "Welcome to Jamrock" wasn't exactly a tourism anthem for the island, but rather a commentary on the violence, crime, and corruption in the Caribbean nation.

5. **"Love Is My Religion" by Ziggy Marley.** This is the title track from his second solo album after leaving the Melody Makers, an album that won Ziggy Marley a Grammy Award in 2007 for Best Reggae Album. The acoustic version, also on the album, is a quiet masterpiece that evokes images of his late father as few other songs do.

PART FOUR:

PURPOSE

▼

CHAPTER 19

FINDING PURPOSE: HOW BOB GELDOF MADE MILLIONS BY HELPING OTHERS

Music moves us—sometimes, physically. We dance, play air guitar, and pound out a drum rhythm on the steering wheel. We sing along, however terrible our singing may be. We are physically moved.

Quite often, songs also emotionally move us. We are stung by the lyrics of a breakup song, drawn into the depths of a personal confession, and inspired by the powerful visions of an anthem. We are emotionally moved.

Songs can inspire us to take action and even change our own behavior. They can bring us together, united around a common cause. Through the stories they tell and the visions they create, songs have been storytelling tools since the dawn of time. In the same way that books and movies tell stories that teach us lessons, so do songs. The most memorable songs are often the songs that move us—physically and emotionally—the most.

On the evening of October 23, 1984, Bob Geldof of the Irish band the Boomtown Rats was doing what many of us do at the end of the day: he was watching the evening news on TV when a report came on about famine in Africa. BBC reporter Michael Buerk had been assigned to cover the developing story in Ethiopia, where a confluence of drought, government mismanagement, and civil war had conspired to create the worst famine that nation had seen in a century. The catastrophic circumstances were killing people at record rates, and there was nothing happening to stop it.

The visual images in Buerk's seven-minute report from Ethiopia were hard to watch and remain painful to see. Emaciated children clung to emaciated mothers, all of them distraught and confused. Families from hundreds of miles around had come to these camps hoping to find food and refuge from the drought, and instead they only found themselves awaiting a slow and painful death. Buerk called the Ethiopian refugee camps "the closest thing to hell on earth" as another child or adult died every twenty minutes. According to Buerk, of the fifteen thousand children living in the camp, one in three were starved to the point of near-death. And each day, hundreds more people were arriving at the camp hoping to find relief from the famine.

Bob Geldof was moved. He called his good friend, Midge Ure of the band Ultravox, and together they wrote a song about the famine and drought. Then they set out to change the world. Bob already had a new album coming out, and he had been booked to do a series of radio interviews to promote it. Instead of using those interviews to talk about his new album, he used them to solicit the biggest and best British and Irish musicians to come together and help him record the song that he had written about Ethiopian famine. Almost exactly a month after first watching Michael Buerk's report from Africa, more than forty of the biggest music stars in the UK gathered at a studio in Notting Hill to record "Do They Know It's Christmas?" under the name Band Aid.

The list of stars taking part reads like a UK music chart from late 1984. Duran Duran was there, along with various members of U2, Culture Club, Wham!, Spandau Ballet, Genesis, Bananarama, The Police, Boomtown Rats, Status Quo, and Ultravox. The producers started working at dawn on November 25, getting the background tracks together. Around nine o'clock a.m. the musicians started arriving. Boy George was late, having slept in and missed his flight from New York. He jumped on a Concorde and made it to London that evening to record his parts. Phil Collins brought his drums, and using an African rhythm lifted from a Tears for Fears song, the drum tracks were laid down. Each singer took a turn singing the entire song all the way through, and then the entire group sang the chorus. When the recording was done, the producers began the long process of editing their work and finding the right voices to sing each line.

Midge Ure was leading the production team, and as the musicians partied into the night, Ure worked away on the song. He worked all through the night, finally finishing the song at eight o'clock a.m. on Monday morning, November 26, 1984. He and Geldof had been working on the song for twenty-four straight hours.

Immediately the track was rushed to the record pressing plants, with their promise to have it ready by Tuesday. They lived up to that commitment, and on Thursday, November 29, 1984, the song went on sale, going straight to #1 on the charts. It became the fastest-selling and best-selling single in British history, outselling every other song on the chart combined. "Do They Know It's Christmas?" was a #1 hit in the UK for five straight weeks.

The song generated unprecedented reaction. I remember hearing the song for the first time on the radio and being blown away by it. I wasn't alone. My friends were all equally captivated by this cool new song! I recorded it on a cassette off of the radio, and together with my friends spent hours stopping and rewinding the tape trying to break down each individual voice. Being North American, it was tough to pick out some of the British artists who were less famous on my side of the Atlantic, but it was easy to find the big names like Simon Le Bon, Boy George, Bono, and George Michael.

DJs on BBC Radio played the song every hour from the moment it came out. Until that time, new songs were usually played six to eight times per day, but this song changed all of that. Musician Jim Diamond, whose song "I Should

Have Known Better" was the #1 song at the time, urged people *not* to buy his song and instead to buy the Band Aid song. The song even changed government policy when public outcry led the British government to agree to drop the taxes on the single so that every cent could go to the cause of helping starving children in Africa.

A year later, during the Christmas season of 1985, the song reappeared on the UK charts and rose as high as #3. Two subsequent re-recordings, Band Aid II in 1989 and Band Aid 20 in 2004, also went to #1. The Band Aid project also inspired artists in North America, where America's biggest stars recorded "We Are the World" as USA for Africa, and Canada's top acts, under the name Northern Lights, created "Tears Are Not Enough."

The songs raised millions of dollars to help ease the pain of famine in Africa, but as the cold winter of 1984–85 went on, Bob Geldof began to realize that the songs alone, while noble, would never raise enough money to really make a difference. Once again, he called his friend Midge Ure to help him bring together an even bigger idea. Instead of a song, Geldof envisioned a concert. Not just a single concert, rather a worldwide concert event that would take place simultaneously in both the UK and the USA and be beamed into the homes of music fans everywhere via satellite. The concert would involve all of the biggest artists in the world. It was an unprecedented undertaking, but once again Bob Geldof pulled it off. On July 13, 1985, at Wembley Stadium in London and John F. Kennedy Stadium in Philadelphia, the world's most famous musicians performed at the Live Aid concerts. Billed as "The day the music changed the world," the show reached a massive audience. Both stadiums were sold out, with 72,000 watching at Wembley and 100,000 crowding into JFK Stadium. The live coverage became one of the most-watched TV events worldwide, beaming into 150 nations and the homes of 1.9 billion people.

Like most teenagers in the 1980s, I spent the entire day glued to the TV watching rock star after rock star perform. It was unlike anything I had ever seen before. In many ways, it felt like my generation's Woodstock. Unfortunately, I wasn't there in person, but technology allowed millions of people to share in the experience simultaneously.

While Boy George made use of the supersonic Concorde during the recording of Band Aid's "Do They Know It's Christmas?", it was Phil Collins who took advantage of the jet for Live Aid. Collins performed a solo set at Wembley Stadium, then hopped on the Concorde and arrived in time to play a set that evening in Philadelphia. In addition to two solo sets, Collins also played drums for Eric Clapton's set and took the place of the late John Bonham for a Led Zeppelin reunion.

Beyond Phil Collins's ocean-hopping, Live Aid was remarkable on a number of other fronts. It was a turning point for many music careers. Their London performance established U2 as mainstream superstars for the first time, and they spent the rest of the decade developing a reputation as the biggest rock band on the planet. There were emotional reunions, as Crosby, Stills, Nash, and Young, Black Sabbath with Ozzy Osbourne, and the founding members of Led Zeppelin all reunited for the first time in years (although both Zeppelin and their critics hated their performance). Queen played what many have called one of the all-time greatest live music performances, electrifying Wembley Stadium with "Bohemian Rhapsody," "We Are the Champions," and a chill-inspiring "Radio Ga Ga" in which 72,000 fans were held under the spell of Freddie Mercury. Brian May of Queen told *Mojo* magazine that the audience clapping along in perfect unison to "Radio Ga Ga" was one of the most spectacular sights he had ever seen. "I'd never seen anything like that in my life, and it wasn't calculated either," he said. "How did they know? Nobody told them to do it." The concert revitalized Queen's career, although sadly it would be only a few more years until Freddie Mercury's deteriorating health and eventual death in 1991 would end the band's magic. His performance at Live Aid is a shining example of why he remains such a powerful figure in rock history.

There were also notable absences, including Bruce Springsteen, who was arguably at the peak of his career in 1985. Springsteen apologized for not appearing, saying he simply didn't realize how big the whole thing would be. Prince didn't attend, nor did Michael Jackson. Annie Lennox got sick, and the Eurythmics had to back out. Tears for Fears and AC/DC both declined, despite their immense popularity at the time. Frank Zappa was invited, but he took a more cynical view of the event, calling Live Aid "the biggest cocaine money laundering scheme of all time."

Indeed, there were cynics and there were criticisms. There

were accusations of misuse of funds. There were issues with some of the nongovernmental agencies in Africa who disbursed the money and suggestions that some of them were under the control of criminals. But in the greater picture, the Band Aid and Live Aid projects will go down in history as game-changing moments when music helped to improve the world. Certainly there had been benefit concerts before, including George Harrison's famous Concert for Bangladesh in 1971, the Amnesty International "Secret Policeman's Ball" concerts, and a nuclear disarmament march in New York in 1982 that culminated in a concert featuring Jackson Browne, Linda Ronstadt, and Bruce Springsteen. But Live Aid was the first time that such a diverse groups of artists came together on such a huge scale to perform for the benefit of a charity. It marked the first time concerts were held simultaneously in different cities, on different continents, and linked together by satellite. Live Aid was the first rock 'n' roll event that was designed not just for the ticket holders at the venue, but also for the nearly two billion people who watched it on TV. The broadcast and stage configuration pushed the limits of technology at the time. And ultimately there was just something very special about millionaire rock stars donating their time, skills, creative work, and popularity in order to make a positive difference in the lives of others. By simply watching, you felt like you were making the world a better place.

His work with Live Aid and Band Aid earned Bob Geldof a knighthood from Queen Elizabeth II in 1986, and he has continued his charity work ever since, a career path that long ago eclipsed his musical fame. Thanks to a career most famous for his contributions to the lives of others, his personal wealth is immense, valued at $1.2 billion in 2011.

Bob Geldof has spent nearly thirty years using his music, fame, connections, and vision to help make the world a better place, but he was inspired by a very simple event. Early in his career, Bob and his band the Boomtown Rats were invited to perform at an Amnesty International event called The Secret Policeman's Ball. Along with Sting and Bono, Bob Geldof cites that event as a turning point, planting the seed of an idea: that he could use his music to make a positive difference in the world.

THIRD WORLD SHOES

Blake Mycoskie had a similar epiphany while on vacation in Argentina in 2006. He took a day off of his vacation to volunteer to deliver shoes to impoverished children in the villages outside of Buenos Aires. The shoes were a simple canvas slip-on style that Argentinians had worn for generations, and right away a light went on for Blake. He suddenly realized that he could market these shoes in America, and he could create a real business, not a charity, that would give back to those in need. Blake founded and became Chief Shoe Giver at TOMS Shoes. TOMS is based on "tomorrow," as in "shoes for tomorrow."

The idea for TOMS Shoes was simple: for each pair of shoes they sold, they would donate a pair of shoes to a child in need. When the *Los Angeles Times* ran a story about

Blake's company, the concept instantly exploded. Within the first six months, TOMS had sold over ten thousand pairs of shoes. Five years later, TOMS Shoes has donated over two millions pairs of shoes to children in need, and the brand is sold at five hundred retailers globally. That success has enabled the company to launch TOMS Eyewear, a company with a similar foundation. For every pair of glasses that TOMS Eyewear sells, they contribute a portion of the profit on that sale to saving or improving the eyesight of someone in the developing world. The TOMS business model has been called "One-for-One," and it is a wonderful example of a business using "purpose maximization" (as author Dan Pink called it) as the guiding instinct instead of the traditional profit maximization. Blake and his team at TOMS believe that profit will flow naturally if they focus first on the purpose. While most companies and careers are based on putting yourself first, Bob Geldof and Blake Mycoskie both prove that putting your mission ahead of your money can actually pay off handsomely.

CAREER OR CALLING?

Although One-for-One is a tremendous concept, you don't have to give 50 percent of your profit away to charity in order to have a purpose. And you don't have to start an international shoe store or organize a multicontinent concert spectacle to integrate purpose into your career. No matter what you do, purpose starts with your perspective. Think carefully about what you do for a living or what you aspire to do for a living. How do you view your work? Do you have a job, a career, or a calling? Author and leadership consultant C. Clinton Sidle put it in the context of a teacher in a January 13, 2010, blog post on the *Huffington Post*. A teacher with just a job is a teacher who thinks they teach history, writes Sidle as he explains the difference between a "career" and a "calling." A teacher with a career views teaching history as the business of education. But a teacher who has a calling is a teacher who believes that they are teaching young minds how they can make history themselves. Most of us have jobs or careers, and not enough of us look at what we do as a calling.

An architect with a calling could spend a portion of his time designing affordable housing for those in need. An accountant with a calling could take on only clients who agree to contribute a portion of the money he saves them to a charity. A chef with a purpose could open a restaurant committed to using only locally sourced and organically grown foods. In each case, they are likely to attract clients who have a similar worldview and who wish to make purpose part of their lives.

Having a strong sense of purpose in your career can also help refocus your mission in difficult times. When you encounter a situation that challenges your ethics, you can fall back on your purpose as a filter for what the best course of action might be. When you have a clear purpose in your career, you make decisions with a heightened sense of clarity, and you can act with a higher degree of confidence and courage.

The Rock Star Playlist: The Five Greatest Live Aid Moments

1. **Queen Rocks the World.** Not only did Queen play the gig of their lives at Live Aid, they put together a musical performance that many experts rank as the greatest achievement in live rock 'n' roll. Behind the scenes, Queen's sound engineer secretly switched out the audio limiters backstage, making the band's performance louder than any other. Still, it wasn't the volume that made Freddie Mercury's momentous performance speak so loud.

2. **Phil Collins Crosses the Ocean.** Having played Wembley Stadium in London early in the day, Collins hopped on the transatlantic Concorde jet to land in Philadelphia in time to perform again for the American audience. You can love Phil Collins or hate him, but you can't deny that his effort that day was pretty damn cool.

3. **Madonna Refuses to Get Naked.** Her career was on fire in 1985, and pictures had recently leaked to *Penthouse* and *Playboy* showing a young Madonna completely nude. When she walked on stage, she immediately informed the crowd that "I ain't takin' off shit today."

4. **Bono Saves a Life.** U2's performance at Live Aid was a sort of coming-out party for the band. It established them as bona fide stars, but few of us watching had any idea just how much of an impact their performance was having. At one point during the song "Bad," Bono jumped off the stage into the crowd to dance with a girl. Only twenty years later did that girl reveal that she was in the process of being crushed to death by the throng of fans rushing toward the stage. Bono attempted to get the ushers to help her, but when they didn't respond, he took matters into his own hands.

5. **Bob Dylan and Ronnie Wood.** As Dylan played, he broke a string on his guitar. Ronnie Wood of the Rolling Stones handed Dylan his guitar, leaving himself without an instrument. Not to be left out, Ronnie Wood played air guitar until a replacement was found.

6. **(Honorable Mention) Bob Geldof Rides High.** At the end of the show, Pete Townshend of The Who and Paul McCartney carried Bob Geldof on their shoulders. It was a fitting tribute to a man who, through music, brought the world together for a day.

▼

CHAPTER 20

GIVE A LITTLE BIT (OR EVEN A LOT): HOW THE GRATEFUL DEAD CASHED IN ON THEIR GENEROSITY

No band has given away as much of their music as the Grateful Dead. As crazy as it sounds, this legendary jam band from San Francisco made giving away their music a pillar of their business plan. Without the benefit of widespread radio airplay or mainstream media coverage, the Grateful Dead used the power of generosity to spread their music and their brand, making them consistently one of the top-grossing touring acts of their era. From April 1965, when they formed in Palo Alto, California, until July 1995, just prior to the death of founder Jerry Garcia, the band played more than 2,300 shows together. Aside from a short hiatus in 1975, they were perpetually on tour. The Grateful Dead makes the entirely unsubstantiated but highly believable claim to have played more free concerts than any band in the history of music.

The Grateful Dead turned their little jam band into a marketing machine, selling millions of concert tickets, over thirty-five million albums, and raking in tremendous profits by licensing their music, image, and artwork. The band was inducted into the Rock and Roll Hall of Fame in 1994 and are ranked fifty-seventh on *Rolling Stone* magazine's list of the Greatest Artists of All Time. Without question, the Grateful Dead will go down in history as one of rock's greatest bands. What makes their story so compelling is that they accomplished all of this without the usual tools: they had essentially no radio airplay; their songs hardly made an impact on *Casey Kasem's American Top 40* chart; they didn't make music videos. Instead, the Grateful Dead leveraged their generosity to create a community, and the community supported the band.

Long before illegal file sharing and downloading, music was pirated through bootleg tapes, essentially live recordings of concerts. If you ever read the tiny print on the back of a concert ticket, you probably would have read a paragraph about how any recording of the concert was prohibited by law. The music industry has always been extremely vigilant in preventing the recording and distribution of tapes of live shows, believing that these recordings would eat into album and ticket sales. The Grateful Dead had a different idea, one that went completely against conventional business and industry wisdom. The band believed that if the fans could record and share their concerts, they would bring new fans into the community. Since most radio stations and mainstream media ignored the eclectic band, they believed that they could use bootleg tapes to help them spread the word.

Instead of preventing taping and prosecuting "tapers" who recorded concerts, the Dead decided to encourage the process. They invited tapers to set up their recording equipment in special sections, often allowing them to plug directly into the soundboard to get the best possible quality. While other bands confiscated recording devices from their fans to prevent them from bootlegging their concerts, the Grateful Dead actively facilitated it. The band helped people record the shows, and then they encouraged people to share the tapes, asking only that they be given away, and not sold for profit.

To make every tape more valuable, the band played a unique set each night, altering their song selection for every concert. As a result, certain shows became monumental collectors' items. When the band played a particularly rare selection or had an unusually great show, fans clamored to get the tapes. While most bands played the same basic set list each concert, the Grateful Dead went out of their way to do something fresh each show. Sometimes it worked, and the results were electric. Sometimes it didn't turn out as well. But no matter what the outcome was, the uniqueness of each concert created a demand for their music that would never have existed if the band had played the same set night after night.

The band's logic contradicted the prevailing wisdom of

the music industry, which was still very much hung up on preventing bootlegs from taking away album and ticket sales. It turns out that, at least in their case, the Grateful Dead was right. Throughout the 1970s as the band toured relentlessly, their fan base grew exponentially. Despite having very little exposure on the radio or TV, the network of Deadheads stretched around the globe, ensuring that the band could sell out nearly every city on every tour. The tapes were a key part of the band's growth, since you could seldom hear the Dead on the radio. Friends who discovered the band shared their tapes with their friends. Older brothers played their tapes for younger brothers. Those already in the tribe of Deadheads used the tapes to invite new members into the group, thereby creating an exciting sense of community around the band's music.

To enhance the experience, the Grateful Dead actively sought out the mailing addresses of their fans and invited them to be a part of the group's fan club. All they did was put a simple note inside the sleeve of an album, asking fans to send them their mailing address. Thousands did. The band responded by sharing special things with them, like advance concert news or samples of music they were working on. This tiny seed grew into the largest "fan club" in rock history, the Deadheads.

Once firmly in the tribe, some fans would embark on a quest to see the band as many times as possible. Thousands of Deadheads would follow them from city to city, all summer long. Taking a few months off work to follow your favorite band across America isn't free, so the band took steps to help these hard-core fans make money. They created an area called "Shakedown Street" where the traveling fans could set up booths to sell everything from tie-dyed clothes to burritos. With a source of income, the Deadheads could afford to put their money back into tickets, transportation, and accommodations so they could continue to follow the band on tour. This process continued unabated for decades.

Today, nearly twenty years after the passing of bandleader Jerry Garcia, variations of the band continue to tour. If you get the chance to see Further, The Dead, or even Dark Star Orchestra live in concert, you'll witness the enduring legacy of the Grateful Dead. It isn't quite the same thing, but it definitely is the next-best thing.

The Grateful Dead had only one hit song, a Top 10 hit in 1986 called "Touch of Grey." It came relatively late in the band's career. For the previous two decades, you simply never heard the Grateful Dead on the radio except on some fringe progressive rock radio stations. The band wasn't invited to play on *The Tonight Show*, and they didn't do the soundtrack for any hit movies. They didn't lip synch on *Top of the Pops* or *Solid Gold*. The Grateful Dead achieved their success by giving stuff away and creating a vibrant and powerful community.

WHO WOULD YOU BET ON?

To witness the power of giving in a more modern and high-tech light, imagine you could rewind time by a decade or so and place bets on the odds of success for one business model over another. You could invest in one of two rival encyclopedia companies, rushing to fill the gap as the world moved from paper to digital knowledge storage. Company number one was Microsoft, and their product was Encarta. Microsoft hired some of the brightest minds to compile the world's written knowledge into an electronic version. With Bill Gates's deep pockets, they poured millions of dollars into creating the world's best electronic encyclopedia.

Company number two was a ragtag group of volunteers who assembled information in their spare time for no profit at all. These volunteers approached other experts to share their knowledge on very specific topics, and they all worked diligently to make sure the information was vetted and accurate. They drew no salary, and none of the contributors were paid or even acknowledged for their contributions. They called their project Wikipedia.

After investing and losing many millions of dollars on it, Microsoft finally put Encarta to rest in 2009. Meanwhile, Wikipedia has become the world's go-to source for information on nearly every imaginable subject.

Most of us would have placed a confident bet on Microsoft. We would have doubled down if given the chance: all in. And we would have lost it all.

Encarta seemed like a really good idea. Microsoft wasn't crazy at all; they built Encarta by purchasing the digital rights to various print encyclopedias and combining the printed word with multimedia sounds and videos. It was a giant leap forward in how we digest information, and Microsoft was the perfect company to lead it. Encarta was a respectable product, and at its peak it boasted more than 62,000 articles.

Today Encarta is long gone, and Wikipedia has more than twenty-four million articles, including 4.1 million in English alone, edited by a team of over one hundred thousand active volunteer collaborators. The entire project is overseen by the not-for-profit Wikipedia Foundation. It is created, maintained, updated, moderated, and promoted entirely by volunteers. For free.

We live in changing times, and sharing is more practical and prevalent than ever. The connectedness that the Internet has brought about has facilitated sharing at a level never before seen in human history. Want to install a dishwasher? Don't call a plumber or an electrician; just Google it. There are dozens of YouTube videos on the topic. Or you can easily find step-by-step instructions on hundreds of different websites. Looking for a recipe to replicate McDonald's' famous and top-secret Big Mac sauce at home? The not-so-secret recipe is right there online, put there by McDonald's themselves, for you to attempt right in your kitchen. From the dangerous to the invaluable, almost every piece of knowledge you need is being shared right now on the Internet.

As an author, I learned firsthand how to maximize sharing. In the spring of 2009 I began work on my first book, *Brand Like a Rock Star*. In those early days, I didn't realize I was working on a book. It was just a blog about the lessons we could learn from rock 'n' roll that could be applied to business. A few months after I started blogging, I received an email from David Meerman Scott, author of the best-selling books *The New Rules of Marketing & PR* and *Newsjacking*. David had read a piece on my blog (about the Grateful Dead, coincidentally) and emailed to let me know that he enjoyed my perspective. It was David who suggested that I turn the ramblings into a book. By simply freely sharing my thoughts on a topic I was passionate about, I found myself writing a book.

The blog continued to evolve over two years, and in 2011 I began to refine and improve on some of the more relevant blog posts. From almost one hundred posts I was able to pare it down to the most powerful and popular twenty posts. With plenty of editing and expanding, those posts became the twenty chapters that make up *Brand Like a Rock Star*.

Sharing those chapters online first was vital to the book's success. The feedback I received from readers allowed me to improve on every topic. In some cases, readers corrected information that was inaccurate. In other cases they changed my thinking on certain topics. In every case the input from my readers allowed me to think about what I was communicating in a fresh way, which no doubt improved the final product.

Like the Grateful Dead, I continued to share my work online as this book came together. Early versions of several chapters were posted on my blog at www.brandlikearock star.com, and readers commented extensively on what I was writing. Sharing these chapters-in-progress not only made the finished book substantially better, but it also helped to build a community of like-minded people who had made a material investment in the book. Instead of just another book, this became a book that several thousand people had a hand in creating. I am extremely grateful to all of them.

Are there risks involved? Absolutely. I have read many pieces that have either blatantly or subtly ripped off something I wrote. In some cases, I've had to talk myself down from calling my lawyer! In most cases, I make a point of reminding myself that the benefits strongly outweigh the risks, and I continue to share and give, knowing that—as the New Radicals sang—"*You get what you give.*" Or, as the Beatles said, "*In the end / the love you take / is equal to the love you make.*"

GIVING GOING ON AROUND YOU

Here are some fantastic examples of how people are benefiting every day from giving and sharing:

- ▶ The fitness instructor who posts new exercise videos every week on her blog, giving away, at no cost, advice on how to live a healthier and more active life. Those free videos lead to plenty of new customers who pay her for in-person fitness instruction. Do some people just watch the videos and do it themselves? Certainly. But that's a small price to pay for the leads the videos generate.

- ▶ The home improvement store that conducts how-to seminars every Saturday morning, covering everything from how to build a patio to how to install your own hardwood flooring. Every Saturday there are people who attend the how-to seminars at the store and then buy their building supplies somewhere else. The store doesn't worry about those people, instead benefiting from the much larger number of customers who attend the seminar, benefit from the knowledge and empowerment, and purchase all of their building supplies on the spot. Those same customers, knowing they can trust the store for solid advice, come back time and time again as new home improvement projects arise.

▸ The advertising sales professional who maintains a daily blog with advice on how to make marketing stand out. Although he makes his living selling newspaper advertising, his blog provides guidance on making any advertising stand out, not just newspaper advertising. Once again, some people read and benefit without ever paying it back. But the benefit to the advertising sales executive is in the leads that inevitably come from business owners who are grateful for the marketing advice and turn to him for future marketing purchases.

▸ A car dealership that follows its biggest and most loyal customers on social media and sends its most dedicated customers periodic gifts based on the their interests: tickets to baseball games, rounds of golf, and spa visits top the list of tailor-made gifts. It would be easier to send them generic thank-you gifts, but by using the power of a community, the car dealership can give

with specific purpose, making their gifts more personal and powerful.

Sometimes giving involves spending money on actual gifts,
as in the car dealership example. But many other times, giving
isn't about hard objects but instead about knowledge, advice,
guidance, friendship, and support. In every case, however, the
act of giving is a direct link to future business success.

The home improvement store gives away knowledge realizing that, when empowered with the knowledge, you are
infinitely more likely to come back to that store to purchase
the material you need to complete your home improvement
project. Notice that they do not make purchasing your
material from them a deal-breaker. The knowledge is given
away free, with no strings attached. That's what makes it
powerful! If the knowledge is conditional ("buy your mate-
rials here and we'll show you how to install them") it can
never carry the same punch. People are suspicious of such
giving, because it really isn't giving at all. It is selling. It is a
gift-with-purchase, not an honest gift.

The best giving is when you give away something of value,
whether it is knowledge or product. It needs to be free, with
no strings attached. And the best giving is personal, never
generic. A gift that matters to the recipient delivered in a
personal way from the giver is always the most powerful.

When the Grateful Dead gave their fans the powerful
and personal gift of music, with no obligations attached,
it helped a quirky band with little mainstream appeal build
the biggest and most influential fan base in rock history.

WHAT DO YOU HAVE TO GIVE?

As an individual, what can you give away? Your time and your knowledge. Your spirit, energy, and enthusiasm. Your expertise and experience.

Where can you give it away? At home, at work, with friends. You can give it away to total strangers.

You can, quite literally, change lives if you are willing to treat your knowledge, experience, creativity, and spirit with an abundance mindset. Stephen Covey famously coined the "abundance mindset" in his landmark book *The 7 Habits of Highly Effective People*. It is in contrast to the mindset that most people seem to have, which is a scarcity mindset. We often use the scarcity mindset to convince ourselves to hoard our possessions and our knowledge, for fear that there won't be enough to go around. If I share my knowledge with you, it is no longer mine . . . and therefore I am no longer indispensable to the company. The abundance mindset rejects that notion and allows us to look at the potential for a win-win situation. When I share my knowledge with you, not only do you get better at what you do, but I also improve in the process. Both of us become more indispensable to our employer. Once you adopt the abundance mindset, you throw the idea of a zero-sum game out the window and become willing to share and give without expectation, knowing that ultimately you will benefit.

Covey believes that people with a higher sense of self-worth are more likely to have an abundance mindset. Their lack of insecurity allows these types of people to not concern themselves with the threat that sharing might present and instead celebrate the positives that come to all involved, including the organization, when knowledge, experience, and energy are shared.

It certainly worked for the Grateful Dead. The fans got free music. The band got rich. And the world was left with a sonic legacy that will never disappear.

The Rock Star Playlist: Five Dead Songs I Am Personally Grateful For

1. **"Casey Jones" by The Grateful Dead.** From arguably their most famous album comes this song apparently inspired by real-life train engineer Casey Jones, although history bears no evidence that Jones was ever high on cocaine.

2. **"Touch of Grey" by The Grateful Dead.** It was their only hit song, but it managed to reach the Top 10 without compromising the band's sound. The song's status as a mainstream pop hit surprised even the band, who never expected to see their name at the top of the charts.

3. **"Sugar Magnolia" by The Grateful Dead.** This is the ultimate hippy Dead song, conjuring up images of dancing in fields, swimming in rivers, and savoring the wonders of nature while enjoying high times.

4. **"Uncle John's Band" by The Grateful Dead.** Quite possibly the best example of the band's harmonic abilities, "Uncle John's Band" has become a popular cover song for many artists, including Jimmy Buffett.

5. **"Truckin'" by The Grateful Dead.** Acknowledged by the Library of Congress as a national treasure, "Truckin'" captures life on the road and stood up for seventeen years as the band's biggest hit until "Touch of Grey" came along in 1987.

▼

CHAPTER 21

FIND YOUR MENTOR: YOU'LL NEVER WALK ALONE

Eric Von Schmidt passed away in his sleep on a cold New England winter night in 2007. You didn't read about it on the front page of the newspaper and it wasn't on *TMZ*. Sadly, considering the impact Eric Von Schmidt left on music history, his death went relatively unnoticed.

Millions of people were impacted by what Eric Von Schmidt did in his lifetime. And while he made music and painted extensively, the accomplishment that Eric is most fondly remembered for is his mentorship of a young singer/songwriter from northern Minnesota.

Eric Von Schmidt was an artist from his earliest days. His father was a painter who did illustrations for the *Saturday*

Evening Post. As a teenager in Bridgeport, Connecticut, young Eric started selling his own artwork, and after high school he won a scholarship to study art in Florence, Italy. Painting fascinated him, but so did music. In 1957 he returned to New England, settling in Cambridge, Massachusetts, where his mutual artistic passions flourished in the Boston coffeehouse scene. Von Schmidt was a rarity, with a rugged, outlaw persona that was uncommon in both the painting and folk music circles.

Around that same time, a young man from Duluth was setting out on his own journey of discovery, moving to New York City to write and perform his music. Robert Zimmerman quickly began playing, networking, and learning from the burgeoning folk scene in Greenwich Village. One weekend he took a side trip to Cambridge to see a singer that he had been hearing about named Eric Von Schmidt.

This young kid calling himself Bob Dylan was captivated with Von Schmidt's rebellious attitude and musical talent. The two quickly became friends, and legend has it that they drove around Boston, trading harmonica licks and looking for people to party with. Von Schmidt recounted for the *Boston Globe* the day they met, recalling that they consumed a bottle of red wine, smoked some grass, and then played croquet, a game that Dylan was apparently terrible at. The day ended back at Von Schmidt's apartment, where they played music, sang each other songs they were working on, and built up a tremendous rapport. "It was a wonderful meeting," Von Schmidt told *The Globe*; "I sang him a bunch of songs, and, with that sponge-like mind of his, he remembered almost all of them when he got back to New York."

Bob Dylan remembered his time with Von Schmidt equally fondly, and on his debut album he included a lyric that referenced meeting him "in the green pastures of Harvard University" over the guitar opening of the song "Baby, Let Me Follow You Down." A few years later, on the cover of the 1965 album *Bringing It All back Home*, Dylan appears with a collection of albums scattered around him. Among them is Eric Von Schmidt's album *The Folk Blues of Eric Von Schmidt*. And that wasn't the last visual tip-of-the-hat Bob sent Eric. On the cover of 1969's *Nashville Skyline*, Dylan appears in the same pose as Von Schmidt did on his own album.

Like many mentors, the extremely talented Eric Von Schmidt never achieved the same level of success as his understudy did. But Bob Dylan never forgot the influence that Von Schmidt had on his development as an artist. In 1972, Dylan contributed to the album liner notes for Von Schmidt's album *2nd Right 3rd Row* and wrote about his mentor's talent:

> *For here is a man who can sing the bird off the wire*
> *and the rubber off the tire. He can separate the men*
> *from the boys and the note from the noises. The*
> *bridle from the saddle and the cow from the cattle.*
> *He can play the tune of the moon. The why of the*
> *sky and the commotion from the ocean. Yes he can.*

Eric Von Schmidt wasn't Bob Dylan's only mentor; there were obviously many others who influenced him, most notably Woody Guthrie, whom Dylan befriended when he first moved to New York. He was also deeply influenced by poets like his namesake Dylan Thomas, and by generations of folk and roots singers. What makes the story of Eric Von Schmidt so interesting is that without his connection to Bob Dylan, he would be almost entirely unknown. Woody Guthrie, Dylan Thomas, and many of Bob Dylan's other influences became famous in their own right, but when Eric Von Schmidt passed away at age seventy-five, he was a small footnote in music history. He wasn't famous. That's the difference between a mentor and an influencer. Mentors give of themselves in order to share, teach, and grow. Profit isn't the motivation. They don't ask for anything in return, and, sadly, most often they get nothing in return aside from the unending gratitude of their protégés and the personal satisfaction that comes from making a significant, positive impact on the life of another human being.

LIVES CHANGED

Actor James Earl Jones and nine other celebrities celebrated their own mentors in the 1999 book *The Person Who Changed My Life* (Matilda Cuomo, Rodale Books). Jones remembered a teacher, Professor Crouch, who discovered that he had a stutter. When Jones presented his teacher with poetry he had written, the professor didn't believe it was his. The piece was simply too good, the professor told him, to have been composed by a student. In order to prove it was not plagiarized, the professor had Jones recite the poem, by heart, in front of the entire class. Jones completed the challenge, surprising himself by doing so without a single stutter. He credits Professor Crouch with not only building his confidence and improving his speaking ability, but also with fostering his lifelong love of words. Imagine if Professor Crouch had not been there for James Earl Jones. Who would have growled out "This is CNN" for so many years? More critically, could anyone have portrayed the intensity of Darth Vader quite like James Earl Jones? On behalf of *Star Wars* fanboys everywhere: thank you, Professor Crouch. You helped turn a nervous boy with a stutter into one of the most recognizable voices in entertainment history.

The forty-second president of the United States received an early mentorship from a teacher as well. For Bill Clinton, that mentor was music teacher Virgil Spurlin. The two met at Hot Springs High School in Arkansas in the early 1960s, when Clinton was a student and Spurlin was the band director. Spurlin helped to teach Bill Clinton how to play the saxophone, an instrument that Clinton played in public many times during his eight-year presidency. That sax helped build Clinton's image, portraying him as a music-loving, carefree baby boomer. But saxophone lessons weren't the greatest lesson that Virgil Spurlin taught Bill Clinton. It was another set of skills that Clinton valued more, skills that would later help build the young student into one of the most influential people of his generation. Spurlin asked Bill Clinton to help him organize the school's band trips, an exercise that gave the future president an appreciation for finding skilled people and helping them focus on doing great work. From those experiences Clinton developed a sense that he could marshal people around a common cause, a skill that would serve him immensely well in politics.

"He thought that everybody was good at something, and if he looked hard enough he could find it, he could convince them of it, and he could raise their aspirations and hopes," said Clinton. "He was unbelievable. I thought of him all my life." Bill Clinton and Virgil Spurlin didn't stop being friends when Bill left high school. The two kept in touch and remained friends until Spurlin passed away.

THE TRUE BENEFITS OF MENTORSHIP

Mark Simpson of the Institute of Entrepreneurship and Community Innovation is a big fan of the mentorship process. He told *The Globe & Mail* newspaper that the true benefit in mentoring is sharing stories and experience, of both success and failure. In fact, by sharing stories of failure, we are reminded that perfection is unrealistic. Even the most successful people made plenty of mistakes along the way, and by sharing those moments with understudies, they can foster confidence and build future success.

Simpson and many others note that many mentorship relationships aren't always verbalized and sometimes work best when they are entirely informal. Sometimes relationships form casually, the way Bob Dylan met Eric Von Schmidt, and friendships build from there. Sometimes they are relationships that are forced upon us through work or school, like Bill Clinton's encounter with Virgil Spurlin and

James Earl Jones's meeting with Professor Crouch. Other mentorships are consciously crafted through networking events, mentorship programs, and business development groups. No matter how they get started, there is no denying the immense value they can have on both parties.

The traditional mentorship involves an older, more experienced person mentoring a younger, less experienced individual. Bob Dylan was ten years younger than his mentor. Bill Clinton and James Earl Jones were both students mentored by teachers. But the Internet has fundamentally changed the way things work. Knowledge has never been more accessible, as long as you are comfortable with technology. Some of the most influential thought leaders today are not older or more experienced. Many brilliant thinkers in social media and marketing are in their twenties and thirties, mentoring CEOs in their fifties and sixties on how to adapt to fast-changing times. This "reverse mentoring" is becoming more prevalent as the older generation recognizes that they can learn from the youth of today and that their relationship can be of mutual benefit instead of a one-way street.

THE BIG PICTURE

The benefits of mentoring can go beyond simply learning from each other. In the case of Lloyd Banking Group in the UK, they believe that mentorships can help rebuild a stagnant British economy. The bank has partnered with the British Banker's Association to establish a formal business mentorship program, pairing small business owners with knowledgeable veterans who can help guide them through the difficult start-up phase of a new business. While exact statistics vary, there is no question that a high number of businesses fail early. Some reports claim that nearly 90 percent of small businesses fail within the first five years! When a higher percentage of new business start-ups are successful, the entire economy benefits.

Welsh business team Sharon Stephens and Rachel Bryan have experienced this firsthand. They set up an international translation and interpreting company during a recession. The two recent university grads began with nothing but a laptop computer at Sharon's dining room table, and a few years later they've built Veritas into a growing company with clients around the world, success they attribute to a mentorship package they won through Lloyds. What did they find most useful in the mentorship process? Knowing that they were getting real-world advice from those who had been there and experienced similar challenges to the ones they were facing. According to Sharon, "No business degree can teach you real-world experience."

MENTORSHIP FOR MONEY

Music is full of stories of so-called mentorship, but often they are clouded by the fact that the mentor stands to benefit from the relationship. Sure, Justin Bieber was discovered by Usher, who then mentored the young singer along a path to becoming the biggest teen sensation in years. But was Usher really a mentor, or was he a smart businessman who wisely seized an opportunity to use his knowledge and experience for profit?

Was Sam Phillips of Sun Records in Memphis a mentor? He was running a nearly bankrupt recording studio on Beale Street, working with black artists like Ike Turner, B. B. King, and Howlin' Wolf, when a young white boy from rural Mississippi walked in the door to sing for him. Elvis Presley gave Sam Phillips exactly what he was looking for: a white boy who could capture the black sound. It was the perfect music for racially divided America, and Elvis took off. Sam Phillips sold Elvis's contract to RCA Records for the pathetic sum of $35,000 and then went on to sign Johnny Cash, Carl Perkins, and Jerry Lee Lewis. Sam never got as rich as he should have from his rock 'n' roll protégés, but he certainly made a living discovering and developing legendary musicians. Is that really true mentorship, or is it just good business?

The Rock Star Playlist: Five Mentor/Student Collaborations

1. **"The Wanderer" by U2 and Johnny Cash.** Bono had long been a fan of American roots music and a longtime fan of Cash, so the band invited Johnny Cash to sing the track during his visit to Dublin in February 1993. While the producer Brian Eno wanted Bono to sing the song, Bono insisted on Johnny Cash. He claims to have written the song with Johnny Cash's deep voice in mind. "The Wanderer" is one of the rare U2 songs that doesn't feature Bono on lead vocals.

2. **Jason Bonham Joins Led Zeppelin.** Jason grew up watching his father John play drums in Led Zeppelin, and he even appeared in the band's movie *The Song Remains the Same*, playing a mini-drum kit. He was fourteen when his

continued on following page

father and mentor died. Although he has played in many bands over the years, in December 2007 Jason Bonham joined Led Zeppelin for an emotional reunion for the legendary concert that formed the basis for the *Celebration Day* album and film.

3. **"Unforgettable" by Natalie Cole and Nat King Cole.** Natalie Cole was able to sing a duet with her father and mentor, Nat King Cole, in 1991. Producer Joe Guercio took the original Nat King Cole song from 1961 and remixed it with Natalie's new vocal, allowing the daughter to sing together with her late father. The tune won Song of the Year at the 1992 Grammy Awards.

4. **Keith Richards and Chuck Berry.** In the 1987 film *Hail! Hail! Rock 'n' Roll*, Rolling Stone Keith Richards has the chance to play alongside his idol Chuck Berry. Berry and Richards don't exactly get along in the rehearsals, but once Richards retreats and lets Berry take over, the elder bluesman teaches the younger Stone a few lessons. It was tense, but it was a learning experience for both the mentor and the teacher.

5. **"China Girl" by David Bowie.** When Iggy Pop met David Bowie in 1971, Bowie was already famous. Pop was struggling as the lead singer of The Stooges. Bowie took Iggy under his wing, helped him kick his drug addictions, and produced the next Stooges album. When Iggy fell back into drugs and checked himself into a mental institution, the far-more-famous David Bowie was one of his only visitors. The two remained friends and collaborators for years, resulting in many songs, including "China Girl." Iggy recorded "China Girl," featuring Bowie's backing vocals, in 1977. It would eventually become a massive hit when David Bowie re-recorded it on his 1983 album *Let's Dance*.

▼

CHAPTER 22

THE ROCK 'N' ROLL COMEBACK: EVERY STATE IS TEMPORARY

George Harrison's first album after the Beatles broke up was an ambitious *triple* album called *All Things Must Pass.* That notion—that every state is temporary—is so simple yet so brilliant, and incredibly valuable to your career and the development of your personal brand. It was also central to George's life at the time, starting a solo career after the most successful band of all time broke up. Indeed, all things *must* pass. Every state is temporary, no matter how euphoric or how dismal. Success gives way to failure. Failure gives way to success. A lake turns to ice in the winter, and the spring sun releases it to become water again. Rock stars have learned this lesson the hard way.

Rock 'n' Roll is a temporary world where songs rise meteorically up the charts, only to begin a downward spiral a few weeks later. It is a cruel world where the killer sold-out show from tonight will end, and tomorrow night's show in a different city might not be anything like it. The moment your great new album comes out, the pressure is on to create the follow-up amid ridiculously high expectations. Rock stars live in a world where everything changes, sometimes every four minutes, like a song coming to an end. Eventually, what you do so well goes out of style, and your flame starts to flicker. What was once the next big thing becomes the greatest that once was. Although success may be fleeting, the desire for it isn't, and thus comebacks are born.

When you think about comebacks, often your first thought is an aging athlete attempting to return to glory or an over-the-hill rocker fighting to reclaim the spotlight. But comebacks aren't just for rock stars or athletes. To be a true rock star in your career, understanding how to rise up after failure should be a key part of your career plan. After all, every career will naturally experience highs and lows. At some point in your career you will very likely come into a deep valley, staring up at the mountain called success and wondering how the hell you are going to get back up there. Rock stars who have already made the descent and the ascent can give you the framework around which to plan your own personal comeback when times get tough.

A SLICE OF MEAT LOAF

No rock 'n' roll career was as up-and-down-and-up-again as Meat Loaf's. His rise began in the early '70s, singing in the cast of *Hair* in Los Angeles. His success there led to a role in *The Rocky Horror Picture Show.* As that movie took off, Meat Loaf turned from theater to music and started working on the album *Bat Out of Hell* with collaborator Jim Steinman. Although Meat Loaf and Steinman felt they had a great album, it didn't sound like anything else on the radio, and nearly every record company rejected them for that very reason. Finally a small record label, Cleveland International Records, decided to release *Bat Out of Hell.* The album instantly took off, blowing away everyone's expectations and eventually becoming the fifth-best-selling album of all time. Not bad for a first try.

But that incredible success came at an incredible price. The popularity of *Bat Out of Hell* created a rift between Meat Loaf, the voice and face of the album, and Jim Steinman, the behind-the-scenes genius who created much of the music. Meat Loaf toured relentlessly to promote the album, and the touring took a toll on his voice and his body. At a concert in Ottawa, Ontario, Meat Loaf fell from the stage and broke his leg. During the recovery, he turned to drugs to ease the pain. By the time the tour was over, Meat Loaf was heavily addicted to cocaine and suffering from near-suicidal depression. To make a follow-up album even more chal-lenging, Meat Loaf suddenly lost his ability to sing. Doctors diagnosed the ailment as psychological, but it didn't change the fact that Meat Loaf couldn't sing. Steinman decided to continue to work on the album, *Bad for Good*, without the drug-addicted and suicidal Meat Loaf.

Without Steinman, Meat Loaf's follow-up albums were expensive failures, and by 1985 he was bankrupt. His finances weren't the only part of his life in ruins; Meat Loaf's collaborative musical relationship with Steinman was over, and his girlfriend suffered a nervous breakdown and checked into rehab.

The road back to the top started there, at the very bottom. Cleaning up his personal life, Meat Loaf began to tour on his own, without an album to promote. His shows were small, nothing like the massive stage productions of the *Bat Out of Hell* era. The tours stopped at small clubs and bars all over America. In order to keep costs down, Meat Loaf's wife became a travel agent and took care of their tour planning. Over the course of a few years of working hard every night to put on a great show, the crowds began to grow. He began to get booked into larger and larger venues. By the late 1980s, Meat Loaf was a strong concert draw in North America, Europe, and the Middle East. While he was still nowhere near the star he was in the *Bat Out of Hell* days, after a terrible decade, things were finally looking good for Meat Loaf.

That's when Jim Steinman came back into the picture. The two started working on a sequel called *Bat Out of Hell II: Back into Hell*. Much like the first time around, record companies weren't that interested at first. Most in the music industry looked at the project as a joke, but Meat Loaf and

Jim believed once again that they were onto something special. And they were. Today *Bat Out of Hell II* is widely regarded as one of rock music's best comebacks. Sixteen years after first topping the charts, Meat Loaf was finally back! He won a Grammy Award, had a #1 song in twenty-eight countries, and sold fifteen million copies of *Bat Out of Hell II*. What an inspiring comeback.

CROSBY'S CRAZY COMEBACK

There is no shortage of rock 'n' roll comeback stories, but few people have risen and fallen more often or more publicly than David Crosby.

Crosby first came to our collective consciousness in the mid-1960s as a member of the Byrds. With hits like "Turn, Turn, Turn," "Eight Miles High," and "Mr. Tambourine Man," the Byrds became one of the hottest bands of their era. However, David's political opinions (particularly his habit of expressing them onstage) hit a sour note with the other members of the band. He was fired from the band in 1967. Rise and fall #1 complete.

Still well-connected within the California music scene, Crosby connected with another unemployed musician, Stephen Stills, and the two started playing together. At a 1968 party at Mama Cass Elliott's house, the two invited friend Graham Nash of the Hollies to play a song with them. Immediately, the trio recognized that their vocal collaboration was something special. Nash elected to leave his band, and Crosby, Stills, and Nash was born. The group's first live gig? A little festival in New York called the Woodstock Music and Art Fair. Not a bad start.

The rise of CSN was quick, and so was the fall. A year after their debut, Crosby's girlfriend died in a car accident, sending him into a downward spiral of drug abuse. Appearances by the band became more sporadic, and bickering within the group more prevalent. By 1976 they were no more. They didn't reunite again until they were invited to play Live Aid in 1985.

Crosby was notorious for his abuse of drugs and alcohol, and over the next two decades those addictions would impact his world repeatedly. In 1982 he was sentenced to nine months in a Texas prison for possession of heroin, cocaine, and guns. Only three years later he was arrested after a hit-and-run accident in San Francisco. After the accident, police found cocaine and a .45 caliber pistol in his car. Another incident in 2004 came about when he forgot his luggage at a hotel. When a hotel employee opened the bag to search for some ID, the employee discovered a .45 caliber pistol and marijuana. Crosby escaped jail time and paid a $5,000 fine.

He has also battled his weight and health, contracting type-2 diabetes and receiving a highly publicized liver transplant in 1995.

Today, despite all of the challenges he has faced, a leaner and healthier David Crosby continues to perform all over the world as a key member of Crosby, Stills, and Nash. He is a legend in rock 'n' roll and a two-time inductee into the Rock and Roll Hall of Fame, once as a member of the Byrds and once for his work in CSN.

OLD SPICE AND UGLY SHOES

The idea of a comeback isn't limited to rock stars. Companies and products have returned from near-dead status to once again dominate their category.

Back in 1938, Old Spice was the hottest new men's aftershave, and for more than a few decades their nautical-themed bottles were extremely popular. But by the 1980s, Old Spice was overshadowed by a rush of designer brands like Ralph Lauren's Polo, Lacoste, and Calvin Klein. The brand faded away in the 1990s and by most accounts was nearly worthless when Procter and Gamble acquired it 1990.

Procter and Gamble experimented with various scents and concepts, creating more youth-oriented body washes and shower gels. They also took a more edgy and humorous approach in their marketing. Recognizing that many perceived Old Spice to be "their grandfather's" product, one marketing campaign noted, "If your grandfather hadn't worn it, you wouldn't exist." In 2010, Procter and Gamble struck advertising gold. Teaming up with ad agency Wieden + Kennedy, Old Spice created the now-famous "Man Your Man Could Smell Like" campaign. That campaign became an instant viral hit on the Internet and dramatically boosted Old Spice sales. Today the brand remains one of the top men's bath product brands in the world. Even *Sesame Street* has parodied the ad, with Grover playing the role of the leading man. Personally, I think the moment that you are parodied by *Sesame Street*, you're famous.

While Old Spice was an eighty-year-old brand when it

made a comeback, the rise and fall happened much faster for Crocs. The unusual colorful clogs took off overnight in 2004. Thanks to a love/hate relationship, everyone knew about the quirky shoes. Within three years Crocs was selling fifty million pairs a year and generating $850 million in revenue. But by 2008 the market became saturated with similar shoes. "Too many people have the same product, selling it to the same consumers, and just our inability to evolve as a brand caused a turn of fortunes in the business," CEO John McCarvel told CNN. In just one year, the company went from $200 million in profits to $200 million in losses. They weren't just struggling to sell shoes; they were struggling to meet payroll.

McCarvel and his team decided to innovate their way out of their funk, creating new shoes that expanded beyond the notoriously ugly designs that initially caught people's attention. They turned out flats, boat shoes, sneakers, and winter boots in fresh designs that were unlike anything Crocs had created before. Today those new lines account for more than 50 percent of the company's business, and Crocs is once again on a growth pattern. Last year, Crocs pocketed $150 in profit from $1 billion in total sales.

As McCarvel told CNN in 2012, "[These] ups and downs have taught us about how to compete and how to have a comeback."

THE ARCHITECT OF A PERSONAL-BRAND COMEBACK

Michael Brooke was a terrible sales person. He had no trouble getting sales jobs, though, since he gave a great job interview.

But a few months into each new sales job, Michael would be let go. Sales was the only area where Michael had any measurable experience, so he limped his way from crappy sales job to crappy sales job, trying to make ends meet. By 1997, Michael had hit rock bottom. He had given himself three months to find a new job, and he was into the final month. He had a wife, two kids, a mortgage, and car payments. He also had holes in his shoes from fruitless cold-calling. He dreaded coming in to work, listening to voice mail, and suffering through another day of rejection. Suffocated and without hope, Michael did the only thing he knew he was good at: he summoned up yet another great job interview and bluffed his way into a sales position at Xerox, calling on publishers and attempting to sell them on professional DocuTech copiers. He was certain he would fail at the new job, but it was his only option.

Things weren't looking any brighter for Michael at Xerox. By all indications, this sales job would end up at the same dead end as all of the previous ones. Selling massive copiers to publishers is a tough close, and Michael wasn't exactly an ace at the tough close, let alone the easy sale. "I was absolutely *the worst* sales person at Xerox," said Michael. "I can't believe they even hired me."

One day Michael managed to get an appointment to see Nick Pitt at a company called Warwick Publishing. With his usual low expectations, Michael walked into Nick's office. It was evident early in the meeting that Nick wasn't all that interested in the Xerox DocuTech copiers that Michael was selling, but the two seemed to have a certain rapport. The ensuing small talk turned to Michael's hobby, skateboarding and working on a small homemade website about the history of the sport. Suddenly, Nick was intrigued. He leaned forward. "We are looking at doing a book on skateboarding. Can you put together an outline?"

Two weeks later, Michael submitted an outline for a book on the history of skateboarding. Warwick Publishing loved it, and Michael walked out with a check in hand as his advance to write his first book. It was an amazing turn of fortune. Thanks to a chance meeting, Michael was quitting his dead-end sales position at Xerox and embarking on a new career as an author! As you probably guessed, Xerox's sales didn't suffer as a result of Michael's departure.

"The book was a total fluke," acknowledged Michael. "But it has sold over 40,000 copies, and I am very proud to have done it. It launched a whole new career for me."

It certainly did. Turning from writing to publishing, Michael soon launched a skateboarding magazine called *Concrete Wave*. The magazine was the culmination of what Michael saw as missing from existing skateboard publications. Today, boasting over seventy thousand readers in twenty countries, *Concrete Wave* is a success in an extremely competitive and cutthroat industry. After working on the magazine for thirteen years, Michael thrives on the magic of making a living doing something he is passionate about. As he reminds himself on the tough days, "The worst day publishing a magazine on skateboarding is better than the best day selling photocopiers!"

From Old Spice to Meat Loaf, from Crocs to skateboard magazines, it seems that all comebacks have a few components in common.

ONLY YOU CAN MAKE IT HAPPEN

When you are climbing the ladder within a company, a lot of good things can happen from momentum. When you are on the inside, you are on people's radar. But when you are on the outside, things are tougher. As the cliché goes, "Out of sight, out of mind." When Meat Loaf wasn't on the top of the charts, he wasn't on anyone's mind. Comebacks are nearly universally self-engineered. Meat Loaf decided to play small bars relentlessly, and eventually he reestablished himself. It took years; it took pain; it took having a wife trained as a travel agent to save on expenses. It was a far cry from the rock-star life he had been living, but that's what it took, and Meat Loaf was willing to do it. Had Meat Loaf simply sat back and waited for his renaissance, he'd still be waiting.

Michael Brooke encountered his big break by accident, walking into the offices of Warwick Publishing hoping to sell them a Xerox copier and walking out with a book deal. But Michael had to make the book happen. Writing a book isn't easy, and once Warwick cut the advance check and sent Michael on his way to research and write a book, there were plenty of challenges for the aspiring author. The bottom line is that Michael had to make the most of his unexpected opportunity, and he did. "Doors open, windows close," philosophizes Michael about his change in fortune. When the door opened, Michael pushed his way through, big-time.

REINVENTION

For Crocs, the only way out of a downward spiral was to reinvent, to come up with something that would capture the imagination of customers the way their original shoes had a few years earlier. That meant taking a bold leap away from the clogs they were famous for and venturing into uncharted territory . . . no doubt a risky move! It is smart branding strategy to always stay true to what your customers expect from you, and clogs are what most people associated Crocs with. But Crocs understood that ugly-looking clogs were not their *only* brand attribute. Their customers told them that the brand also stood for being colorful, funky, and fun. So Crocs created new shoes that kept the same funky, colorful, and fun attributes as the original Crocs. Crocs also wisely held on to their original designs and didn't completely abandon what they were most known for. It was a risky strategy, but it worked.

Reinventing a bad salesperson as a best-selling author is a different story, but an equally risky one. From his original book deal to the launch of a skateboard magazine, Michael Brooke was also willing to take smart risks. Some of them were born of necessity and the disdain that Michael had for his lack of success in the sales business. After his successful book, Michael saw a niche in skateboard publishing and jumped in. Risky for sure, but based on a combination of industry smarts and strong gut feeling, Michael was able to engineer a success story.

GO BACK TO YOUR ROOTS

Meat Loaf may have worked his ass off, but he certainly didn't reinvent himself. When he embarked on rock 'n' roll's most famous comeback, he actually did quite the opposite.

Meat Loaf's legendary 1977 album was called *Bat Out of Hell*. His 1993 comeback was called *Bat Out of Hell II: Back into Hell*. And his 2006 comeback attempt was called *Bat Out of Hell III: The Monster Is Loose*. Meat Loaf became a comeback success by returning to what made him famous, not by trying to reinvent himself. He partnered once again with writer/producer Jim Steinman. Together they created songs that carried a common sonic thread with the original *Bat Out of Hell*. The new songs were often long, theatrical, orchestral, and filled with double-entendre, just like the songs on the original album. What made the two *Bat Out of Hell* follow-ups successful was their connection to the original album. Meat Loaf's comeback was based on a combination of hard work, determination, and returning to what made him great in the first place.

Michael Brooke's success came from going directly back to his roots, not as a writer or publisher, but as a skateboarder. Having fallen in love with the sport from the moment he saw his first skateboard as a ten-year-old in England in the early 1970s, Michael carried that passion with him into adulthood. When sales job after sales job failed him, Michael's passion for skateboarding gave him the break he desperately needed.

AS JOURNEY ONCE SAID . . .

Don't stop believing. The one thing that all comebacks have in common is an unshakable core belief that it can be accomplished. That holds true in music, business, and personal life. Sometimes that belief seems almost insane to hold on to, yet it stoically remains. Meat Loaf, even during his darkest nearly bankrupt days, believed that he could be a star again. When Procter and Gamble took over Old Spice, they obviously believed the brand could rise again. And John McCarvel and his team at Crocs believed that with careful reinvention, they could turn their nearly $200 million in losses into profits once again.

As a sales person, Michael Brooke always believed . . . that he was in the wrong career. He just didn't know a way out. Once he found his exit strategy, there was never any doubt about his ability to make a living in skateboarding. "When you realize that it is all about connecting the dots and getting creative, you can take on the world," says Michael. "I teach people to take that first step."

The Rock Star Playlist: Five Famous Triumphant Rock 'n' Roll Comebacks

1. **"Paradise by the Dashboard Light," by Meat Loaf.** From *Bat Out of Hell*, "Paradise by the Dashboard Light" is the song most people remember. The account of teenaged backseat antics while listening to a baseball game on the radio became a massive hit, despite being more than eight minutes long.

2. **"I'd Do Anything For Love (But I Won't Do That)" by Meat Loaf.** It was fifteen years after the runaway success of *Bat Out of Hell*, and Meat Loaf was finally back on top with *Back Out of Hell 2: Back into Hell*. The lead song was another lengthy anthem that went straight to #1 in twenty-eight different countries.

3. **"Suspicious Minds" by Elvis Presley.** In a discussion about comebacks, it is impossible not to acknowledge Elvis Presley's 1968 comeback. After spending the 1950s watching every song go to #1, Elvis hadn't reached the top of the charts since 1962 with "Good Luck Charm." That streak ended abruptly in 1969 when "Suspicious Minds" went straight to the top. Combined with his late 1968 comeback TV special, "Suspicious Minds" gave the King's career new life.

4. **"What's Love Got to Do with It?" by Tina Turner.** After the fall of the famous Ike & Tina Turner Revue in the mid-1970s, Tina Turner found herself simultaneously rebuilding her life and her career. She put aside her Las Vegas–inspired revue show and evolved into a more gritty rock 'n' roll performer. At the insistence of David Bowie, Capitol Records signed Turner to a record deal and tested the waters with a version of Al Green's "Let's Stay Together." Capitol

continued on following page

immediately recognized the talent they had and went to work on recording a new Tina Turner album. *Private Dancer* was completed in just two months, "What's Love Got to Do with It?" was the first single, and Tina Turner's comeback was complete.

5. **"Hurt" by Johnny Cash.** Johnny Cash was long gone by 1994. His glory days as a rebel in the country music world were thirty years in the rearview mirror. He was too old for the youth movement in country, and recognizing that, Columbia Records dropped him from their label. Nobody saw Johnny Cash as a viable artist in 1994. And then along came Rick Rubin. Rubin, better known for hip-hop and hard rock, guided Johnny through a set of songs that became *American Recordings*. Recorded in Cash's living room, the sparse songs highlighted Johnny Cash's storytelling ability and won the singer a Grammy. Over the next few years, the two would continue to collaborate, with Rubin often choosing contemporary songs for Cash to perform in his unique style. The most awe-inspiring of those songs was "Hurt," a song originally by hard rock band Nine Inch Nails. Cash stripped the song down and poured his heart into it. Released shortly before his death in 2003, "Hurt" stands as a moving epitaph for a legendary singer.

▼

CHAPTER 23

KNOWING WHEN TO QUIT: AVOIDING THE CURSE OF INXS

As much as true rock stars are champions of fighting back against adversity, the smart ones also know when to throw in the towel. Knowing what to quit, when to quit, and what to turn your attention to can be vital to your success.

On November 11, 2012, at a stadium in Perth, Australia, INXS officially quit. After thirty-five years together, the band decided that while their classic music would live forever, they would no longer be making new music or touring. Reaction from around the world was largely disbelief: many people didn't realize that INXS was still together.

To most music fans, INXS died in 1997, when charismatic

lead singer Michael Hutchence committed suicide. On that November day, the band that once reigned as one of the world's most popular lost its visual and musical identity. Hutchence was a poet, a sex symbol, a unique voice, and a larger-than-life character. He was impossible to replace, and the world was in shock when he died. INXS should have ended it then. Unfortunately for them, they didn't.

They recruited 1980s two-hit wonder Terrence Trent D'Arby, whose musical claims to fame were "Wishing Well" and "Sign Your Name," to be their new lead singer. After a few months with D'Arby filling in, they found a new lead singer and continued to play live and make new music, which was widely ignored.

REALITY BITES

In 2004, seven years after Hutchence's death, the band found fleeting fame as the centerpiece for the reality TV show *Rock Star: INXS* in which various singers competed for the chance to lead the band. The ultimate winner of that contest was a young Canadian singer named J. D. Fortune. At the conclusion of the show, INXS announced that they would soon be heading out on tour and recording a new album with their new lead singer/reality TV celebrity.

That album, *Switch*, gave us "Pretty Vegas," a decent song and a minor hit everywhere except in Canada, where government regulations mandate radio airplay for Canadian music. Thanks in large part to a maple leaf on J. D. Fortune's passport, "Pretty Vegas" became a significant hit in Canada.

The next time INXS was in the news was when Fortune went public with his firing, claiming the band simply shook his hand in the Hong Kong airport and said goodbye and thank you, leaving him stranded and broke. The band countered that Fortune was a contract employee, and his contract had expired. It was simple business.

J. D. Fortune reappeared with INXS a few years later when the band released an album of re-recorded versions of their earlier hits, each song featuring a different guest vocalist. The band announced that Fortune was back in the fold and would be touring and working on new music with them. It wasn't long before that arrangement fell apart. Again.

In 2011, INXS named a new lead singer and posted new songs on their website, promising a new album that never came. It is probably for the better. By the time they got around to announcing that they were kaput, nobody cared.

THE SAD FALL

It was a massive nosedive for a band that was so epically huge in the 1980s. Consider their string of hits: "Original Sin," "What You Need," "Need You Tonight," "Devil Inside," "Never Tear Us Apart," "Suicide Blonde," and many others. Their album *Kick* was a defining '80s record, and for several years there were very few bands as popular around the entire world as INXS.

What would the career of INXS look like if they had quit when Michael Hutchence died? We would probably look back on their music with a much stronger affinity. There wouldn't be fifteen years of mediocrity attached to their name. The band could probably maximize their back-catalog of music for far greater profit than they ever made on any post-Hutchence album or tour.

To be fair, the band's status was already well in decline when Hutchence took his own life, but when he died it should have been evident that INXS was dead as well. The decade-and-a-half spent rotating through faceless lead singers attempting to replace someone who most fans felt was irreplaceable only served to diminish what the band represented. Despite a tremendous track record of great music, the INXS brand will be forever tarnished by their inability to quit. Like a party guest who just doesn't know it's time to go, INXS refused to leave when the lights came on and the bar stopped serving drinks.

REPLACING THE IRREPLACEABLE

The list of bands that have successfully replaced high-profile lead singers isn't a long one. AC/DC comes to mind, replacing the late Bon Scott with Brian Johnson in 1980 and going on to even greater success. That is the rare exception. Van Halen would qualify in the "almost" category for their transition from David Lee Roth to Sammy Hagar, but their attempt to three-peat with Gary Cherone on vocals was a disaster. And the ensuing decade of off-and-on reunions with Hagar and/or Roth have turned Van Halen into a music industry joke.

However, in the case of both AC/DC and Van Halen, there was another factor. Both bands have highly visible characters in the band beyond the lead singer. For Van Halen, it is guitar phenomenon Eddie Van Halen and his signature finger-tapping style. For AC/DC, it is Angus Young, famously dressed in his schoolboy uniform. For both AC/DC and Van Halen, replacing a lead singer was made easier because their brands were not one-dimensional. Most bands, including INXS, don't have that luxury. After the lead singer, most members are relatively invisible.

There are nostalgia bands that have successfully made the lead singer replacement. Most notable among them is Journey, who replaced Steve Perry with a Filipino You-Tube sensation named Arnel Pineda who sounds exactly like Perry. Journey continues to tour and profit from their catalog of hits. Fans often come to hear Journey because of Pineda and his eerie similarity to Steve Perry. You can put Foreigner in that same column, replacing Lou Gramm with Kelly Hansen and continuing to tour. But no fans are clamoring for a new Foreigner or Journey album. Lynyrd Skynyrd tried to keep it in the family, replacing Ronnie Van Zandt with his younger brother Johnny and carrying on, but it was never the same band and there never was another "Sweet Home Alabama" or "Free Bird."

THE ZEPPELIN MODEL

There remains, thirty-two years after they broke up, an astounding amount of brand equity in Led Zeppelin. When drummer John Bonham passed away in 1980, the band immediately quit. They issued a heartfelt press release indicating that they could not fathom the thought of carrying on without their dear friend. That was it. Led Zeppelin was done.

When Led Zeppelin announced that they would be playing one show together in December 2009, they immediately broke all records for ticket demand. The O2 arena in London, home to the concert, could hold about twenty thousand people. When tickets went on sale, there were twenty million online ticket requests, crashing the system. The show, with John Bonham's son Jason replacing him on drums, was a massive success. In late 2012, just in time for huge Christmas season sales, Zeppelin finally released the video and audio recordings of the show.

Despite the obvious demand, lead singer Robert Plant steadfastly refuses to take the band on a world tour again. They could make millions and millions of dollars, overnight. But he says "no way." He refuses to go into the studio and make a new Led Zeppelin album. Although he hasn't ruled out future one-off Led Zeppelin concerts, he's made it pretty clear that he has no interest in turning a rock legend into a nostalgia circus.

The value in the Led Zeppelin brand is strong, not simply because of the music they made in their 1970s heyday, but also because of the music they *didn't* attempt to make after Bonham's death. They didn't record a weak album. They didn't become a shell of their former selves. They didn't parade out a string of new drummers in the manner that INXS did with singers.

The same wisdom was applied by Nirvana, who never played together after the suicide of troubled lead singer Kurt Cobain. When Nirvana drummer Dave Grohl formed a new band, he desperately wanted to invite Nirvana bass player Krist Novoselic to join him, but chose not to so fans wouldn't perceive his new band as Nirvana without Cobain. Grohl knew that without Kurt Cobain, there was no Nirvana. The catalog of Nirvana songs would only have been diminished by music made with a different lead singer, no matter how strong the music may have been.

SPRINGSTEEN THE HEDGEHOG

Jim Collins wrote about the idea of quitting in *Good to Great* (HarperBusiness, 2001). In that classic business book, Collins described the triangle that's formed when you merge three circles together. In one circle are the things you are great at doing, the things you can do better than almost anyone else. In another circle are your passions, the things you love to do and derive intense pleasure from accomplishing. In the third circle are the things that make you money. The intersecting circles form a triangle in the middle, and in that triangle are the things that accomplish all three goals: they are things you are great at, that you love doing, and that can make you rich.

According to Collins, you increase your chances of success if you simply eliminate the things that don't fall into that triangle. The things you love to do but can never be great at? Eliminate them. Things that make you money but you aren't passionate about doing? Forget it. Jim Collins calls it the "hedgehog concept," because hedgehogs are only good at one thing, but they do that one thing exceptionally well. I prefer to call it the "Springsteen concept," since Bruce has been known to record a lot of songs that sound alike. He's been accused of recording too many songs about working class union towns and closed-up factories. Sure he does; that's what makes him great! He's better at it than anyone else, he's passionate about it, and it makes him wealthy.

What can you quit doing today? Look around you at work, and take note of the things you do that you aren't great at, aren't passionate about, and aren't making any money from. Make a list, and one by one start to eliminate those things from your routine. Eliminate the distractions that prevent you from focusing on that triangle where excellence, passion, and profit intersect. You will need to delegate tasks, assuming you have the authority at your job to do so. If you don't have that freedom, maybe you'll need to meet with your boss and see if your responsibilities can be shifted. You might need to coordinate with someone else at work to handle certain tasks. Or you might need to quit altogether and find a job that you are great at, passionate about, and can earn a living from.

And certainly there will be things on your list that you choose to keep doing that you aren't great at but you love. For example, I continue to play ice hockey, despite the fact that I'm not great at it—and getting worse with age. I'm a goalie, and the morning after a hockey game my knees hurt like crazy. I know I'll never make the NHL, but I continue to play because I love doing it. I'm not suggesting you eliminate your passionate hobbies. We all need positive distractions to clear our mind.

But if your goal is to be remembered from the great things you accomplished, you need to avoid the fate of INXS. Know what and when to quit, and know what you want to do with all of the free time and energy you have, thanks to your first-rate quitting skills. Very few people have ever become happy, successful, and wealthy doing something they are bad at, aren't passionate about, and derive no profit from.

The Rock Star Playlist: Five Defining INXS Songs

1. **"Original Sin," by INXS.** It was 1984, and INXS had just recorded their fourth album, *The Swing*. The band was already successful in Australia, but the song "Original Sin" became their first #1 hit in their homeland and their first song to crack the US pop charts, peaking at number thirty.

2. **"What You Need," by INXS.** A year after "Original Sin," INXS managed to score a Top 5 hit in America with "What You Need." Taken from the album *Listen Like Thieves*, "What You Need" gave fans a sense of the unique funk-rock-pop that the band was capable of making.

3. **"Need You Tonight," by INXS.** When the album *Kick* was released in late 1987, it sent INXS into the rare air as one of the biggest bands in the world. The album sold over six million units and spawned four Top 10 hits, including the number one song, "Need You Tonight."

4. **"Elegantly Wasted," by INXS.** Released in 1997, *Elegantly Wasted* was the final album with Michael Hutchence. He passed away six months after the album's release.

5. **"Pretty Vegas," by INXS.** With reality show winner J. D. Fortune singing lead vocal, in 2005 INXS released their first album since the death of Hutchence. It gained them some significant press coverage, but the resulting song wasn't a hit outside of Canada, where J. D. Fortune is from. In reality, though, it wasn't all that bad a song.

▼

PART FIVE:

PROFITS

▼

CHAPTER 24

YOUR OBSTACLES WILL DEFINE YOU: HOW A ONE-ARMED DRUMMER IS CHANGING THE WORLD

He was twenty-one and on top of the world. The band he had joined as a fifteen-year-old drumming prodigy had skyrocketed to fame, bringing him endless wealth and notoriety. *Pyromania*, their third album, had spent the previous year selling over 100,000 copies a week, and their song "Rock of Ages" had knocked off Michael Jackson's "Beat It" as MTV's most-requested music video. Life had been very, very good to Rick Allen and Def Leppard.

With so much money coming their way, the band relocated to Dublin, Ireland, early in 1984 so that they could take advantage of lower taxes while they worked on the follow-up to *Pyromania*. There was tremendous pressure on the band to create another successful album, and things had become stressful. Original producer John "Mutt" Lange started the project but dropped out early on when he was overcome with exhaustion. They brought in Jim Steinman, the writer behind Meat Loaf's *Bat Out of Hell* album, but his raw style didn't gel with the band's vision of a slicker sound. After Steinman left, the band took a crack at producing their new album on their own, but that plan fell apart as well. As winter arrived and 1984 came to a close, the band decided to scrap everything they had done and take a break over the holidays. The plan was to start fresh in the new year and record the album of their lives.

On the last day of 1984, Rick Allen was driving his Corvette to a New Year's party in Sheffield, England, when the driver of the Alpha Romeo in front of him refused to let the Def Leppard drummer pass. According to Allen, he became frustrated and ended up recklessly passing the sports car. Going far too fast, he missed a turn in the A57 highway and lost control of his car. The Corvette tore off the road, flying through a stone retaining wall and coming to rest upside down in a field. In the passenger seat, his girlfriend was unhurt, held firmly in place by her seat belt. Allen wasn't so fortunate. He had been thrown from the vehicle. Although he was alive, the seat belt had severed Rick Allen's left arm as he flew out of the car. He lay in a field, conscious but in total shock, unaware of the trauma his body had just experienced.

A nurse who lived nearby heard the accident and ran out

to help. She attended to Rick and put the severed limb on ice, hoping that it could be reattached. At the hospital, doctors initially reattached his arm, but in the days after it became clear that persistent infection prevented it from taking. Rick Allen suffered quite possibly the cruelest punishment that a drummer could suffer: he lost his left arm at the shoulder.

Like anyone in that circumstance, Allen's immediate reaction was depression. He was in disbelief, and the reality of losing his arm took a few weeks to really sink in. As he began to rehabilitate, he slowly started to come to terms with the devastating fact that he would never again be able to play drums in Def Leppard. The pity didn't last long, though. Rick immediately immersed himself in rehab and refused to waste any time feeling sorry for his situation.

As he was healing, Rick's brother brought a portable stereo to his hospital room. At first the music angered Rick, because it was a constant reminder that he was not going to be able to continue as a musician. But over the course of a few days, the music in the background gave Rick an interesting realization. As the songs played, Rick found himself laying in his hospital bed playing along to the drum tracks, using only his feet and his right arm. While he was pretty sure he'd never play with a band like Def Leppard again, he was encouraged that someday he might be able to play drums.

When the band's manager stopped by the hospital to see Rick, he braced himself for the news that Def Leppard was going to look for a new drummer. Instead, he was told to get better and rejoin the band! The album was in limbo and they figured they would be working on it for at least another year, so there was plenty of time for Rick to heal. "Get well," they said, "and when you are ready to rock, we'll be waiting for you."

As soon as he was able to leave the hospital, Rick Allen was meeting with engineers and drum experts to create a custom drum set that he could play with two feet and one arm. It wasn't always easy, but Rick was determined beyond description. When the band gathered to continue to work on their new album, Rick would lock himself away in a soundproof room for hours on end, playing and perfecting his parts. Meanwhile, the band would work on their portions using an electronic drum to keep the time. When Rick was ready, he revealed his work to the rest of the band . . . and blew them away. Def Leppard was back! They spent months together creating an album that they were proud of. Still, they had been gone for a few years. Would their fans remember them? Would they embrace a drummer with only one arm?

To test the waters, the band's management booked a series of small concerts. The shows would be a test to see if the fans were receptive and if the band was ready for a world tour. To augment their one-armed drummer, Def Leppard hired Rick's friend Jeff Rich of Status Quo to help out. For those first few shows they would alternate drums, with Rick doing the bulk of the work on his new custom drum kit and Jeff filling in where needed. But a few shows into the tour, Jeff had a commitment to Status Quo and couldn't make the Def Leppard concert. That night, Rick Allen played all of the drum parts, and Jeff Rich happily handed in his resignation as part-time assistant drummer for Def Leppard.

The first major show the band played was the Donnington Festival, and it was an emotionally overwhelming event for all involved. Rick called it one of the most moving experiences of his life, looking out at eighty thousand fans and knowing he was really back. When Joe Elliot introduced the band to the audience, the crowd went wild when Rick's name was called. The drummer stood up, and overcome with emotion, tears streamed down his face. Those powerful emotions washed over the whole band and many in the audience. When the band headed out on tour, a similar reaction greeted Rick Allen in every city in which they played.

MORE THAN A DRUMMER

Today, Rick Allen is still the drummer in Def Leppard. He has been playing drums with one arm for much longer than he ever played with two. The band continues to tour and draw thousands upon thousands of fans to every show. While his unique setup is no longer a novelty, it is still an amazing sight to see and sound to hear. Rick Allen creates a unique rhythmic thunder despite what would traditionally be called a "handicap."

Rick is more than a drummer. He is the cofounder of the Raven Drum Foundation, a nonprofit group created to serve, educate, and empower veterans and people in crisis. Using drums and rhythm as their focal point, the charity has had tremendous success. He also oversees the One Hand

Drum Company, a company that funds the foundation through the sale of Rick's personalized merchandise. His signature item is his hand-drawn stick figure self-portrait known as StikRick. All of the One Hand Drum Company profits support the Raven Drum Foundation charity.

Although Rick Allen is a fantastic drummer, he isn't as famous as he should be for his percussion skills. He isn't remembered for the cool cowbell that opens "Rock of Ages." His fame didn't come from the fact that he was a child prodigy, joining Def Leppard at age fifteen. Rick Allen is famous thanks to the obstacle he conquered.

Is Rick Allen unusual? Yes, inasmuch as there aren't a lot of one-armed drummers out there, especially ones that lost their arm at what appeared to be the height of their fame. But he really isn't that unusual. His story isn't all that different from many other stories. Overcoming obstacles and doing incredible work under difficult circumstances is a hallmark of the human spirit.

FLY ME A RIVER

Captain Chesley Sullenberger was just another pilot at US Airways until January 15, 2009, presented him with the opportunity to do incredible work under difficult circumstances. "Sully" was the captain of US Airways flight 1354, scheduled to fly from New York's La Guardia Airport to Charlotte, North Carolina. As the pilot in the left-hand seat, Sully was in charge of the plane and its passengers, and he was assisted in that role by his copilot, Jeffrey B. Skiles, and a crew of flight attendants. On this particular leg of the flight, the copilot was doing the actual flying and Sully was working the radios and navigation equipment. This was nothing unusual, as it is common practice for pilots to trade off duties throughout the day.

Shortly after taking off from La Guardia, the unthinkable happened: the plane flew into a flock of geese, ingesting several of them into the plane's engines. Planes hit birds quite frequently, and normally it isn't a major issue. On this day, it was. Something that had never happened before occurred: both engines were overwhelmed by the impact of the birds on their turbines, and both engines simultaneously died. The plane, only a few thousand feet into its climb, was suddenly left powerless above America's largest and most densely populated city.

Like bird strikes, engine failures happen from time to time on airplanes. That's why having two engines is so vital. Almost every type of aircraft can conduct normal operations on one engine. Under normal circumstances, with one engine failed, the pilot would have plenty of thrust available to keep the plane aloft until he could safely land at the nearest airport. But with both engines dead, Sully was forced to act.

He immediately took control of the aircraft and leveled the plane. Had the plane continued to attempt to climb without engines, it would have lost speed and stalled, sending it tumbling uncontrollably to the ground. With the plane level, he began to weigh his options.

The first option was to return to La Guardia, but to accomplish that he would need to fly in a pattern over the city to line up with the runway. There was no way his plane would maintain altitude long enough to return to La Guardia, and crashing into New York City would be devastating.

Sully's second option was more promising. A few miles to the west, off the right side of the plane, was Teterborough Airport in New Jersey, a popular airport for executive jets and private planes. Sully and his copilot could see the runway, and air traffic was ready to reroute everyone else to accommodate the disabled US Airways flight, but the math didn't work. Turning to the right would create an immediate loss of altitude, and there was no way they would make Teterborough.

The third option wasn't really an option at all, but at this point it was all they had left. As the plane steadily lost altitude and speed, Sully surveyed the icy cold Hudson River below. Landing his plane in the water was the only way he had any chance to save the lives of the 155 people on board.

There is no checklist or manual for landing a fully fueled and fully loaded Airbus 319—without any engine power—on the water. It had never been done before—ever. Nobody had ever even contemplated such a thing.

Sully picked his spot carefully, far enough away from the many boats and ferries crossing the river as to not cause them harm, but close enough that they could help with the rescue operation. He struggled to keep the wings level. If one wing hit the water first, the increased drag could send the plane cartwheeling, surely killing everyone on board. As the plane neared the water, Sully raised the nose in order to slow it down. He wanted to hit the water at the slowest possible speed.

With 150 passengers bracing for their lives, Sully gently let the plane touch the water. Both engines made contact, simultaneously, and immediately the friction dragged the belly of the plane down into the water. For a moment it looked like it might submerge, and then the big jet slowed down, veered slightly to the left, and peacefully came to rest. From the air, it looked as if Sully had done this same maneuver a hundred times before. In that historic footage that most of us will never forget, the doors opened and passengers began to emerge, walking out onto the wings in the frigid air and stepping into the boats that had rushed to the rescue.

What Captain Sullenberger did that January afternoon made him a hero. He became an overnight celebrity. In his many years of flying, Captain Sullenberger had previously taken off and landed safely thousands of times. His record was impeccable. He had flown combat missions in the air force, had given young pilots the gift of learning how to fly, and had applied his skills as a glider pilot. For decades, he had been safely delivering our friends and family back to us with the seemingly routine skill of an expert pilot. But Captain Sullenberger will not be remembered in history for all of those noble yet ordinary accomplishments. He will be forever defined by the day he safely landed a disabled passenger jet on the Hudson River.

INVISIBLE RAILWAYS

To listen to him on the radio, you would think that Shilo Bellis is just like any other radio personality. He hosts a daily show on Canadian radio station CJXL-FM, known as XL Country 96.9, in Moncton, New Brunswick. For years, Shilo has been entertaining his listeners and playing music by the country stars he loves. You would assume that the bulk of a radio host's job happens when the microphone is on, but that's not the case with Shilo. Most of his listeners have no idea about the incredible workload that Shilo faces when the microphone is turned off.

Behind the scenes, while songs by Tim McGraw, Brad Paisley, and Taylor Swift are playing, Shilo is listening intently, but not to music. Shilo is listening to a software program that reads back the text on the many computer screens around him. Shilo is blind; he can't look at the list of songs he is about to play. He can't glance down and see that a listener has texted him requesting the new Lady Antebellum hit. He can't even look out the window to check the weather and remind you to turn your headlights on in the evening fog.

Using a special text-to-speech program, Shilo listens and gathers all of that information while the songs are playing. He collects it and stores it all in his hard drive of a memory and then flawlessly shares it with his listeners on the air without referencing any notes. Because he doesn't use any written material, Shilo has a way of speaking from the heart and connecting on a very human level with his audience. Nothing he says to you is ever written down.

When you are listening to someone on the radio, there is no such thing as "blind" or "sighted." You can't tell if someone is tall or short, gay or straight, black or white, in a wheelchair or standing upright. And none of it matters to the listener. That's one of the beautiful things about radio; a voice can be your friend without being judged.

However, within his industry Shilo is undoubtedly defined by the way he has overcome the obstacle of his blindness. It is what separates him from those who have succeeded without conquering an obstacle, or from those who have conquered a different kind of obstacle. There is nothing wrong with that! Certainly we should judge his talent as a broadcaster without giving special consideration to the challenges he has faced. Being a world-class radio host takes skill and talent, and vision or no vision, Shilo has both of those attributes. But there is nothing negative about respecting and recognizing him for the way in which he has conquered his obstacle. People within the radio industry have an increased level of respect for Shilo in the same way that aviators have an increased respect for Sully, and drummers have an increased respect for Rick Allen. Overcoming obstacles isn't easy. Often it is easier just to give up than it is to fight.

Rick Allen fought and won, and created incredible music as a result.

Sully fought and won, and saved hundreds of lives in the process.

Shilo Bellis fought and won, and entertains thousands of people every day.

Your obstacle might not be visible to others. It might not be, comparatively, very big. Maybe it hasn't appeared to you yet, but it will. It's out there, and when it does appear, remember that you will forever be defined by how you handle it.

Even if you don't win, it is far better to be remembered as one who fought to the death than one who surrendered.

The Rock Star Playlist: Five Earth-Shaking Def Leppard Classics (Meant to Be Played Loud!)

1. **"Bringin' on the Heartbreak."** This was the biggest hit on their breakthrough album *High 'n' Dry*, an album that made them famous but not-quite-world-famous. Their next album would catapult them into world fame.

2. **"Rock of Ages."** With its famous gibberish beginning and cowbell intro, "Rock of Ages" was the song that opened *Pyromania*, the album that truly launched Def Leppard's career.

3. **"Photograph."** This single from *Pyromania* was arguably their most radio-friendly hit and opened the band up to an entirely new audience. With frequent video play on MTV, Def Leppard was everywhere in 1983–84.

4. **"Pour Some Sugar on Me."** After their lengthy hiatus and Rick Allen's recovery, the band returned with *Hysteria*, their biggest-selling album ever. Despite a slow start in sales, it went on to sell over twenty million copies and spawn seven hit singles, including this, the biggest hit from the album. The album's name was suggested by Rick to describe the media coverage of his accident and the band's long disappearance.

5. **"Love Bites."** This track from *Hysteria* originally started out as a country-sounding song that the band objected to recording. But producer Mutt Lange insisted. The end result was a classic late-eighties power ballad with heavily layered harmonies and a thick production style that had become a signature part of Def Leppard's sound.

CHAPTER 25

▼

ROCK STAR LEADERS: HOW JAGGER, BONO, GROHL, AND BON JOVI RANK ON THE CEO SCALE

They strut confidently across the stage. They captivate the audience, direct the band, and turn a concert into a spectacular show. Beyond their voices, lead singers are like CEOs when they are on stage, setting the tone for their company with their directions and decisions. But are they Level 5 Leaders?

The concept of "Level 5 Leaders" was first introduced by author Jim Collins in his 2001 book *Good To Great*. It emerged from a study of 1,435 different companies and their leaders. Collins determined that eleven of the 1,435 companies were truly exceptional, and all eleven of them were led by what he called "Level 5 Leaders," those who exuded these six specific traits:

1. They develop a sense of humility.

2. They aren't afraid to ask for help.

3. They take personal responsibility for their actions.

4. They develop discipline.

5. They surround themselves with the right people.

6. They lead their teams with passion.

So how do the lead singers of legendary rock bands stack up against Jim Collins's legendary defining leadership traits?

HUMILITY: BE DAVE, NOT AXL

Arrogant leaders tend to lead their businesses into the ground, but Collins discovered that leaders who have a strong sense of humility have the ability to lead their teams to higher levels of success. On the surface, this is a tough one for lead singers, since so much of their over-the-top rock 'n' roll persona depends on coming across as self-confident and cocky. But when you dig a little deeper, you start to find lead singers who appear cocky on stage but ultimately possess deep humility.

Axl Rose is a perfect example of an arrogant singer who drove his band into the ground. While the collapse of Guns N' Roses wasn't entirely Axl's fault, his extreme arrogance was pivotal in the band's fall from rock royalty to industry joke. Guns N' Roses exploded onto the scene in the summer of 1987 with *Appetite for Destruction*, an album since certified eighteen times platinum, selling more than thirty-five million copies worldwide. Not bad for an album produced on a budget of $370,000! Songs like "Sweet Child 'O Mine," "Welcome to the Jungle," and "Paradise City" became huge hits and rock classics. The album scored five stars from AllMusic.com and consistently ranks among the greatest albums of the '80s in many publications.

When the original lineup disintegrated in the mid-1990s, Axl Rose set to work on a new album. He boasted to anyone who would listen about the great music he was working on. So did his friends. Skid Row singer Sebastian Bach heard some of the songs Axl was working on in 2006 and called them "fucking epic," suggesting that they had the power of *Appetite for Destruction* combined with the grandiosity of the song "November Rain." Axl worked for nearly twenty years, off and on, with a variety of musicians coming and going, to create *Chinese Democracy*. It became one of the most delayed and most expensive albums in rock music history, with Axl Rose apparently burning through $13 million on the project.

Over the course of the two decades spent working on *Chinese Democracy*, Axl made a habit of showing up late for concerts, not showing up at all, or starting shows hours after the scheduled start time. He initiated numerous lawsuits. On stage and off, he blamed his troubles on his former band mates in Guns N' Roses, band mates who, for the most part, had gone on to be part of other successful bands. In a 2012 interview with *USA Today*, Rose discussed how he didn't even write any music for years in the mid-1990s because of criticism from former Guns N' Roses members Slash and Duff McKagan.

When it finally came out in late 2008, reaction to *Chinese Democracy* was disappointing, to say the least. It could never have lived up to the lofty expectations of a twenty-year wait.

Thus, Axl Rose's astounding lack of humility played a major role in the eventual destruction of one of rock's coolest bands.

On the other hand, Dave Grohl has taken a completely different approach to his career. Grohl was the drummer in Nirvana. After Kurt Cobain's suicide, he moved out from behind the drum kit and started a new band, Foo Fighters. The Foos have gone on to create a reputation as an A-list rock band and could well be headed for a place in the Rock and Roll Hall of Fame someday.

Grohl is famous for being one of the most personable and genuine people in rock 'n' roll. He doesn't overestimate his own self-worth, referring to himself as "somewhat of a blandish drummer" when asked by *Blender* magazine about his work in Nirvana. He recorded his last album in his garage, surrounded by his family and friends. When the album became a hit, Grohl wrote a personal thank-you note to his fans and shared it on his website. "It makes us feel like the luckiest band in the world," he wrote. "So thanks. It means everything to us."

Grohl's humility was witnessed by nearly twenty thousand fans at a Foo Fighters concert in New Orleans in August 2012. He was mid-concert when he noticed a fan in the front row with an empty beer. Being out of beer at a Foo Fighters concert sucks, and it sucks even worse when you have to give up front-row seats in the middle of the show to get a refill. Knowing this, Dave took a beer from his stash on stage, opened it up, and poured it into the fan's empty beer cup. He refilled a fan's beer! That's how much humility runs through the veins of Dave Grohl. Can you even imagine Axl Rose refilling a fan's beer?

ASK FOR HELP: FREDDIE MERCURY AND MICHAEL JACKSON

Level 5 Leaders are never afraid to appear weak by asking for advice. They are wise enough to know that they aren't necessarily the smartest person in the room, and there might be a better way to do something. While musicians generally love to collaborate, they are also notoriously ego-driven. Is it possible for the lead singer of a band to ask someone else for advice?

Freddie Mercury of Queen, onstage, was the ultimate lead singer. He was bold and brash, charismatic and engaging. He could hold an audience in the palm of his hand. Offstage, he was a quiet introvert who hated giving interviews and generally kept to himself as much as possible.

Queen's biggest-selling song of all time is a great example of Freddie Mercury's ability to accept help from others. "Another One Bites the Dust" was the brainchild of John Deacon, the band's bass player. He was inspired by Chic's "Good Times," and created a bass riff borrowed from the classic disco song. In the studio, Deacon played most of the instruments and did much of the work himself. While the band liked the song, nobody really saw it as a hit single.

Backstage after a concert in Los Angeles, Freddie wasn't afraid to ask for help from Michael Jackson, a man known for having his fair share of hit songs. Michael told Freddie that Queen should absolutely release "Another One Bites the Dust" as a single. Michael Jackson was right, and the song became a #1 hit. The song sold seven million copies and won Queen an American Music Award and a Grammy nomination. If Freddie Mercury had not been willing to accept help from Michael Jackson, Queen would have never experienced the incredible success of "Another One Bites The Dust"!

TAKE RESPONSIBILITY: BONO OWNS U2'S FAILURES

Throughout the 1990s, U2 started to leave their 1980s blueprint for success behind. Their songs became more experimental, incorporating industrial noises and tape loops to create entirely new sounds. From 1991's *Achtung Baby* onward, U2 became increasingly experimental. Albums like *Zooropa* and *Pop* took them further away from their original core sound, and at one point they recorded an album so unusual that they released it under a different name! That album, credited to the band the Passengers, was nothing at all like what U2 fans were accustomed to hearing.

During this unusual time in the band's history, fans became more polarized. Some embraced the new sound, while others started to give up. The majority appeared to be in the latter group. While the band's concerts continued to sell out and their albums sold reasonably well, there was palpable uncertainty among fans when it came to the future of U2. They missed the jangling, sparse guitar sound of The Edge and the passionately restrained voice of Bono. They craved a return to the straight-ahead rock 'n' roll sound that made U2 famous.

That's when Bono took personal responsibility. Following the disappointing critical reaction and sales numbers to the 1997 album *Pop*, the band regrouped. They went back into the studio and rediscovered their core sound. When the album was ready, Bono publicly stated that U2 was "reapplying for the job of the best band in the world."

All That You Can't Leave Behind was released in October 2000, and it was an immediate hit with fans who had lost the band in their 1990s experimental phase. *Rolling Stone* called it U2's "third masterpiece" along with *Joshua Tree* and *Achtung Baby*. The song "Beautiful Day" went straight to #1 in twenty-two countries and won three Grammy Awards. Just over a year later, in the wake of the September 11, 2001, terrorist attacks on New York City, the band played what *Sports Illustrated* ranked as the best Super Bowl halftime show in the game's history.

The years since Bono took personal responsibility for his band have been exceptionally productive, culminating in July 2011 with the conclusion of the most profitable tour in rock history. That's what happens when a leader steps up and takes personal responsibility for the team around him.

DEVELOP DISCIPLINE: JON BON JOVI, CEO

There are few lead singers who have bridged as many changing times and fads as well as Jon Bon Jovi. His band, Bon Jovi, rose to fame in the early 1980s with big hair, power chords, and sing-along choruses. They ruled the decade and then continued their string of hits into the '90s while most bands of their era faded away. Today, Bon Jovi remains a powerful force in rock 'n' roll, and they continue to sell out stadiums around the world.

A major driver behind the band's success is Jon Bon Jovi's personal discipline. He is a relentless worker: writing, recording, and touring for long stretches at a time. But beyond simply working hard, Jon Bon Jovi has the ability to use his discipline to work with purpose. His role as leader of Bon Jovi has been compared to the way a CEO runs a company, with, as *Billboard* noted, a "personification of that delicate intersection of art and commerce."

According to those close to the singer, he takes his role at Bon Jovi Inc. very seriously. He has a better handle on the business of the band than almost anyone involved. He lives and breathes the band from the time he wakes up until the moment he falls asleep. AEG president Tim Leiweke told *Billboard* that without question, "Jon is a CEO. That's the way he views his role."

Steve Bartels, president and COO of Island Def Jam Records, was equally impressed by Jon's business discipline. "His business acumen and instincts are unparalleled," he told *Billboard*. "Jon Bon Jovi drives hard, and the entire organization feels his energy. It rubs off, and therefore much gets done in an efficient manner. The success speaks for itself due to this approach."

FIND THE RIGHT PEOPLE: GEORGE HARRISON AND FRIENDS

Great leaders surround themselves with great people. It has been said that A players attract A+ players, while B players attract C players. Rock star leaders possess the self-confidence to create a team of people who are as smart and skilled as they are, and maybe even more than they are.

George Harrison was that kind of musician. He was never afraid to surround himself with genius, even when it meant that he might look worse in comparison. Such fears never stopped George Harrison from surrounding himself with the very best.

He was the first Beatle to record a solo album, putting out two instrumental albums prior to the band's breakup in 1970. He worked extensively with R&B artist Billy Preston and slide guitarist Delaney Bramlett. Both influenced Harrison's later work. When he wanted to learn the sitar, he worked with the world's best, Ravi Shankar, and developed a deep friendship with the Indian artist.

That relationship led Harrison to organize one of the world's first big benefit shows, the Concert for Bangladesh. The two shows, on August 1, 1971, featured some of the biggest artists of the day on stage together at Madison Square Garden. Harrison surrounded himself with legends like Bob

Dylan, Eric Clapton, Badfinger, Leon Russell, Billy Preston, and fellow ex-Beatle Ringo Starr. The Concert for Bangladesh became a model for future benefit concerts, including 1985's Live Aid, providing an opportunity for brilliantly talented people to play together for a greater cause.

Perhaps the clearest example of George Harrison's ability to build a team of greatness around him was the Traveling Wilburys, a band he put together along with his producer, Jeff Lynne of Electric Light Orchestra. Harrison and Lynne were having lunch with Bob Dylan and Roy Orbison and planned to spend the afternoon jamming together. The idea was to record a fun little song that Harrison could use as the B-side of a new single. At lunch, Harrison realized that he had accidentally left his guitar at Tom Petty's house. He left to retrieve it and returned a short while later with both the guitar and Petty. The five musical greats recorded a song together called "Handle with Care." Both the musicians and the record label felt the song was far too strong to be buried as the B-side of a single, and the decision was made to record an album together.

For ten days in 1988 the five men collaborated, working at a studio in the home of another brilliant musical mind, Eurythmics leader Dave Stewart. There were no egos. Each of the great musicians involved took part as equals. The resulting album was fantastic, and the songs "Handle with Care" and "End of the Line" both peaked at #2 on the *Billboard* Hot 100 chart. The album was nominated for numerous Grammys and won the 1989 Grammy Award for Best Rock Performance by a Duo or Group.

Roy Orbison died of a heart attack at age fifty-two, just

two months after the *Traveling Wilburys Vol. 1* was released. He never got to savor the rejuvenation his career received, thanks to the project. Early in 1989, while the Traveling Wilburys were peaking, the haunting album *Mystery Girl* was released. It contained the Top 10 hit "You Got It," marking twenty-four years between appearances on the Top 10 for Roy Orbison. That's a pretty cool story, and George Harrison had a role in it, thanks to his desire to work with the very best and brightest in the Traveling Wilburys.

LEAD WITH PASSION: MICK'S RELENTLESS DEDICATION

So many lead singers exude passion, but few more than Mick Jagger. He was, and is, one of the most popular and influential figures in rock music history. His vocal style, stage manner, fashion sense, and visual look changed the way music is made and heard. So many of today's most popular musicians name Mick Jagger as a major influence. Without Mick Jagger, there would be no Steven Tyler, no David Bowie, and no Jon Bon Jovi.

Among Mick Jagger's chief attributes is an incredible passion: for the music, his band, his relationships, and his fans. He has had passionate love affairs with Linda Ronstadt, Jerry Hall, Carly Simon, Pamela Des Barres, Carla Bruni (now the wife of French politician Nicholas Sarkozy), Margaret Trudeau (at the time the wife of Canadian Prime Minister Pierre Trudeau), and even Angelina Jolie.

But Mick Jagger's true passions are music and the Rolling Stones. He helped found the band, along with classmate Keith

Richards. His look and sound helped shape and define both the band and the generation who grew up listening to them. Their tours were relentless and epic in scope. With massive stage sets and sound systems, the Rolling Stones toured nearly every corner of the world. In the 1990s and 2000s their tours grew even longer, despite the band's advancing age. Jagger led his boys on several tours that stretched well over one hundred concerts and often close to two years long.

His passion has sometimes resulted in conflict with his band mates, and his relationship with Keith Richards is notoriously shaky. The two go through phases where they appear to get along quite well, and then things go cold again. Yet after fifty years, they still have the passion to find a way to work through their differences and create amazing music.

Apart from the Stones, Jagger has passionately explored his own musical muse with several solo albums. Recently he teamed up with a diverse group of musicians to create a new group. Damian Marley, Dave Stewart, Joss Stone, and Indian film composer A. R. Rahman joined Jagger in a band called Super Heavy. The project began when Dave and Mick were talking about the incredible music that Dave was hearing in the hills of Jamaica, where he lived. He and Mick decided that it would be a blast to create a global fusion, blending their music together with the soulful voice of Stone, the reggae DNA of Marley, and the eastern influence of Rahman. The concept never included going on a world tour together or making millions; they simply wanted to explore their musical passions.

From daily meditation and yoga to vocal exercises and workouts, Mick Jagger leads a life dedicated to his craft.

Although some might say he has earned the right to take a day off, he is relentlessly passionate about what he does. Even as he nears seventy, he continues to set the standard for what the passionate leader of a legendary band should look like.

The Rock Star Playlist: Five Songs by CEO-Worthy Lead Singers

1. **"Runaway," by Bon Jovi.** This is the song that founded the band. Jon Bon Jovi actually did much of the work himself, but when the song became a regional hit in New York he was forced to quickly assemble a band to play live. The band Bon Jovi came together and remains a powerful force thirty years later.

2. **"Learn to Fly," by the Foo Fighters.** Dave Grohl is the nicest guy in rock 'n' roll. He has no pretense or ego. His humility is legendary. This Foo Fighters song oozes that kind of friendliness and positivity.

3. **"Another One Bites the Dust," by Queen.** This is the quirky little song that bass player John Deacon created. It was never intended to be a hit single until Michael Jackson gave Freddie Mercury some friendly advice. The rest is history.

4. **"End of the Line," by the Traveling Wilburys.** This Wilburys song came out after the death of Roy Orbison, and the haunting video the band created to promote the song was a tribute to their late friend. Orbison's passing made the song's title even more powerful.

5. **"Miracle Worker," by Super Heavy.** While it was hardly a hit of any great significance, this song illustrates Mick Jagger's passion for music and for collaboration. With diverse partners, Jagger was able to explore Jamaican, Indian, and jazz music in one super cool rock 'n' roll song.

ACKNOWLEDGMENTS

Rock's greatest songs were not created without inspiration, guidance, direction, and leadership. The Beatles had manager Brian Epstein directing them and producer George Martin crafting their work. The Grateful Dead had Hal Kant, a lawyer they called their "czar," working on their behalf to facilitate their greatness. There was Shep Gordon, Alice Cooper's manager, who became an industry legend so large that a movie, *Supermensch: The Legend of Shep Gordon*, was made about him. There are so many people in the process of bringing music to life, from managers, producers, engineers, and promo reps, to drum techs, roadies, and caterers. Without these people, some of the greatest music of all time would never be created or heard. While it would be crazy to compare this book to the works of The

Beatles, Grateful Dead, and Alice Cooper, there were many people behind the scenes who helped it come to life and to whom I owe tremendous thanks.

First, thank you to my family, who put up with a perpetually open laptop for months while this book was being written. They endured hours of verbal ramblings as the book took shape inside my head. My wife Susan and our sons Isaac and Matthew are rock stars in every sense of the word, and I am deeply grateful for their love, support, patience, and input. Thank you as well to my parents, Michael and Stephanie, for supporting my career in the music business even when it didn't look very promising or make a whole lot of sense.

Without the support of Rob Steele, David Murray, Scott Broderick, and everyone at Newcap Radio, this would have been an impossible project. Thank you for allowing me the opportunity to work with the incredible team at Newcap and to apply those experiences toward this book.

I am very grateful to Greenleaf Book Group and their tremendous team for helping to bring this book and *Brand Like a Rock Star* into existence. They have been partners in this project every step of the way, putting their very best editors, designers, and promotions people to work on behalf of the book.

I also owe a debt of gratitude to the giants upon whose shoulders I stand. Authors such as Al Reis, Jack Trout, Seth Godin, Hugh MacLeod, Malcolm Gladwell, Mike Michalowicz, David Meerman Scott, Guy Kawasaki, B. J. Bueno, and Jim Collins have influenced my thinking and perspective immeasurably. Please never stop sharing.

Roy H. Williams and the faculty and cognoscenti of Wizard Academy in Austin, Texas, were pivotal in the creation of this book. Wizard Academy has given me a business education that no school ever could. There is no better place than Wizard Academy to simultaneously clear your mind and fill your brain, and I look forward to returning again and again.

Finally, thanks to you. Thank you for reading, commenting, and sharing your thoughts. The readers of my blogs at www.brandlikearockstar.com and www.startyouupbook.com have been instrumental in shaping this book with their comments and feedback.

If you would like to share your thoughts with me, you can email steve@authorstevejones.com or steve@startyouupbook.com; I would love to connect with you!

Finally, one of the most enjoyable aspects of my career is the chance to speak at conferences of all kinds, all over the world. To inquire about having me speak to your business, conference, or event, please contact Speaker's Spotlight at 1-800-333-4453.

ABOUT THE AUTHOR

Thirty years spent in the music business form the foundation for Steve Jones's observations on business, marketing, branding, and career growth. Having witnessed the rise (and sometimes fall) of countless rock legends, Steve shares their experiences and stories, and shows how to put those lessons into action in order to create a more successful, happier, and rewarding career.

Steve has helped build successful radio brands across the United States, Canada, and the Caribbean. Today he is the vice president of programming at Newcap Radio, one of Canada's largest radio broadcasters. He is a highly sought public speaker, sharing the "rock star" philosophies and strategies with companies and conferences worldwide. As an author, Steve made his debut in 2011 with *Brand Like a Rock Star:*

Lessons from Rock 'n' Roll to Make Your Business Rich and Famous. *Start You Up* is his latest book.

Steve is based in Halifax, Canada, where he lives with his wife, Susan, and their two boys, Isaac and Matthew. When not immersed in music, Steve is a passionate traveler, avid scuba diver, private pilot, and hockey player. Steve cheers for the Boston Red Sox and the Edmonton Oilers, both of which can be immensely frustrating.